FOCUSING: SELECTED ESSAYS

1974-1999

FOCUSING: SELECTED ESSAYS

1974-1999

Neil Friedman

Copyright © 2000 by Neil Friedman.

Library of Congress Number: 99-91758
ISBN #: Hardcover 0-7388-1232-3
Softcover 0-7388-1233-1

All rights reserved. No part of this book may be reproduced or transmitted in any form or by any means, electronic or mechanical, including photocopying, recording, or by any information storage and retrieval system, without permission in writing from the copyright owner.

This is a work of non-fiction. Some names have been changed, and any resemblance to any actual persons is entirely coincidental.

This book was printed in the United States of America.

To order additional copies of this book, contact:
Xlibris Corporation
1-888-7-XLIBRIS
www.Xlibris.com
Orders@Xlibris.com

CONTENTS

BOOKS BY NEIL FRIEDMAN 13
A NOTE ON A NAME 15
A NOTE ON THE PUBLICATION DATE 15
INTRODUCTION :
    AN OVERVIEW OF THIS BOOK 17

PART ONE : IN THE BEGINNING

PROLOGUE 29
1. HOW FOCUSING CAME INTO MY LIFE 33
2. FOCUSING. EUGENE T. GENDLIN. NEW YORK:
    EVEREST BOOKS, 1979. 35
3. FROM THE EXPERIENTIAL IN THERAPY
    TO EXPERIENTIAL PSYCHOTHERAPY:
    A HISTORY 37

PART TWO : FOCUSING

PROLOGUE 57
AN OPENING STORY 59
4. EXPERIENTIAL FOCUSING 60
5. FUNDAMENTAL CONCEPTS OF FOCUSING 90
6. WHAT FOCUSING IS AND WHAT IT IS NOT 95
7. INNOVATIONS IN HOW I LEAD
    A ROUND OF FOCUSING 101
8. A TYPOLOGY OF FELT SHIFTS 107
9. BENEFITS OF FOCUSING 109

PART THREE : FOCUSING AND PSYCHOTHERAPY

PROLOGUE 123
10. FOCUSING-ORIENTED
     EXPERIENTIAL PSYCHOTHERAPY 128
11. THE MAN WHO NEVER SAID
     WHAT IT WAS ABOUT 133
12. EXPERIENTIAL LISTENING 135
13. HOW I DO FOCUSING-ORIENTED
     EXPERIENTIAL THERAPY (1982) 168
14. GENDLIN AND ANGYAL:
     FOCUSING AND HOLISTIC INSIGHT 199
15. HOW I USE FOCUSING FOR SELF-THERAPY 209
16. FOCUSING-ORIENTED
     HEMINGWAY-INFLUENCED THERAPY 222
17. BOOK REVIEW: BODY THERAPIES 225
18. THE INTEGRATION OF FOCUSING
     IN VERBAL FOCUSING THERAPY (1996) 228
19. THE INTEGRATION OF FOCUSING WITH OTHER
     BODY-CENTERED INTERVENTIONS (1996) ... 247

PART FOUR : FOCUSING AND MEDITATION

PROLOGUE 281
20. MEDITATION AND FOCUSING:
     ONE COMPARISON 283
21. A FOCUSING APPROACH TO MEDITATION 285
22. HOW I COMBINE FOCUSING AND
     MEDITATION 288
23. MICHAEL JORDAN, IMPROVISATIONAL ACTING,
     AND NONTRADITIONAL MEDITATION:
     FURTHER REFLECTIONS ON MEDITATION
     (ESPECIALLY) AND FOCUSING (1999) 291

PART FIVE : FOCUSING AND MIRACLES

PROLOGUE 305
24. FOCUSING, TOPISTICS, MEDITATION,
    AND ALTERED STATES: ONE EXPERIENCE 307
25. CANCER. FOCUSING. MIRACLE 313
26. FOCUSING, METANORMAL CAPACITIES,
    AND TRANSFORMATIVE PRACTICE 317

CONCLUSION 321
END NOTES 324
REFERENCES 341
ACKNOWLEDGEMENTS 349
ABOUT THE AUTHOR 350

*for
my
mother*
HOPE
*and
my
daughters*
ZOE
and
KYRA

*and
for
focusers
of the
21st
century
and
3rd
millennium*

BOOKS BY NEIL FRIEDMAN

Focusing: Selected Essays 1974-1999
Focusing and Listening
A Remembrance: Spring Hill and Opening the Heart
On Focusing
You Cannot Stay on the Summit Forever: Talks and Stories From
 The Opening The Heart Workshop
Therapeutic Essays
Experiential Therapy and Focusing
The Social Nature of Psychological Research

A NOTE ON A NAME

The name of the man who discovered focusing is Dr. Eugene T. Gendlin. I have known him for twenty-five years. When I think about him, talk to him "in my head" (e.g., "Now, listen. . . "), or write about him informally, he is "Gene." When I write about him formally, he is either "Gene Gendlin" or "Gendlin." All these different ways of referring to him have found their way into this book.

A NOTE ON THE PUBLICATION DATE

I had intended for this book to be my last publication of 1999. Life intervened. It is my first publication of 2000. I like the symbolism. What began as an ending, ends as a beginning. It is a promising way to kick off the 21st century.

One of the most wondrous discoveries of all [in therapy] was the slowly dawning awareness of the presence of a formerly subliminal, continuously changing stream of inner experience. The range, richness, Heraclitean, and awesome nature of this internal universe amazed and continues to amaze me. Here was an ever-present, but formerly unsuspected veritable internal universe. After a couple of months, I began to perceive more clearly a constant flux of visual images. One of the most exciting of many exciting memories is that of the sudden recognition that these images exquisitely symbolized what I was feeling and experiencing in each moment. Here was a previously unsuspected gold mine of information about myself and the meaning of my experiences.

—Roger Walsh

I, on my side, require of every writer, first or last, a simple and sincere account of his own life, and not merely what he has heard of other men's lives.

—Henry David Thoreau
Walden

Only Ernest could cure Ernest, and the remedy was at hand. He need only begin again to write. . . Therein lay the cure.

—Michael Reynolds
Hemingway: The Final Years

INTRODUCTION : AN OVERVIEW OF THIS BOOK

Since 1976 I have written thirty-eight pieces on focusing. Twenty-six are collected in this volume. Thirteen have appeared in *The Focusing Connection*, three in *The Focusing Folio*, two in *Experiential Therapy and Focusing*, two in *On Focusing*, two in *Focusing and Listening* and one each in *Psychotherapy: Theory, Research and Practice, The Journal for Humanistic Psychology*, and *The New York Chapter for Humanistic Psychology Newsletter*. One is dressed up to go out in public for the first time in this book. They are "Neil Friedman's Best Writings Thus Far on Focusing."

    I did not set out to make a mini-career writing about focusing. Ann Weiser Cornell deserves an assist. In 1982 she asked me to be on the Editorial Board for the *Focusing Connection*. I accepted. I have been there ever since. I have done little to nothing toward editing the newsletter. But the position has given me a stake in it. I have sent Ann fourteen mostly handwritten pieces. She has published thirteen.[1] She has provided me a remarkably reliable outlet for writing on focusing. She is about to find out how important she has been.

    Here is what happens under less auspicious circumstances. In 1980 I wrote "Experiential Listening." I submitted it to *The Person-Centered Review*. The editor sent it to two readers. Germaine Lietaer loved it. The second reader gave a detailed critique and voted against its being published. The editor asked me to incorporate the criticisms and cut the length by one-third.

I did not agree with the critique. I liked the essay at its original length. I never re-submitted it. I published it as one chapter in *Therapeutic Essays* (1987). I put it in the back of my file cabinet. I never sent another piece to the *Review*. I have never sent the piece to any other journal.

The story has a happy ending. In 1998 Joan Klagsbrun used the paper in her training-group for focusing-oriented therapists. They loved it. I re-read it. It had always been for me a companion piece to "On Focusing" (1986). I suddenly saw how to change the opening of "On Focusing", with which I had never been satisfied. I rewrote it. Together I self-published the two essays as *Focusing and Listening* (1999)— seventeen years after I had submitted the Listening piece to the *Review*.

The point is that there was a time in my life when I lacked a stubborn persistence, rapid recovery from rejection, and flexible determination about resubmitting my writing to someone else's notion of what deserved publication.[2] That period lasted from 1968 to, well, now. Ann Weiser Cornell's near-total acceptance of my writings has helped keep the flow going. I have had an outlet for my writing about focusing.

Thanks, Ann.

II

This book consists of twenty-six focusing-related writings. I have had some fun and some headaches deciding how to organize them. After a combination of playfulness of spirit and despairing travail, I decided on five categories:

- **In The Beginning** refers to my time in New York (1973-1981) during which I met Gene Gendlin, focusing, and—as he called it then—experiential psychotherapy. I was living in New York City, building a private practice and commuting to teach at the School of Social

Welfare at Stony Brook, on Long Island. I describe how focusing came into my life. I reprint my review of FOCUSING. And I include the very first piece I ever published that was influenced by Gene's work: a history of the experiential in psychotherapy.

- **Focusing** is a collection of articles that could be called A Focusing Manual. They are about the basic concepts and processes of focusing. They are my contributions to the teaching of focusing. It is interesting to me that the oldest article in this section was not published until 1986—twelve years after I met Gene. It was that long before I felt confident that I had something to say about teaching and learning focusing.

- **Focusing and Psychotherapy** was the most difficult section to organize. This was partly because of the number of things I have written on the topic. It was partly because my writings stretched from 1976 to 1999. It was partly because during that time Gene changed what he called his therapy from Experiential Psychotherapy to Focusing-Oriented Psychotherapy. And it was partly because I wanted to introduce yet another term for our therapy: Focusing-Oriented Experiential Therapy.

    The essays are all over the place. They include a theory piece, case reports, a comparison with another theory of therapy, pieces about different aspects of my therapy, and descriptions of how I do therapy. There is no summary piece. In the prologue to the section I do attempt a road map to help the reader through the thicket.

- **Focusing and Meditation** consists of three pieces I wrote between 1988 and 1991 and a brand-new piece looking back at them and the subject of focusing and meditation again. I was struggling in the earlier essays to carve out a clear distinction between focusing and meditation and then to comment upon their compatibilities and incompatibilities. Being on the Internet focusing discussion list helped me do the fourth article.

I am a sporadic, erratic, and eclectic mediator. I am not an expert at meditation. Yet the first three articles just came tumbling out. Natural childbirth. The fourth was definitely Caesarian.

- **Focusing and Miracles** was the last section to get named. A miracle is something good that cannot be explained by one's governing paradigm of explanation. There are events in these papers that I cannot explain. Mostly I don't feel a need to explain them. They all happened. They are or are about miracles. And they are related to focusing.

There is, Dear Reader, no reason whatsoever for you to read these pieces in order or, for that matter, to read all of them. (I do expect my mother to do so.) To everyone else—read the ones you are drawn to. Read the ones that speak to you. Read the ones you missed. Read the new ones. Read the ones that match your special interest. Read the ones that don't match your special interest. Read your favorites.

There will be no final exam.

III

To put together this book I have had to re-read twenty-five years of my writings on focusing. The task has been daunting but relatively painless. I still like a lot of the articles. Or, perhaps I should say, I don't dislike too many of them too much. I am talking about the writing qua writing. I have made revisions in several articles. I have corrected spelling, punctuation, and typos. I have changed some titles. I have added and deleted sentences and paragraphs. I have improved (I hope) the writing. (I have also retained slight differences in style: e.g., roman numerals between sections in some essays; sub-headings in others; nothing in others.)

My changes in literary style have been consistent and instructive.

Compound sentences have become simple sentences. Complex sentences have become simple sentences. Semicolons have become periods. Commas, 'ands,' and 'buts' have been removed. Subordinate clauses have either disappeared or become whole sentences. Adjectives and adverbs have been reduced by 25%. Sentences have become shorter. Words shorter. The total number of syllables per paragraph has been reduced. Monosyllabic words have increased by 15%. One, two, and three word incomplete sentences have multiplied. Except where they haven't.

The paring down is not 100%. I have kept some 'club-sandwich' size sentences. They are among my favorites.[3] Although I have generally put my writing on a diet, the remaining plump sentences stand out more now against the background of slim, spare, crisp, plain, simple English.

The reasons for this change are autobiographical. My 'un-self-conscious' writing style has always tended towards the down-to-earth, unpretentious, and first-person singular. My early writing role models were Henry David Thoreau and James Baldwin.

Thoreau is a master of the first-person singular:

> I, on my side, require of every writer, first or last, a simple and sincere account. . .
>
> I would fain say something, not so much concerning the Chinese and Sandwich islanders, as you who read these pages. . .

And the short aphorism:
> The mass of men live lives of quiet desperation.
> That government is best which governs not at all.

James Baldwin is also a first-person writer:
> I am the man. I was there. I suffered.
> I want to be an honest man and a good writer.

But he is also given to flourishes of lyrical, complex, and sometimes murky elegiac writing:

> And now—now it seemed that they were all equal in misery, confusion, and despair... And something in him was breaking; he was, briefly and horribly, in a region where there were no definitions of any kind, neither of color, nor of male and female. There were only the leap and the rending and the terror and the surrender. And the terror: which all seemed to begin and end and begin again—forever—in a cavern behind the eye. And whatever stalked there *saw*, and spread the news of what it saw throughout the entire kingdom of whomever though the eye itself might perish. What order could prevail against so grim a privacy? And yet, without order, of what value was the mystery? *Set thine house in order* . . .

In 1987, at Coki Beach, in St. Thomas, I read Ernest Hemingway's *For Whom the Bell Tolls*. The ending left me crying into my goggles while snorkeling.[4] It was the first Hemingway I had ever read. I soon read six more books by him. And then I stumbled upon *Ernest Hemingway on Writing*. It is a collection of simple sentence or single paragraph entries on the writer's craft:

— The secret is that it is poetry written into prose.
— Good writing is true writing.

— The hardest thing in the world to do is to write straight, honest prose on human beings.
— Write the truest sentence that you know.
— On *The Star* [a newspaper], you were forced to learn to write a simple declarative sentence. This is useful to anyone.

Hemingway pushed Baldwin a little to the side. Hemingway's lean prose became the ground to my writing—just as focusing is the ground to my doing therapy. My more lyrical flourishes—and my soft spot for sometimes well-chosen adjectives and adverbs—stand out more now from their Hemingway-ish background—just as my more expressive interventions do in my focusing-oriented therapy. I do Hemingway-oriented writing.

I have gone on at such length because writing matters to me. Writing ought to come from the heart. Writing ought to be an extension of one's focusing. I put on the page what I have 'seen' in my focusing. I include the 'I.'

Writing matters to me in at least three senses. It matters to my mental health whether I am writing or not. (It is much harder for me to be neurotic when I am writing.) I cannot read bad prose even when the content is rumored to be important. And I take pride in my own writing. Like doing therapy, writing is also my craft and vocation. In my not-so-secret heart of hearts I am a writer almost as much as I am a therapist.

IV

This book is a "summing-up-thus-far." In the Conclusion I have some things to say about where I see focusing going now as the century turns. Here I want to be more personal.

I started therapy in 1973 at the age of thirty-three. This was one and one-half years before I met Gene. My life was in shambles—as it has been periodically. I think of myself before 1973 as my "pre-therapy, relatively unconscious self." I think of myself since 1973 as my "in therapy, becoming more conscious self." I am a work-in-progress.

There have been three major influences on my therapized-and-becoming-more-conscious self.

The first was Leida Berg. I began seeing her on April 13, 1973. She was a seventy-five-year-old Park Avenue psychiatrist who always wore what I thought of as opera clothes. She smoked cigarette after cigarette through a long, black, ever-so-delicate cigarette holder. When I asked her—accusingly—why she smoked, she replied, "Because I love it!"

Leida was a tough, confrontational existential therapist. She had been analyzed by Abraham Kardiner. At some point she had thrown out her psychoanalytic textbooks and become herself. She was haughty, tough, and absolutely right-on. She had x-ray vision. She was the first person to lovingly assault me with the question, "And what are you feeling?"

My therapy with her was very cathartic, very helpful in getting me to reclaim and express my anger, and led to large life-changes rather quickly (Friedman, 1981).

You will see in a minute why I now skip to the third influence on my therapized self. It was the Opening the Heart workshop at Spring Hill, in Ashby, Massachusetts. It found me in 1982. I was at another ebb tide. I had been there for eight months.

The Heart workshop is a loud, intense, body-centered, cathartic experience. It is a weekend marathon that wears down mind and body and opens the heart (Friedman, 1987).

My first experience as a participant in the Heart workshop ended my depression. The depression did not return for ten years. During that time Spring Hill remained in my life as I became a Heart staff member (1983-1998) and, for a while, co-director of Spring Hill (1985-1988).

In between these two intensities stands focusing. It was the second influence on my becoming more conscious self. It began with Gene in December, 1974, and has continued to this day to be absolutely central to who I am and what I do. I am a focusing-oriented therapist and a focusing-oriented person. Focusing—a quiet, inward, non-violent way to befriend and accurately symbolize fine discernments of felt senses—focusing is basic to my self-therapy and professional therapeutic work. The more expressive and cathartic work that comes from Leida and the Heart workshop depends upon and grows out of the ground of focusing.

I resonate with focusing more than I do with the other two. I am not like Leida. I do not relish and take delight in an angry-exchange therapy. I am not as confrontational. I can't be her.

And after two open-heart surgeries of the medical kind, my body is not as at home with the Heart work as it once was.

Another way to say all this: Leida died. Spring Hill closed down. And through it all, focusing and I keep on truckin'.

Come along with me now as I share my life in focusing with you.

PART ONE
IN THE BEGINNING

PROLOGUE

He will hate the connotations of the next sentence.

In the beginning there was Gene Gendlin.

I met him on December 12, 1974. He came and demonstrated focusing to a supervision group I was leading. It was one of the most fateful meetings of my life.

Actually, I had visited with him for about a half-hour, nine years before. In 1974 neither of us remembered that meeting.

In 1965 I was finishing my Ph.D. thesis at Harvard. I was considering a first teaching job. The candidates were Miles College, in Birmingham, Alabama, (a Black college) and the University of Chicago.

I was pretty sure I was going to Miles. I wanted to do civil rights work. I wanted to be part of history.

The University of Chicago flew me out for a look-see. I remember next to nothing of that trip.

I met Gene on that trip.

How do I know that? I was in the process then of finishing my first book. Footnote 15 of my *The Social Nature of Psychological Research* reads:

> Actually, as Eugene Gendlin first suggested to me [my results] can be seen as an attempt to suggest the interpersonal dimensions which might have to be considered in a definition of empathy (1968, p. 108).

It was one time when I was re-reading my book and found that footnote that I remembered Gene sitting on a sofa, in Chicago, below a non-representational painting that was primarily a white canvas with small size rectangles and perhaps other shapes in various bright colors. Gene confirmed the existence and the site of such a painting. He was one of the Chicago faculty that I had met.

I went to teach at Miles. Had I taken Chicago's offer, it is intriguing to speculate that I might have been involved in the very beginnings of Changes.

I remembered none of this, that Friday afternoon in 1974.

The first piece in this section, "How Focusing Came Into My Life," begins with that Friday morning class.

The second piece is my review of the hardcover edition of *Focusing*, published by Everest Press. I am struck by how much of that early review has become part of my standard way of introducing focusing. I always cite the research from which focusing came. My flyer for a focusing workshop always has a sentence that uses the structure "Focusing is an A, B, C way of getting in touch with one's whole felt sense of an X, Y, Z, and through steps, achieving a felt shift, a piece of bodily resolution of the issue." You will meet that sentence structure again in this book. And you will meet it in the review.

The review also indicates how much Gene and focusing had already come to mean to me. The review was probably written in 1977. Gene had already left New York. I had had about three years' experience with focusing.

The mini-focusing I do in the review, in which there are tears and "love and gratefulness," is about how I felt then towards Gene and focusing.

The third and longest piece in this section is my very first published piece on Gene's work. I wrote it with his help. As editor of the journal *Psychotherapy: Theory, Research, and Practice*, he was able to accept it for publication as soon as one reader just barely voted for its acceptance!

If you aren't into the history of experiential psychotherapy, skip it.

The article gives a good picture of where I was vis-a-vis the psychotherapy world at that time.

I had had an existential/experiential therapy with Leida Berg.

In conjunction with my work with Leida I had read some existential writings on psychotherapy, of which Rollo May's *Existence* and Mullan and Sanguillano's *The Therapist's Contribution to the Treatment Process* were the most memorable.

At the same time (1975-1977), I was teaching "How People Change: Theories of Psychotherapy" in the MSW program at Stony Brook. In the course, I began with Freud and the Freudians, touched on the Interpersonal School and ended with Rogers and Gendlin. Gene helped me organize the course around the role of the experiential in therapy.

At the same time, I was still quite outspokenly political. I had written "Inequality, Social Control, and Educational Reform" (1972). I had taught a course on Imperialism. Two women students had asked me to be their advisor for a thesis on Women's Consciousness-Raising groups.

All these influences can be seen in the paper. It was also a lecture for my How People Change course.

Further lectures[1] indicate that I was working towards an academic, theoretical, and historical book on Experiential Therapy—which is what Gene called his work then. The lectures come from 1978. The next year I took a leave to build up my clinical practice. The following year I sought to extend the leave. The Dean said no. I was a tenured faculty member. I had to either come back to academia full time or quit a lifetime-guaranteed job.

I quit.

The academic book never got written. I became a full-time Focusing-oriented experiential psychotherapist.

I have never regretted that decision.

I left Stony Brook in a student's car. The car was a convertible. The building that housed Social Welfare was the one tall building in the area.

Driving away, I said that I was going to take one look back at the building and never look at it again.

I turned in my seat. I took a look. I turned back towards the front. My new life was ahead of me. I did not look back again.

HOW FOCUSING CAME INTO MY LIFE

It was December, 1974. I was living in New York City. I had been in therapy for a year. The therapy had already led to a career move. I was a beginning therapist. I was volunteering my services at a men's counseling center. The receptionist was in therapy with a friend of Gene Gendlin's. He told me that Gene was in New York, teaching at Richmond College, on Staten Island.

There is a gap here. Somehow I got from this contact to calling Gene. I was teaching at the School of Social Welfare, in Stony Brook, New York. I was leading a supervision group in New York City for students at the school who lived in the city. Would Gene come to one of our sessions? Yes. No question of fee was raised. After I told him the group's needs, I remember Gene saying, very caringly, that I should be sure to get something for myself as well.

Gene came and taught focusing. I was impressed. Afterward, he was in a rush. I got into Gene's car and drove cross-town with him. I asked if he would supervise my therapy work. He said yes. We agreed on an incredibly reasonable fee. I began supervision the next week.

Thus began my romance with focusing.

In supervision, I remember listening to about three minutes of a tape with Gene indicating how he would slip in focusing questions and listening responses. I could feel myself learning how to do good therapy.

A few months later, I terminated the therapy I was in and began therapy with Gene. I saw him for a year and a half.[2] Mostly,

I experienced focusing and listening as a client learning from a master practitioner.

During this time Gene was hosting "focusing soirees" at his apartment, one Friday evening a month. Gene would teach focusing. People would pair up and practice. There would be discussion.

These evenings led to a core group of focusers who helped Gene start a Changes group at the McBurney YMCA. On Thursday evenings, anywhere from 15 to 50 people would come for free. I began to lead the newcomers' group.

Watching Gene was an education. One evening, a guy wandered in off the street. He was out of it. Strange, weird. Gene asked for a volunteer. He came forward. I recall thinking, "Uh-oh."

Within minutes, Gene and the guy were in deep contact, like two normal people, one guiding and one following. Gene had him focusing. The hush in the room was profound. I marveled that, in the right hands, such a simple technique could do so much. At about that time I committed myself to focusing.

FOCUSING, EUGENE T. GENDLIN. NEW YORK: EVEREST BOOKS, 1979.

This is an important book. How do people change? What must the client be able to do in order to get something worthwhile out of therapy? To research these questions, Gene Gendlin and his associates listened to thousands of hours of therapy tapes. They concluded that for therapy to work the client must talk in a certain way, a special way. Gendlin calls this way "focusing." Focusing is happening when words come from and point to one's experiencing process.

Having identified focusing as the essential ingredient in successful therapy, Gendlin proceeded to conceptualize it as a skill that could be taught. In simple, vivid, demystified language, this book presents the wisdom accumulated in his [at that time] fifteen years of teaching focusing.

Focusing is a quiet, to-oneself, inward, quasi-meditative way of getting in touch with one's whole *felt sense* of a problem or issue, and, through steps, achieving a *felt shift*, a piece of bodily resolution of the issue. Focusing teaches a person how to stay in a friendly way with the fuzzy, as-yet-unclear felt edge of a problem and, through asking open-ended questions of it, to find symbols for what has been implicit, not yet fully formed. This "carrying forward" of one's experiencing process becomes the basis for therapeutic change.

A "felt sense" is not just an emotion and a "felt shift" is not just a discharge. The concepts refer to the more subtle, finely differentiated internal acts, which Gendlin is masterful at describing. For example, my felt sense right now is one of excitement. . . a special kind of excitement that is more than just excitement. As I write the word "excitement" I feel sensations more sharply in my stomach. . . and then tears start to rush toward my eyes. Along with the tears the words "love and gratefulness" come. The felt sense now has shifted. Were I to stay now with that "love and gratefulness" feeling I would get further movement, more of a sense of "all about that." Such is the basic idea of focusing: I have immediate access to my concrete, bodily felt existence and can use it as a resource.

The book begins with a discussion of how focusing originated and what it is and is not. Then comes a focusing manual designated to be used by the reader in a self-help way to learn how to focus. This is followed by four troubleshooting chapters which describe various ways of dealing with typical focusing blocks. Four chapters on listening and the wider social implications of focusing conclude the main text. (The listening chapters are not quite adequately integrated into the book.) An appendix consists of a skimpy philosophical note, a review of the research on focusing, a nationwide directory of people who teach focusing, and a short form to use while focusing.

What makes the book so valuable? Foremost, if Gendlin is correct, he has made available to professionals, clients and the general public the one skill common to all good therapy.[3] Second, he has presented it in basic, pictorial, homey English spiced with tasty examples. Third, except for four terrible hype sentences, the book has a positive but not boundless tone that makes it to me more believable than most self-help cure-all books. Finally, it is refreshing to read a distinguished philosopher and therapist debunking experts and talking about the wisdom in us all.

The book is no substitute for experiencing focusing and listening. It may make them seem easier to learn than they are. But when combined with experiential skill-training, the book may just give the reader most of what it promises. And that is saying a lot.

FROM THE EXPERIENTIAL IN THERAPY TO EXPERIENTIAL PSYCHOTHERAPY: A HISTORY

> There are two modes of knowledge, through argument and through experience. Argument brings conclusions and compels us to believe them, but it does not cause certainty nor remove doubts in order that the mind may remain at rest in truth, unless this is provided in experience.
>
> — Roger Bacon, 1268

Experiential therapy aims to "stay in touch at all times with the person's [client's, patient's] directly felt concrete experiential datum. . . and help the person also to stay in touch with that, and get into it" (Gendlin, CC & ET, 13). In experiential therapy the touchstone of therapeutic intervention is the feeling process in the client. The goal is for therapist and client to achieve a deep resonance with the client's felt experiencing at the moment, going with it, getting deeper into it, moving with it, keeping it company, helping the client to open himself to his experience, embrace it, take a friendly stance towards it, and beckon it to teach him. Experiential therapy is not primarily another school, another method, but a meta-orientation, a certain way of using various vocabularies, theories, and procedures. "A therapist calls himself 'experiential' if the emphasis is on the concrete, lived, and felt steps of the patient" (Gendlin, ET, 321). Experiential therapy focuses on being rather than talking about, on the ongoing, lived, present flow of experience, what *is* rather than what should be, could have been, or may be. The client's whole felt sense of the "now" with its implicit richness—such is the focus of the experiential orientation in psychotherapy.

Before there was an experiential therapy there was the experiential in therapy. It has always been there in good therapy. It is not the possession of any one school. I want to call attention to the continuity in the history of therapeutic technique by tracing the experiential theme through the works of several theorists of individual therapy. Then I want to touch upon five general cultural trends which also contribute to the historical matrix from which the current experiential therapy is emerging. To this end I will construct a history that makes reference to Freud, Rank, Ferenczi, Reich, Fromm-Reichmann, The Sullivanians, Horney, Angyal, Gendlin, Rogers, play therapy, the encounter movement, existentialism, consciousness-raising, and 'transpersonal' disciplines.

Freud

The debate over the role of the experiential in therapy begins with Freud. For him, in the beginning, there was no need for the patient to experience anything: purely intellectual self-knowledge, impersonal insight, was sufficient for change. Enlightenment could come from outside. Freud wrote:

> In the early days of analytic technique it is true that we regarded the matter intellectually and set a high value on the patient's knowledge of that which had been forgotten, so that we hardly made a distinction between our knowledge and his in these matters. We accounted it specially

fortunate if it were possible to obtain information of the forgotten traumas of childhood from external sources, from parents or nurses, for instance, or from the seducer himself, as occurred occasionally; and we hastened to convey the information and proofs of its correctness to the patient in the certain expectation of bringing the neurosis and the treatment to rapid end by this means. It was a bitter disappointment when the expected success was not forthcoming (Coll. Papers, Vol.2, 362).

From this disappointment Freud groped towards and emerged ultimately with a somewhat more experiential conception of therapy. In *Beyond the Pleasure Principle* he wrote that "Twenty-five years of intense work have had as their result that the immediate aims of psychoanalytic technique are quite other today than they were at the outset." Freud goes on to state that neither direct interpretation of the unconscious nor even interpretation of resistances will force the patient to "*remember* the whole of what is repressed in him" (my emphasis). Thus, Freud comes to a more experiential conception of therapy. The patient "is obliged to repeat the repressed material as a *contemporary experience* . . . the patient must *re-experience* some portion of his forgotten life" (Freud, BPP, 12-13, my emphasis).

We shall see that this *reliving of past experience in the present* is but one of the ways that the experiential can be brought into therapy. However, it is well worth underscoring that in his late writing on technique Freud clearly indicates that his older, primarily cognitive conceptions of therapeutic change must be expanded to find room, side-by-side, for the concept of experience. Hence, Freud's progress is clearly in the experiential direction.

Yet, his *emphasis* remains more cognitive than not. The analyst would still "*prefer* . . . [the patient's] remembering it [the repressed memory] as something belonging to the past" (p. 12, my emphasis). The experiential is granted entrance somewhat reluctantly and only as a repetition of the past. The concepts of resistance, transference, and counter-transference are the Freudian words for talking about what is going on in the experience between therapist and patient. But they are essentially *negative* constructs. The resistance is to be conquered, the transference managed, the counter-transference resolved. Thus, to the extent that the experiential in therapy enters via Freud, it enters as repetition and obstacle, as that which blocks the associative flow, which, rather than the experiential flow, is the psychoanalytic touchstone.

Rank and Ferenczi

A history of advances in the theory of analytic technique after Freud can be constructed around the increased and expanded conception of the role of experience. In 1923, when Rank and Ferenczi published *The Development of Psychoanalysis*, they referred to Freud's work as The Stage of Enlightenment ("making the unconscious conscious") and their own as The Stage of Experience. They emphasized the importance of current realities in treatment. They suggested that to be therapeutically successful an analysis needed to be more than an intellectual reconstruction of the patient's early childhood years. It had also to be a genuine reliving. They wrote, "one might be tempted to ask oneself whether our therapeutic analyses have not up to now been too 'didactic' . . . " (Rank and Ferenczi, p. 60).

Still later, Rank defined the therapeutic purpose to be "to allow the patient to understand himself in an immediate experience which . . . permits living and understanding to become one" (cited in Gendlin, ET, 319). He affirmed that "the feeling of experience is made the central factor in the therapeutic task . . . the therapeutic process is lifted from an intellectual training which every kind of 'making conscious' implies to the sphere of experience" (Rank, p. 5).

Reich

Freud was saying as much but apparently without impact on his followers. Reich complained, on the basis of his experience in the Vienna psychoanalytic seminar, that "while the principles of resistance technique are generally known and acknowledged, in practice one proceeds almost exclusively according to the old technique of direct interpretation of the unconscious. The result is analyses that are didactically rich and poor in success where the patient acquires a good knowledge of psychoanalytic theory but is not cured." He offers a charming example:

> A patient with a number of perversions had been under analysis for eight months during which time he had rattled on incessantly and had yielded material from the deepest layers of his unconscious. This material had been continuously interpreted. The more it was interpreted, the more copiously flowed the stream of associations. Finally the analysis had to be broken off for external reasons, and the patient came to me . . . he knew, for instance, how to give an exact description of the more intricate mechanisms of the simple and double Oedipus complex. I asked the patient whether he really believed what he was saying and what he had heard. 'Are you kidding,' he exclaimed, 'I really have to contain myself not to burst out laughing at all this.' (Reich, p. 26)

Character analysis is designed to focus the analysis on the immediate experience. In order to get emotion into the sessions, to make the analysis really take hold, to keep it from becoming sterile, arid, academic, the analyst is to focus on the way the patient is living with him at the moment: "The way the patient speaks, looks and greets the analyst, lies on the couch, the inflection of the voice, the degree of conventional politeness which is maintained. . . character resistance is expressed not in terms of content but formally, in the way one typically behaves. . . It is not what the patient says and does. . . but *how* he speaks and acts. . . " (Reich, 49-51).

Reich draws the analyst's attention to the present and the

relationship. Yet he still conceptualizes all this present-centered and relationship-centered material negatively. It is still "resistance" whose contemporary meaning needs to be interpreted, so that it can cease blocking the emergence of childhood memories. The sniffing out of the contemporary meaning of the resistance remains merely preparatory work: "Through the analysis of the character resistance, we arrive at the center of the neurosis, the Oedipus complex" (Reich, 55).

Fromm-Reichmann and the Sullivanians

The Interpersonal School contributes a shift in emphasis. The experiential no longer enters therapy merely as resistance or repetition. It is now valued in its own right. Sullivan conceived of the therapist as a full participant-observer in the therapy situation. Freida Fromm-Reichmann is reported to have said, "The patient needs an experience, not an explanation." (cited by May, 81)[4]

It is through *the interpersonal interaction* that experience comes in. Fromm-Reichmann and Sullivan emphasized the therapeutic power of the interpersonal relationship of therapist and patient as experienced by both. As a Sullivanian text puts it:

> The patient's experience of the relationship with his therapist has a direct impact on thoughts available to consciousness, and on the balance of forces within the patient's personality . . (Pearce and Newton, p. 320).
> The exciting process of interaction, of getting progressively more intimate, better and better acquainted with another human being, is a compelling and exciting experience. . . (p. 324).

Cherishing, validation, and tenderness are mentioned as being necessary parts of the experience of the relationship. The relationship facilitates moments of experiential truth. We see a fictionalized version of such a moment in this excerpt from *I Never*

Promised You a Rose Garden. Dr. Fried is Frieda Fromm-Reichmann. Her moment-to-moment sensitivity to what is going on in the interaction with her client, Deborah, leads to a re-experiencing of a crucial childhood event. Dr. Fried begins summarizing where they are:

> 'It was a willing soil then, to which this seed of YR came,' the doctor said, 'The deceits of the grown-up world, the great gap between Grandfather's pretensions and the world you saw. . .'
> 'The gap between the carefully brought up little rich girl with nails and imported dresses and the—and the—'
> 'And the what? Where are you now?'
> 'I don't know', she said, but she was speaking from a place in which she had been before. 'There are no colors, only shades of gray. She is big and white. I am small and there are bars between. She gives food. Gray. I don't eat. Where is my. . . my. . .'' 'Your what?'
> 'Salvation!' Deborah blurted.
> 'Go on," the doctor said.
> 'My. . . self, my love.'
> Dr. Fried peered at her intently for a while and then said, 'I have a hunch—do you want to try it with me?'
> 'Do you trust me with it?'
> 'Certainly, or there wouldn't be this science at all, where the two of us work together. Your own basic knowledge of yourself and truth is sound. Believe in it.'
> 'Go ahead then, or psychiatry will disappear.'
> (Laughter)
> 'Your mother had trouble with a pregnancy when you were very small, did she not?'
> 'Yes, she miscarried. Twins.'
> 'And afterward went away to rest for a while?'
> The light struck the past and there was a seeming sound of good strong truth, like the pop of a hard-thrown ball into a

> catcher's glove. Connect. . . 'The white thing must have been a nurse. I felt that everything warm had left. The feeling comes often, but I thought it could never have been true that I ever really was in such a place. The bars were crib bars. They must have been on my own crib. . . The nurse was distant and cold. . . *Hey! Hey!* The now-friendly light struck something else and its suddenness made the small, prosaic connection seem like a revelation full of greatness and wonder. 'The bars. . . the bars of the crib and the cold and losing the ability to see colors. . . it's what happens *NOW*. It's part of the Pit—it's what happens *Now*, NOW!' The rush of words ended and Dr. Fried smiled. 'It is as big, then, as abandonment and the going away of all love' (Green, p. 98).

Horney

Another analyst whose theoretical system came to emphasize the role of the experiential in therapy is Karen Horney. She first reviews the history of the development of psychoanalytic technique in terms not unlike our own:

> In the history of psychoanalysis intellectual knowledge at first seemed to be a curative agent. At that time it meant the emergence of childhood memories. The overrating of intellectual mastery also showed at that time in the expectation that the mere recognition of the irrationality of some trend would suffice to set things right. [Then] the pendulum swung to the other extreme: the emotional experiencing of a factor becomes all important and has since been stressed in various ways. As a matter of fact this shift in emphasis seems to be characteristic of the progress of most analysts. *Each one seems to need to rediscover for himself the importance of emotional experience.* (Horney, 343n, my emphasis)

Horney goes on to indicate that "mere intellectual realization" on the part of a patient is no *real*ization at all; "it does not become his personal property; it does not take roots in him." He *knows about* but does not really *know* his existence. Horney adds that "only when experiencing the full impact in its irrationality of a hitherto unconscious or semi-conscious feeling or drive do we gradually come to know the intensity and the compulsiveness of unconscious forces operating within ourselves. . . It is not enough [for the patient] to know vaguely that his anger or self-reproach is probably greater than warranted by the occasion. He must *feel* the full impact of his rage or the very depths of his self-condemnation: only then does the force of some unconscious process. . . stare him in the face" (Horney, 343-344).

In notes based on a lecture of Horney, Sara Sheiner writes that in such an experience the person is fully present, integrated, no longer partialled out, and this has an exhilarating and liberating effect. The opposition to the neurosis is mobilized in the fact of fully experiencing it in one's depths (Sheiner, 88-90).

Angyal

In a relatively unknown jewel of a book, *Neurosis and Treatment*, Andras Angyal set forth an entire theory of human nature, personality, development, neurosis, health and treatment, a theory which is at once psychodynamic and existential. In his discussion of therapy Angyal refers to a group of inexperienced therapists whose supervisor left them in the middle of the year. They became cautious. "The zip went out of their work; it became lifeless. Such work, no matter how 'correct', is useless because thoughts in themselves are ineffectual; only emotions, the primal valuative experiences. . . can motivate us for action and change."

Angyal goes on about what he calls "the drama in therapy":

> Whatever else the therapist does, he must see to it that the sessions do not drag and become humdrum. . . A sense of

vitality should pervade the therapeutic hour... the sessions should be maintained at a high emotional pitch... Discussions conducted in generalized abstract terms are more apt to kill feelings than to evoke them... The therapist must help the patient recapture the true drama of being alive, of which his neurosis has robbed him. Every therapist who is keenly aware of what neurosis does to the patient's life will develop his own style of conveying to him that something very important is going on in the sessions, and that we are not here to twiddle our thumbs. If the therapist himself is not alive to this, or lets himself be diverted from his central task by a search for specific connections, or by fascinating discoveries, he is not functioning as a therapist. (Angyal, pp. 247-248)

Rogers and Gendlin

With the work of Carl Rogers and Eugene Gendlin, we move for the first time in this review from the recognition of a role for experience in therapy to the origins of an experiential therapy.

Hart (1973) has divided Carl Rogers' work into three broad periods. The first (1940-1950) is called non-directive psychotherapy. The therapist attempted to facilitate the client's gradual achievement of insight "by creating a permissive, non-authoritarian setting in which the client was free to proceed at his own pace and his own directions... therapist responses such as giving advice, expressing opinions or feelings, interpretations, offering plans, and other interventive activities were eschewed."

The second (1950-1957) is the period of reflective psychotherapy. Feelings are given more emphasis than in the first period. As Hart puts it, "the most striking change... was the therapists' emphasis on responding sensitively to the affective rather than the semantic meaning of a client's expressions." The main—or sole—method during this period is the reflection of feelings. "The counselor makes a maximum effort to get under the skin of the person. . . to get within and to live the attitudes observed. . . to absorb himself completely in the attitudes of the client."

This is not yet an experiential therapy. Three steps are missing. (1) The therapist is limited to one technique—reflection of feelings; (2) The therapist is limited to role-playing a perfectly neutral acceptance of the client; (3) There is no explicit theory of experiencing to underpin the therapeutic work.

Enter Gene Gendlin:

> I came to Rogers' group in Chicago in 1952 from my work in philosophy and my interest in the question: How does raw experience become symbolized? I thought that this happens in psychotherapy. A person struggles with and finds words and other expressions for unclear—but lived—experience. I found that Rogers and his group were not very clear in their own minds just what in the client they were responding to. It was the client's 'message' or 'feelings'. . . In practice the open mindedness and the willingness to let the client lead did usually result in a process of grappling with unclear but sensed experience. However, saying this to therapists usually brought puzzlement. Rogers and others encouraged my theoretical efforts to pin this down. People said things like 'Gene, we're glad you're working on these ephemeral things.' What was felt but undefined by the client was thought to be unmeasurable and incomprehensible and it made people uncomfortable to talk about such a variable. Even when it was included in our research project it was more due to the democratic ways of Rogers' group than to an understanding of the variable. When it correlated with success in therapy while other variables did not, people began to try to understand it more seriously. (personal communication)

Work with schizophrenics combined with Gendlin's theoretical focus on experiencing to move client-centered therapy into a third phase, the phase of experiential therapy:

(1) The client-centered therapist no longer only reflects feelings. The repertoire of therapist responses has been broadened. The therapist may respond expressively to the client. The therapist may share his/her feelings with the client.

(2) The therapist no longer role-plays a perfectly neutral acceptance of the client. As Gendlin puts it, "today client-centered therapists make 'genuineness' the first condition for therapy and therapist-expressivity and spontaneity main therapeutic factors" (Gendlin, E&EP, 210-211). In looking back on his own development as a therapist, Rogers has come to the conclusion that in therapy "*I should be real.* I have come to realize that only when I am able to be a transparently real person and am so perceived by my client can he discover what is real in him. . . " (in May, EP, 86). That is, the therapist's truthfulness to the moment helps the client achieve the same for himself.

(3) What keeps all this from becoming a mere eclectic hodgepodge, a "real" therapist doing whatever he/she feels like, using whatever technique comes to mind without rhyme or reason? *The theory of experiencing underpins therapeutic intervention and the touchstone of effective therapeutic response is the client's own experiencing process.* The question is: Did this particular reflection of feeling or this particular instance of therapist expressivity help the client get in touch with what is real in him/her? As Gendlin sums it up,

> Experiential therapy focuses on the inchoate—the felt sense that someone's words come out of. Therapeutic *movement* (as against mere self-observation or knowing oneself) comes in the act of attending to, responding to, and for some seconds being with what is sensed *under* what is clear. (personal communication)

We shall see below that this explicit theory of experiencing can be combined with various therapeutic modalities and techniques to product an experiential therapy.

Other Influences

Thus far we have reviewed contributions from schools of individual therapy to the emergence of the experiential orientation. Experiential therapy is also being shaped by several other trends—play therapy, the encounter movement, existentialism, consciousness-raising, and transpersonal disciplines.

Play Therapy

A major stumbling block to the recognition of the healing power of "the genuine experience of being" (Sanguillano), has been our cultural bias in favor of reason, knowledge, the intellect, verbal insight—what Roger Bacon called "argument". People will be cured by "talking about." Nicholas Hobbs notes that play therapists have been instrumental in releasing us from this prejudice. He writes:

> In play therapy with young children most therapists do not bother to try to develop insight. Rational formulations are adult fare, a consequence of the adult's addiction to words. Instead, therapists provide children concrete experiences in relationship with a particular kind of adult and get good results (Hobbs, 116).

Strictly speaking, this is not true of all play therapy. Melanie Klein's "play analysis" "was characterized by a very early launching into deep interpretations of the children's behavior" (Dorfman). But most play therapy has been a relationship therapy in which, as Allen puts it, "therapy exists to the extent that it is a meaningful and unique life experience" (213). Verbalizations about presumed internal psychodynamics, profound interpretation of one's psychic machinery, intellectual discussion of one's case history take a back seat to the concrete lived experience—as they do now in experiential therapy. As Gendlin remarks:

> Let us conceive of the individual as not fully formed sentient experiencing, and pay attention to it, respond to it, refer to it, and make room for it, even when silent and without shape. Then let us respond from our own person in whatever way is immediate and plainly real for us, but quickly make room again for attention to the newly moving experiencing in him which we thereby create. For no one can predict what will come next and be referred to next in this newly ongoing further process. How radical this sounds for adult therapy, how obvious it sounds for therapy with children! (Gendlin, E&ET, 233-234)

The Encounter Movement

The Encounter group movement has helped prepare the way for experiential therapy. Through experiences in groups many counselors and counselees alike have seen "how interactions with other persons, unexpected feedback, expression of emotions, and *interaction on the feeling level* have an effect on a person and modify his behavior" (Back, my emphasis). Encounter groups tend to present-centeredness, leader-expressivity, and the facilitation of encounter—defined many years ago by Moreno as "the rare, unforgotten experience of total reciprocity. The encounter is extemporaneous, unstructured, unplanned, unrehearsed... It is 'in the moment' and 'in the here', 'in the now'... " (Moreno in Siroka)[5]

This description of encounter corresponds to the moments of truth (Sanguillano), the existential moments (May), and the peak experiences (Maslow) that experiential therapists consider basic to people-change. The encounter movement enriches our conception of experiential therapy through its emphases (1) that experience does not have to be reliving to be therapeutic; it can be a new living; (2) that the experience of emotional intensity can emerge from interaction with an intensively involved other; and (3) that the self-disclosures of the leader can facilitate the healing process. In return, the philosophy of experiencing offers to the encounter movement an alternative to mere shouting and screaming and crying, divorced from any underpinning in a theory of personal change.

Existentialism

Gendlin (ET, 317-320) has reviewed the contributions of specific existential thinkers to experiential therapy. Here I will confine myself to some observations on how the existential movement in general has helped move therapy in the experiential direction.

A first contribution has been the existentialists' rigorous critique of Freudian metapsychology. The existentialists have generated an alternative to the reductionist view of human nature which has provided an inadequate philosophical basis for much psychoanalytically-oriented psychotherapy. Mullan puts it this way:

> Existence, highlighted by the belief that man is free to choose, is denied and almost effaced by Freudian psychology with its instinctual base and with its emphasis on causality and unconscious motivation. A system which mechanically views the two personalities topographically, dividing them into superego, ego, and id; a system which describes much spontaneous behavior as acting out; a system where transference and counter-transference preempt much of the therapist's thoughts and concerns, and a system which routinely attempts to explain the present on the basis of past experiences is diametrically opposed to existence and an 'existential' method. (Mullan, p. 2).

Existentialism makes several positive contributions too. Its emphasis on the moment, the encounter, "interactional newness" (Mullan and Sanguillano), authenticity, choice, existence preceding essence—all move therapy in an experiential direction. Consider Mullan and Sanguillano:

> ...The immediate experience occurs before (our) knowing the essence of this experience... we view the subjective and the experience as preempting the objective and the explanation. To be sure, both exist concomitantly, but it is only through the... experience that the... explanation becomes genuine. (Mullan & Sanguillano), 1961, p.23)

Consciousness-Raising

The consciousness-raising movement is another force capable of moving psychotherapy in an experiential direction.

Unfortunately, there has been a tendency in both the mental health professions and the women's movement to see consciousness-raising and therapy as opposites. Consciousness-raising groups sometimes have anti-therapy lines; mental health professionals sometimes pooh-pooh "political kaffe klatches."

But there can be a real rapprochement between consciousness-raising and the experiential orientation in therapy. They have much to offer each other. *Both start from a deep respect for feelings.* The Redstockings Manifesto states, "Our politics begin with our feelings... Information derived from our feelings is our only reliable information..." (cited in Eastman).

Two women quoted in a study of the effects of consciousness-raising (Kogel and Wurman, 1975) echo this sentiment. One says of her consciousness-raising experience, "What was new was the fact that they [feelings] were really given importance. I had always had the attitude, 'well, it was just a feeling', if it doesn't make sense on other levels, if it isn't reasonable and logical, then one must somehow get rid of it ... The group made me see that feelings were really important." A second woman adds:

> I think we all got interested in feelings as a phenomenon. We got interested in our own feelings. . . The similarities [to therapy] are definitely around feelings and understanding them and knowing them and leaving space for your feelings and respecting them even and [the same] for your experience. . . therapy and c-r have in common for me sort of grounding me, centering me more. . . if I know my feelings I'm not like a zombie. . .

Both these quotes, of course, could come as well from experiential therapy. In practice, consciousness-raising groups tend to be experiential. But, as in the case of encounter group movement, what is lacking is an explicit theory of how the experience of feelings and the feeling of experience can be curative. Experiential theory can help consciousness-raising explain its own practice.

Transpersonal Disciplines

Finally, a cluster of transpersonal disciplines are also finding a place in that synthesis called experiential therapy. Traditional esoteric psychologies (Zen, yoga, the Sufis), drug-induced altered states of consciousness, schools of meditation and body movement all provide methods, exercises, "ways" for many people to get into their bodily felt experience. These ways minimize the participatory involvement of another. Their inwardness, their emphasis on silent involved self-attention, is thus a modality different from encounter and other group-oriented forms. Their increasing impact on mental health consumers and producers is a further influence in the direction of experiential psychotherapy and a further influence shaping the form of experiential psychotherapy.

Experiential Psychotherapy

From all this there is emerging a rich conception of an experiential orientation in psychotherapy which synthesizes what can be learned from each of the aforementioned sources into a way of being with this particular person just now. During any one hour, the client is now focusing inwardly, in silence, on his/her experiential flow; now describing this experience with feeling to the therapist who chooses either to reflect the feeling back or express what he/she is feeling in response. Now there is a spontaneous interaction between therapist and client as they share this moment between them. Now the client is re-experiencing here and now with this new person feelings from a childhood experience, feelings which will be lived through differently in this particular encounter. Now the flow is blocked. The client loses touch. Client and therapist lose each other. They grope back via whatever avenue they can—inward focusing, reflection of feeling, encountering, therapist expressivity, interpretation etc., to discover what is *now*, that which is *now* sensed but inexplicit, that which can *now* carry the process forward anew.

Such is the emerging way of experiential psychotherapy.[6]

PART TWO
FOCUSING

PROLOGUE

I think of this section as A Focusing Manual. Read it. Follow-up a couple of its references (Gendlin, 1969 & 1981; Cornell, 1996). Find a focusing workshop, class, training, or partner with whom to practice. Bingo! You have begun focusing.

This does not mean that you now know what there is to know about focusing. Far from it. If you focus for a lifetime, you will be learning focusing for a lifetime. Focusing is best related to as a long-term companion. It serves the marathoner better than the sprinter. It may take you ten years to get your black belt in focusing.

This is a start. We all have to start somewhere. There is an art to knowing what and when to start. All focusing veterans were once in the position of staring wide-eyed at some introductory materials.

The first essay, "Experiential Focusing," is my clearest single effort to define, describe, illustrate, and teach focusing. It grows out of—and replaces—an earlier published effort which I have left out of this collection (Friedman, 1986). It is a good starting place.

"Fundamental Concepts of Focusing" was written right after "Experiential Focusing." It is a precis. There is some redundancy. That is not bad. The fundamental concepts:

— the felt sense
— the befriending attitude
— accurate symbolization
— resonating
— the felt shift
— asking and receiving

are worth repeating. One has to 'get' them in one's gut as well as intellectually. Then focusing begins to become part of one's unselfconscious repertoire of habits of daily living. With practice, focusing will become as natural to you as washing, combing your hair, and flossing.

"What Focusing Is and What It Is Not" approaches the same territory from a different angle. It contrasts listening to the mind with listening to the body. It presents focusing as a certain way of relating experiencing and concepts.

"Innovations in How I Lead a Round of Focusing" reviews the eight steps in which I now teach a round of focusing. Then it indicates what seem to me to be my contributions, my particular style, of leading focusing.

"A Typology of Felt Shifts" is also unique. I have never seen anywhere else a specification of intensities and kinds of felt shifts. I hope this essay will help people recognize when a felt shift is happening.

Finally, "Benefits of Focusing" indicates what I think one can get out of focusing. Focusing will not tone the buttocks, shrink an enlarged heart, or rolf the pancreas. But it will do many things. I list ten benefits. There may very well be more.

This section is not complete. There could be a piece on the felt sense. There could be a piece on the limitations of focusing. Some endnotes will touch on these issues.

If you are a practiced focuser, could you skip this section? Sure. Would I suggest you do so? No. Why not? Each of us does and teaches focusing in his/her own way. Whoever your main teacher(s) may be, exposure to others is useful. We each have our own fragrance to add to the realm of focusing.

This is mine.

A story introduces this part.

AN OPENING STORY

I like to begin teaching focusing with a story. Here is the story.

Once upon a time there was a convocation of healers, wizards, sorcerers, therapists, channels, mystics, and disembodied spirits. Each had a time to get up and do his or her particular miracle.

Quite the pyrotechnics! One walked on fire. One hypnotized the entire audience without their knowing it. One foretold the future. One read past lives. One stood on one leg in a bizarre position until his whole body shook. One did medical diagnoses based only on each audience member's name and age.

Then a short, plain-looking man got up. It was his turn. He said, "My miracle is that when I am hungry, I eat; and when I am thirsty, I drink; and I know when I am hungry and when I am thirsty and what I am hungry for and what I am thirsty for."

Then, he sat down.

He was the focuser.

— Adaptation of a Zen Story

EXPERIENTIAL FOCUSING

One of the most wondrous discoveries of all [in therapy] was the slowly dawning awareness of the presence of a formerly subliminal, continuously changing stream of inner experience. The range, richness, Heraclitean, and awesome nature of this internal universe amazed and continues to amaze me. Here was an ever-present, but formerly unsuspected veritable internal universe. After a couple of months, I began to perceive more clearly a constant flux of visual images. One of the most exciting of many exciting memories is that of the sudden recognition that these images exquisitely symbolized what I was feeling and experiencing in each moment. Here was a previously unsuspected gold mine of information about myself and the meaning of my experience.

—Roger Walsh

Growing up, August was my favorite month of the year. My family spent the month at the seashore in Atlantic City, New Jersey.

This was the old Atlantic City, long before the casinos took over. At night we ate out. We walked the boardwalk. We visited the arcades. We played pokerino, skee-ball, and miniature golf.

And—best of all—we spent every sunny day at the beach. I had an ocean ritual that never varied:

We are at the beach by 10 a.m. I run immediately full-speed into the ocean. I get into about four feet of water. I throw myself head-first into the water.

Thud. Splash.

I stay underwater for as long as I can. I come up for air. I shake my hair out of my eyes. I look around. I take in the scene: the seagulls, other bathers, the blueishness of the blue sky. I take in the panoramic view only after my total immersion in the salty Atlantic.

Focusing is our ocean. I am going to throw us right into it. I am going to present one person's full round of focusing step-by-step. Afterward, we will step back, shake the water out of our eyes, and take an overview of focusing.

II

In what follows I am the guide. My client is the focuser. I guide the focuser through the eight steps in which I now teach a round of focusing.

This focuser is quite experienced. He is a virtuoso of his affective life. He is a social worker and a poet. He has come to me for focusing-oriented experiential therapy. This is our twenty-second session. It was tape-recorded. The date is November 12, 1997.[1]

The focuser is sitting in a light tan upholstered chair across from me and to my left. He takes his glasses off and perches them somewhat precariously on the corner of my glass-top table which stands to my left and his right.

In what follows my *focusing instructions* and *listening responses* are in *italics*. His responses and any other comments by me are in regular type face. The words not spoken—my names for the eight steps—are in **bold face**.

He is ready to jump in. He closes his eyes.
I begin guiding:

G: **1. Saying hello**: *Find a comfortable position . . . Relax and close your eyes . . . Take a few deep breaths . . . and when you're ready just ask, "How am I inside right now?" Don't answer. Give an answer time to form in your body . . . Turn your attention like a searchlight into your inside feeling place and just greet whatever you find there . . . Practice taking a friendly attitude toward whatever is there . . . Just listen to your organism . . . (30 seconds of silence)*

F: There is a good feeling—pride—in my chest area. It is about the poem I just finished.

G: *You feel pride in your just-finished poem and the physical feeling is in your chest area.*

F: Yes.

G: Do you want to stay with the feeling or clear a space?[2]

F: Clear a space.

G: **2. Clearing a space . . . Making a list (optional)**: *Now imagine yourself sitting on a park bench. Ask yourself, "What's in the way between me and feeling all fine right now?" Let whatever comes up, come up. Don't go inside any particular thing right now. Just stack each thing at a comfortable distance from you on the bench . . . Take inventory: "What's between me and feeling all fine right now?" [or "What are the main things. . ."] If the list stops, ask, "Except for that am I all fine?" If more comes up, add it to the stack. Stay distanced from your stack. Give me a signal when you're ready for the next step.*

F: I want to acknowledge the good feeling again.

G: Yes, yes. Please do.

F: And now I want to look at . . . the stuff on the bench.

G: Yeah.

F: One imperfect line in the poem . . .

G: Put that on the bench.

F: My fear about money, about having enough to live on.

G: Put that out there.

F: Sadness about aging . . . my adopted child . . . and my wife's withdrawal from me . . . (Big sigh) That is about it right now.

G: So there is . . . the imperfect line from the poem, the fear about money, sadness about—

F: Growing older.

G: —growing older . . . and the adopted child and . . . your wife's withdrawal from you.

F: Yes. (Thirty seconds pause)

G: **3. Picking a problem**: *Now, feel yourself magnetically pulled toward the one thing in your stack that most needs your attention right now . . . If you have any trouble letting it choose you, ask, "What is worst?" (or, "What is best?"—good feelings can be worked with too!) . . . "What most needs some work right now?" . . . "What won't let go of me?" . . . Pick one thing. (short pause)*

F: Our child . . . Maya.

G: OK. (pause: twenty seconds) Ready to move on?

F: Yes.

G: **4. Letting the felt sense form**: *Now ask, "What does this whole thing feel like?" . . . "What is the whole feel of it?" Don't answer with what you already know about it. Listen to your body . . . Sense the issue freshly . . . Give your body 30 seconds to a minute for the feel of "all of that" to form.*

F: (one minute silence; then begins to cry) I DON'T FEEL LIKE SHE IS MINE . . . She is some . . . foreign . . . kid living in our house . . . I mean, she's Indian . . . but that isn't the foreign I mean . . . I have a sick feeling about her in my insides . . . in my middle.

G: *Sick feeling in the middle.* (F: Yes.) *She is foreign to you and it isn't the Indian-ness that is the foreign.*

F: Yes.

G: You may have already done this step but let's just check . . . **5. Finding the handle**: *Find a word, phrase, image,* *sound or gesture that feels like it matches, comes from, or will act as a handle on the felt sense, the whole feel of it. Keep your attention on the area in your body where you feel it, and just let a word, phrase, image, sound or gesture appear that feels like a good fit.*[3]

F: The handle is 'foreign.' She is like a stranger to me (long pause) . . . so is her mother, I mean, my wife. She's so distant.

G: So the child is foreign to you like a stranger and your wife is—

F: Cold.

G: *Cold . . . you are out in the cold vis a vis both of them and the feeling is in the middle of your body.*

Let's just check all that . . . **6. Resonating the handle**: *Say the word, phrase, image, sound or gesture back to yourself . . . Check it against your body . . . See if there is a sense of "rightness," an inner "yes, that's it" . . . If there isn't, gently let go of that handle and let one that fits better appear.*

F: The handle is right . . . It is now about both of them . . . I mean, and me. It is important that it is BOTH of them. Yeah. That gives me a little shift inside.

G: *The "both" gives you a little shift.*

F: Yes.

G: **7. Asking and receiving**: *Now we are going to ask the felt sense some questions. Some it will answer. Some it won't. Receive whatever answers it gives. Ask the questions with an expectantly friendly attitude and be receptive to whatever it sends you.*

Ask, "What's the crux of this feeling?" "What's the main thing about it?" Don't answer with your head; let the body feeling answer.

F: (after thirty seconds) I've never felt like I belonged anywhere . . . not even in my own family of origin.

G: Not even—

F: No.
G: *And ask, "What's the worst of this feeling?" "What makes it so bad?" Wait...*
F: It is the "anywhere"... I've never belonged anywhere.
G: *The worst is the never having belonged "anywhere."*
   And ask, "What's wrong?" Imagine the felt sense as a shy child sitting on a stoop. It needs caring encouragement to speak. Go over to it, sit down, and gently ask, "What's wrong?" Wait...
F: (talks slowly, with pauses, some effort to get the words...) I've always wanted to belong... and no one has ever 'belonged' me.
G: *You've yearned... but no one has ever 'belonged' you.*
F: Yeah.
G: *And ask, "What does this feeling need?"*
F: It needs to feel like I do belong somewhere.
G: *That you do belong somewhere...*
   And now ask, "What is a good small step in the right direction for this thing?" "What is a step in the direction of fresh air?"
F: I just got an image of moving my chair right into the circle... not sitting outside... alone.
G: *A good small step is moving your chair into the circle.*
F: Yes... that's interesting.
G: Something interesting there... (I pause for thirty seconds to see if he has more to say. He does not and so I go on.)
   Ask, "What needs to happen?" "What actions need to be taken?"
F: Moving the chair into...
G: *Moving the chair into...*
F: The circle.
G: *The circle.*
   And now ask, "What would my body feel like if this thing were all better, all resolved?" Move your body

into the position or posture it would be in if this were all cleared up. This is called looking the answer up in the back of the book. Now, from this position, ask, "What's between me and here?" "What's in the way of it being all OK?" Wait . . .

F: You know . . . there is a space in the circle . . . like it is waiting there for me . . . and I"m the one who isn't . . . joining. They're not keeping me out. I'm keeping me out.

G: So if this thing were all better . . .

F: No. No. I didn't follow your instructions.

G: Oh. OK. I see.

F: It is the truth of how it is right now.

G: Oh, I see . . . The issue shifted.

F: Yes.

G: *It is you who doesn't join rather than them keeping you out.*

F: Yes! (strong affirmation)(pause)

G: *Finally, ask your felt sense space to send you the exactly right focusing question you need at this moment . . . Now ask the felt sense that question. Don't answer with your head. Just hang out with the felt sense, keep it company, let it respond. Wait . . .*

F: I want to make sure . . . "Why am I not in the circle?" (chuckles) Because I keep myself out of it. It's a habit. Brilliant! Just brilliant! (laughing) I'd rather bitch, moan, and complain . . . HA! HA! HA!

G: What? (I'm not sure what 'HA! HA! HA!' refers to.)

F: Don't you see?

G: Not yet.

F: It is all MAYA. (Hindu term for illusion) (He breaks into tears for a few minutes.) It is a good name for her . . . yes it is . . . but it is "my maya."

G: You like her name . . .

F: It fits.

G: *The name fits . . . but it is your maya.*
F: You got it.
G: *(A summary statement) Your maya is that THEY keep you out.*
F: YES (a strong YES affirming that he feels really heard and understood).
G: 8. **Coming back**: *OK, now you have a minute to use however you'd like. Some people find it useful to retrace the steps they've come. Some like to stretch and relax. Some find it useful to underline the furthest place they've come to; pitch a tent there so you can come back to it if you want . . . Use this minute however you would like and then open your eyes . . . and this round of focusing is over.*
F: (Yawns . . . stretches hands over head . . . shakes out torso . . . opens eyes . . . puts on glasses.) That was quite a trip!

III

Focusing is quite a trip.

As you have just seen, for me, a focusing round in its entirety is an eight step eyes-closed process through which a guide leads a focuser.

Let us look back now at this example to see what it teaches us about the focusing process.

First, notice what I, the guide, do and don't do.

Mostly I give *focusing instructions* and *listening responses*.

My focusing instructions are printed in full at the end of this essay. There are different types of instructions (e.g., Gendlin, 1981; Cornell, 1996). No set of instructions is sacred. It is good to experience a few different sets and see what works best for you. My set is simply the instructions that I use now. It has evolved over time. I like these instructions.

I will take up listening in detail later. For now, suffice it to say that a listening response is an attempt to say back to another person the felt essence of what he or she has just said. Listening is a way of showing one has understood what has been said. It is a way of keeping a person company.

Now, note what I do not do as the guide. I do not interpret, give advice, fix the problem, tell my own story, or give a mini-lecture on what it is like for a couple to adopt an Indian child. I take pains not to in any way, no matter how subtle, *mangle* the focuser's process.

I give focusing instructions and listening responses.

And I do other things too: I keep pointing out the **bodily** nature of the experiencing ("the physical feeling is in your chest area"); I reinforce the focuser's wanting to acknowledge the good feeling again ("Yes, yes. Please do."). I notice and verbalize when a 'shift' has occurred. ("The 'both' gives you a shift.") I am happy when the focuser ignores my instructions and does something better for himself. ("Oh, I see . . . The issue shifted.") When I don't understand something that seems important ("HA! HA! HA!"), I ask for clarification. And I allow myself a summary statement that stays very close to the focuser's own formulation ("your maya is that **they** keep you out").

Let us look now at the focuser. What does he do? He stays on track. He does not go off into intellectualizing, explaining, friendly chit-chat, tangents, or obsessive ruminations. Had he done any of these—as all focusers sometimes do—I would have gently brought him back to what he is doing now—focusing.

The example does not show that the focuser has already at times 'dealt' with the adoption issue in therapy. He has talked *about* this issue in earlier sessions. He has *inferred* various things about it ("It must be that . . . "). He has offered various interpretations of his behavior ("I don't get closer to her probably because . . . "). And he has gone over some hand-me-down answers about feeling like his kid is a stranger to him ("My wife says . . . ").

But in focusing I ask him to do something radically different: to approach the issue freshly, to experience it directly, to let it talk to him.

When the issue is approached directly via focusing ... it changes in content, and there are changes in his bodily state. First, it is not just the child who is foreign, but his wife is far from him too. The recognition that it is 'both' begins to let something move—shift—in his body. More happens: he did not belong in his family of origin. He has never belonged anywhere. And then: it is **he** not **they** who are keeping him out now. This last is a major new insight that is accompanied by a physical release—laughing. In a way that is usual for focusing but is particularly dramatic in this example the problem has mutated (Gendlin, 1964). At the end of the session he recognizes that he has come a long way. He sees the matter differently (insight) and he feels better (felt shift).

IV

Now it is time to step back from this example and get an overview of focusing.

Focusing is a quiet, eyes-closed, affective, direct sensing into one's bodily experience so as to find one's whole FELT SENSE of a problem, issue, or situation and, through asking the felt sense questions, to achieve one or more FELT SHIFTS, bodily resolutions of the matter.

Focusing instructions lead the focuser towards the bodily felt sense of a something, which is then symbolized. The symbol may be a word, phrase, image, sound or gesture.[3] The symbol is checked against the bodily felt experiencing. When the symbol is accurate there is a beginning felt shift. The felt sense is then asked in a friendly way open-ended questions so as to bring new insights and physiological release and a feeling of well-being.

Focusing is a process of finding felt senses, being friendly to them, symbolizing them, and allowing them to shift. A self-propelled feeling process carries forward the focuser's experiencing until a stopping place is reached. One half-hour of continuous focusing is a lot.

Focusing was developed in the 1960s by Eugene Gendlin partly out of his philosophy of experiencing (1962) and partly out of research on the process and outcome of psychotherapy (1961, 1967, 1981). In the research Gendlin asked, 'What distinguishes successful from unsuccessful therapy?' He found that it was not what clients talked about. Research showed that the *content* of the sessions did not distinguish successful from unsuccessful therapy. Nor was it the orientation of the therapist. Rather, it was *how* the clients talked. Those clients who spoke from their own experiencing process were more likely to profit from their therapy than those who did not.

Gendlin then reasoned that if we know what clients have to do to profit from therapy—make symbols for their own experiencing process—can we teach people how to do this? From this question Gendlin crystallized out and then refined the technique of focusing. Focusing is a precise specification of what successful clients do in therapy. They focus. They know how to make touch with a conceptually vague but bodily felt sense. They stay with it. They let unexpected stuff emerge from it. The ability to focus correlates with success in psychotherapy (Hendricks, in press).

For thirty years now Gendlin has been teaching people how to focus. As we have seen, focusing is a skill that a guide teaches to a focuser. It proceeds in steps. We have seen a complete round of focusing including all eight steps as I now teach it. My complete instruction sheet follows this essay.

V

Focusing is an aesthetically appealing but subtly nuanced and difficult-to-be-completely-grasped process. Examples help teach it. Here are some. I will share with you four examples of focusing for self-help and four examples of focusing in therapy. Each example illuminates one or more aspects of the focusing process.

The first example comes from Gendlin's book, FOCUSING. It is my favorite example from that book. In it, what is being focused upon is a troubling incident, the kind of thing with which clients sometimes start therapy sessions. Here it is being worked upon for self-help.

The example illustrates particularly well both the "clearing a space" movement of focusing and the changing and deepening of an issue when focusing is applied to it.

In the example, Peggy works part-time. Her husband, John, comes home one evening jubilant. His bank has plans to promote him. In his excitement, he knocks a piece of Peggy's china off the table. It breaks. Peggy flies into a rage, refuses to cook dinner, and runs upstairs in tears:

> She was surprised and upset by her . . . outburst. Stormy scenes were not usual for her. So she focused . . .
>
> She began by getting as comfortable as possible, removing all unnecessary physical irritations that might have masked what her body wanted to tell her. She washed her face because it felt hot and itchy after crying. She took off her shoes, propped a pillow against the headboard of the bed, and leaned back against it.
>
> She stacked all her problems to one side, as though making a space for herself in a jumbled storage room. "Why don't I feel terrific right now? Well, there's that big pile of dog-eared school papers I still have to finish. And there's that problem about Jeff getting sent home from kindergarten. And of course there is this lousy new thing about the broken dish . . . ."
>
> **The felt sense.** Now she let her attention go to the problem that, at the moment, seemed to be the worst: the stormy scene involving that broken dish.
>
> She asked, "What does **all that** feel like?" and then she let the unclear sense come to her in its own way—large, vague, formless at first, lacking words to describe it, lacking labels or identifying marks of any kind.
>
> **Finding a handle.** Now, very gently, she asked what the

quality of the felt sense was. She tried to let the felt sense name itself, or to let an image come and fit it . . . .

She had asked: "What is the worst of this?" The feeling came, "Anger at John." A further question: "Over the broken dish?" The wordless reply, "No. The dish has hardly anything to do with it. The anger is over his air of jubilation, the way he radiates confidence about his future."

Thus did the problem change. The inner shift was unmistakable.

She received this fully and sensed it over and over, feeling the change going on in her body. When her body had finished changing, she went on. . . .

Again, she got the felt sense, the changed way the whole problem was in her body at this moment. "His jubilation . . . . What now is the **whole sense** of that?" . . . .

Resonating. She took the word "jealous" and checked it against the felt sense. "Jealous, is that the right word? Is that what this sense is?" The felt sense and the word apparently were a close match, but not a perfect one. It seemed that the felt sense said, "This isn't exactly jealousy. There's jealousy in it somewhere, but . . . ."

She tried "sort-of-jealous" and got a tiny movement and the breath that let her know that was right enough, as a handle on the felt sense. She did it again, and . . . yes.

Asking. Now she asked the felt sense itself: "What is this sort-of-jealous? What about the whole problem makes for this sort-of-jealous?"

She let the question reach the unclear felt sense, and it stirred slightly. "What is **that**?" she asked, almost wordlessly. And then, abruptly, the shift came. "Sort-of-jealous . . . uh . . . it's more like . . . a feeling of **being left behind**."

"Ah!" That "ah!" came with a large, satisfying sense of movement. Peggy's body was telling her that she was unhappy over the fact that her own career was stalled . . . .

But this quality—the feeling of being left behind—was

only the tip of the iceberg. Peggy wanted to see if it could lead to more change and movement.

And so she went through the cycle of focusing movements again. "What is this left-behind feeling? What's really in it for me? What's the worst of it?"

This focusing session lasted for perhaps 20 minutes. When it was over, Peggy felt enormously refreshed. The shape of her problem had changed, and **she** had changed. She and John then talked calmly about their lives and their futures. The broken dish was forgotten.

That one focusing session had not made Peggy's motherhood versus career problem vanish, but it had started a series of beneficial changes inside her. Further sessions told her more about herself and helped her to move from where she was stuck. (Gendlin, 1981, pp. 46-50)

Notice that through focusing Peggy has used an everyday experience as a teacher. She does not have to keep reacting to broken dishes. She learns the lesson. She gets the message.

Here is another *self-help* example.

Maria and Lawrence have just formed a focusing partnership.[4] They have taken a workshop with Gene Gendlin and practiced focusing under supervision from me seven times. It is a Tuesday in the Spring and this is their fourteenth meeting:

L: You want to be the guide or the focuser?
M: I'll focus. I really need it today.
L: OK. Close your eyes. Bring your attention into your body. See what is there.
M: It is like I am crying and screaming inside.
L: Crying and screaming. . . . Do you want to put things out on the bench? (Notice the option.)
M: No. I'll stick with where I am . . . . It just changed!
L: So, what is the whole feel of—
M: Now, I want to shake and throttle him.

L: Shake and throttle—
M: My fucking father! He wouldn't send me a penny towards the down payment on the new house.
L: He wouldn't send you a—
M: I'm really pissed.
L: Yes, you are! Is there a question you want to ask the "pissed"?
M: (Much more slowly) Yes . . . . A couple: Do I deserve the money? . . . Do I need the money?
L: So ask your inside feeling place, "Do you deserve the money? Do you need the money?"
M: (deep silence; then, laughter)
L: Something is funny.
M: I don't **need** his money. I just wanted to get his goat. I **wanted** him to turn me down—again—so I could feel self-righteous (laughing).
L: There seems to have been a felt shift. (understatement!)
M: You know it! God, I'm still playing that game with him. The game of "punished-unjustly brat." Enough of that!
L: That **is** different.
M: Yes, it is. Let me take a bathroom break. Then it is your turn. Thanks.

Notice how Lawrence reflects back to Maria the emotional essence of what she has said and then gives her a focusing direction. Maria's speech starts quickly, slows down (typical of focusing) and her "crying and screaming" turn first into quiet and then laughter. Her whole sense of what is going on changes radically as does her feeling state.

Just as the "Peggy" example is my favorite from FOCUSING, this next is my favorite from FOCUSING-ORIENTED PSYCHOTHERAPY. Gene says it is an instance when in order to explain focusing he turned to doing it. He is on the radio. The interviewer (who becomes the focuser) is the talk show host. The example deals only with finding the felt sense. Why do I consider it so important?

The interviewer brings up two subjects—race and condominium prices—which a socio-politically oriented therapist might readily latch onto. Gene recognizes that these can be important factors. But, by staying with finding the truly felt sense, he helps the interviewer find what is true for him right now. They do not go off on an ideologically fueled, but not-felt tangent:

> Interviewer: I'm having trouble understanding, and I think our audience probably does too, what this unclear felt sense is, that you talk about.
> Gendlin: Well, if you would be willing, choose some problem of your own, for a minute. You need not say what it is, just pick one in your mind.
> I: That's easy. I'm right in one. My building is being turned into condominiums, and we have to move. It makes me so angry. That whole way of squeezing people's money out of them—so very much money for just an apartment—and that whole policy is wrong. We're black, of course, and that has something to do with it too. And I *hate* moving. Everything is disrupted. I'm just not ready to move.
> G: I know that this is a big issue, about condominiums, and I know we could talk about that for a long time. I can understand that you're angry about it. And the race issue that comes into it is even bigger, I know. But I'll ask you, so I can explain focusing, to do something a little different. Could you just sense the whole of your discomfort now, about that whole moving business, and—just as if you didn't know about it already—sense how it makes you feel. See if you can get one word or phrase for *the quality* of it.
> I: Well, I know what I feel. I'm not ready. I'm not prepared for it. It comes as a surprise; I didn't expect it.

G: Just be with the sense of "not prepared." You know a lot of what that means, but just as if you didn't know it, just stay a little while with that uncomfortable sense, that you're calling "not prepared."

(*Silence, . . . it seemed like a long silence because this was on the radio, but it lasted perhaps 15 seconds.*)

G: Probably this is hard to do, right now, you're having to run the program and so forth, but we're only explaining to the audience how this is done, maybe later when you have a quiet minute—
I: (Laughs)
G: Why are you laughing?
I: *I've got it. It answered me. I know what it is. It came.*
G: Now, you don't need to say what it is.
I: Oh, I can say it. It's being middle-aged. that's what it is.
G: Oh—
I: I'm not prepared to carry heavy things. What are the women going to say when that comes out? I'm afraid I'll hurt my back. We haven't moved for years, and I haven't done any heavy carrying for 20 years. I am sure going to look foolish. But, of course, that's nothing. It's getting middle-aged, that's what bothers me. We can move.

(*Relief shows on the interviewer's face.*)

Gene comments: "I . . . want to be clear that I am not trivializing problems about condominiums and certainly not about race. This processing step does not in any way diminish the seriousness that this man feels about social questions. [But] what exactly had this man not known before that he now knows? It . . . was not the well-known disruption of moving that made him feel 'not ready, not prepared.' It was rather [his being middle-aged that] came there when he let the murky sense give the next step." (Gendlin, 1996, p. 95)

The murky felt sense, when attended to, tells us what our experienced difficulties are right now. Without the felt sense we can intellectualize forever. We can talk about our issues obsessively and endlessly. We can clothe ourselves in other people's certainties about what is wrong—or right—with us. Or, we can use focusing and go inside and directly experience 'the rub' of it. Only then can we say that we truly know what is there.

One more example of self-help focusing just came to me. I am the focuser. My journal is my companion. I am guiding myself. Something happened inside me as I finished writing the previous example:

> The feeling is heavy, like, in my gut and in my arms[5] . . . like 'heavy lifting' . . . the guy in the example . . . something in common between him and me and how I'm feeling about this paper.
> (I'm quiet, eyes closed, waiting.)
> It is about being middle-aged.
> What is 'middle-aged' about the paper?
> Oh, I'm taking something I wrote in my forties (Friedman, 1986) and revising it now in my sixtieth year. I feel *nostalgic* for when I originally wrote it . . . *that time* . . . . (tears) A warm feeling inside and an inner smile as I remember 'that time' (more tears).
> I feel softer, refreshed, less heavy, less-middle-aged as I put this example in the paper.

This is 'focusing on the fly.' I have called it 'mini-focusing' (Friedman, 1989). Notice that I do not guide myself through the eight steps. There is nothing sacrosanct about the eight steps. I start right where the 'feltness' is: a heavy feeling in my gut and arms. I follow the felt sense and my visual memories where they take me—to that time in my forties. I cry. The content and the feeling of the issue both change. I allow my nostalgia to be there. I feel lightened.[6]

I go back to the essay.

VI

In the previous examples we have seen more and less practiced focusers working on themselves, sometimes with a guide, sometimes by themselves. Now I want to turn to four examples of focusing in therapy. It is not easy to focus alone. Newcomers who try it are often disappointed and give up. Like meditation, one often needs a guide. The guide may or may not be a psychotherapist. Credentials and profession count less than a certain quality of the person, training in focusing, and psychological acumen. I focus best with a guide who is empathic, unobtrusive, spontaneously liking of me, unhurried, clear, and knowledgeable of the focusing process. A person who has these qualities and is also a therapist is a real find. There aren't many such people.

John Welwood is a therapist who uses focusing in his work with clients. In this example he emphasizes what he calls the "unfolding" quality of focusing. New meanings unfold as the client focuses on an experiencing that is always denser, more highly textured, richer than he or she explicitly knows. The presenting problems take a dramatic turn in his or her surface mind. Focusing gets to the heart of the matter:

> A client comes in feeling miserable and depressed. He knows his feelings have to do with his wife, but he does not know what to do about them. At first he talks about his feelings toward his wife and hers toward him, his blame of her and his guilt about that, and so on. But his words are rather lifeless. He is talking "off the top of his head," without any deep inward reference [i.e., focusing] going on. As the therapist, I guide him to find his felt sense of his situation underneath all his thoughts and emotional upheaval. How does he feel it in his body? I let him feel around inside awhile without saying much about it.
>
> I next ask him what kind of feeling quality it has (such as

shaky, fearful, jumpy, tense, or viselike). "It's a heavy feeling in my stomach," he responds. Now that he is in touch with this heaviness directly, he can begin to inquire into it and unfold its meanings, as presently felt, rather than as he might usually think about them. Such inner questioning is like holding up a frame to this global heaviness, or like shining a flashlight into the darkness. The frame in this case is a question from me: "What is so heavy about this for you?" Again he returns to his felt sense, and we wait for something more specific to unfold.

"It's anger, just sitting in my gut," he now says, "and weighing me down, eating me out from the inside." His words start to gain vigor and intensity. As he feels around in the anger he has now articulated, the next direction appears: "But even more than angry, I feel terribly disappointed in her. She isn't like her old self." Pause. We are now on the edge of something new. "But I'm also disappointed in myself. Things used to be so good between us, and now we don't even listen to each other." He sighs deeply at this point, as he is getting close to the core of his present feeling. I can tell by his shaky tone of voice that he is close to opening up something larger and more significant. He is no longer talking about his felt sense; he is talking **from** it. His next statement really cracks it open: "And, you know, I'm just now realizing that I haven't let her know how much I care about her in a long time. That's what's so heavy, I've locked up my love and sat on it for months now. I don't know how she even puts up with me." Something in his body is now releasing—he breathes more deeply and looks as though blood were returning to him. He is now in a quite different place from when he first walked in half an hour ago. Each step of unfolding—heavy, angry, disappointed, but particularly this last one—provides what Gendlin calls a **felt shift**, which forms the basis of genuine therapeutic change. (Wellwood, 1982, pp. 95-96)

Obviously, something now needs to happen to this man's locked up love. This focusing has not solved that problem. Further focusing rounds—or other experiential interventions—are now called for.[7]

Welwood writes that any life problem usually "has many different strands, but one central tangle (sometimes two or three); many different angles and edges, but one central crux; many irritating aspects, but one central 'rub.' Focusing is not so much concerned with all the twists and turns, ins and outs of a problem or situation so much as its central core." (p. 99) His client's "central core" issue was his blocked love, an issue that pervaded his life. The steps of focusing wended their way to this core issue, as they would have had he started with some other related surface manifestation of the basic issue.

Here is an example from my own work as a therapist. The example illustrates again the use of focusing to identify on a felt level a basic syndrome, a broad attitude, a large issue that underpins several specific problems. When the client is focusing at the level of the general attitude, he or she is working on each of the related problems at once. This is more economical and effective than taking one troublesome area at a time. "People change," wrote Angyal, "in their roots, not their branches." (p. 205) Focusing gets to the roots.

> The client is a 45-year-old former teacher about to go into business for himself. He has had a year of focusing therapy. His eyes are closed. He has put a hefty stack of troubles on the bench and picked one to work on—starting his business. I ask him to attend to the feel of the whole of it.
>
> C: I feel some sort of calm yet urgent and anxious "wanting-to-have-this-done" feeling.
> T: A "wanting-to-have-this-done" feeling?
>
> (Client nods yes and sighs.)

T: (slowly) Let words, images or memories come from that feeling.

C: (After 30 seconds of self-attending) I see myself at the start of a class . . . ah ha! It is the same feeling that I have whenever I start a class. (Client wrinkles his brow, like that isn't quite right.) No, it's more like whenever I start a new class. I feel a deeper calm now. I just got the sentence, "Will I be able to do it?" (Client chuckles) Oh yeah, that's the same feeling I often have before I go to bed with a woman for the first time. (Client is quiet again. Next, he tells me what is happening in his body process.) I feel alive and breathing . . . on the track.

T: (gently) Ask the place where you feel it all—"What's the crux of this?" "What is the main thing about it?"

A minute passes. I sit and wait. My mind is empty. My attention is focused on him.

C: I'm quiet, listening closely to myself . . . . I want to try out a few possible sentences that feel close to right. "Will I succeed?" (Client shakes his head no.) "Am I OK?" (He shakes his head. Again, apparently, this is not it. I sit calmly, not rushing in.)

Ah . . . "Can I sustain it?" (Client is quiet. No head nodding. He has been "hearing" these sentences emerge from the felt sense and then checking them against the felt sense.)

Not quite right, but close . . . . More sentences are coming . . . "Do I have the persistence? Can I overcome the obstacles?" None feels exactly right, but all feel near the core.

T: (softly, taking my cue from his words) Ask it, "**What's the core of this?**" (My client's response tells me I am on target.)

C: As you said that I felt energy swirling in me. And the

> sentence, "I'm not sure that I'm enough" came to me
> . . . . "I'm not sure that I'm enough." (He says it over to check that just **this** is the right sentence, the **name** for the syndrome.) When I said that over I got very still and then really quickly other instances flashed by . . . the first appointment with a new customer . . . the way I feel when I wake up in the morning . . . the way I feel each time before focusing . . . this feeling about myself holds me back in a lot of ways.

We are now in the phase of focusing Gendlin calls "global application": "The individual is flooded by many different associations, memories, situations, and circumstances, all in relation to the [same] felt referent." (Gendlin, 1964) I let the client go on citing instances and then, when the wave subsides, remind him of the key sentence, "I'm not sure that I'm enough." I invite him to begin another round of this feeling process by asking again, "What's the **whole** feel of that?"

Here is yet another example of my using focusing in therapy. An experienced focusing client came into his session newly in love. He spent three-quarters of this session on this very good feeling. He focused on it.

Why? Why would one use a focusing therapy session to focus on a good feeling?

Because therapy is not just about pathology. It is about what is right as well as what is wrong. Angyal notes that "what is right"—what he calls "the healthy system"—gets too short a shrift in most therapy. Therapy needs to demolish the neurotic system and reconstruct the healthy system. (Angyal, 1965) In this session, I am primarily strengthening the healthy system. Gendlin warns therapists not to be too "pathology oriented." He reminds us "a person is a who, not a what." The "life-forward direction," as Gendlin calls it, needs our attention. (1996, chapter 20)

One can learn from good feelings as well as bad. Focusing is not just remedial. It can be transcendental. It is useful for growth wherever the person happens to be at the moment. Focusing is good both for fixing troubled places inside and for experiencing self-transformation.

In the following example, from his good-feeling place an edge emerges that tells the client something new, something not previously clear about himself and his love. The example shows once again how one's experience always has a "more than what one already knows" quality to it. The example also shows the spontaneous occurrence of other inner processes in the context of focusing. I will note this occurrence in bold face, and we will refer to such things again later.

> He comes in, sits down, removes his glasses and shoes, closes his eyes, and begins focusing. He feels a fluttering behind his eyes. His arms want to move. His torso feels spacious, clear. (This is the felt sense.) I ask him for a word, phrase, image, sound or gesture that fits the felt sense.
> "Inspired . . . . I feel inspired . . . ".
> He says the sentence back to himself. "Inspired . . . . I feel inspired . . . ". He says that the-thing-in-his-arms has stopped happening. His arms feel lighter and relaxed. The whole of him now feels still. (This is a felt shift)
> He checks the sentence again: "Inspired . . . . I feel inspired . . . ". The second check deepens the process. His shoulders want to fall a little. He wants to slow down. There is, he reports, "**A swirling of energy right behind my eyes.**" His attention now is being pulled toward his chest area.
> He does not want to put things on the bench. He wants to stay where he is. He asks his chest area, "What is the crux of this 'inspired'?"
> He reports an image of a woman and her son. He asks for the whole feel of this image. He gets a faint smile on his lips. His breathing has deepened. He reports feeling warm all over.
> "Is there a handle for this new felt sense?" I ask. He says he sees the woman embrace him. His body tingles all over. Inside him he hears the sentence, "I'm in love."

I ask him to check that. He says, "Yeah . . . I sure am!" His shoulders relax still more. The tingling stops. There is a feeling of "rightness of fit" between the handle and the felt sense. He wants the felt sense to tell him more. I say, "Let's just tap it and see what it sends us." He sees **his** daughter and the woman's son. They are sitting side-by-side. He feels tears just behind his eyes. "What's that?" he asks himself aloud.

His head jerks suddenly from left to right and back again. A memory from fifteen years ago has popped into his process. He sees himself in his bedroom crying about leaving his little brother. He is going away for a year. Now the little brother joins the image of his daughter and the woman's son and **the three of them are dancing together**. The image is now a moving picture. He feels "a pleasant kind of teary."

"What kind of 'pleasant kind of teary' is it?"

He says aloud the sentence, "It is a fatherly-kind-of-love," and with that the tears are released. He sits and cries and sobs.

After a few minutes the tears stop and he reports feeling calm inside. An image of his own father starts to appear. He is not ready for this next step. So he underlines the phrase "fatherly-kind-of-love" and "something-about-me-and-my-father" as the furthest place he has gone to in this session. About forty minutes have gone by. He puts his glasses and his shoes back on, pays me, and leaves.

Notice in this example the number of felt senses and shifts. What Gendlin calls a self-propelling feeling process has occurred. It has also opened up a slightly altered state of consciousness indicated by the fluttering behind the eyes, the sudden head swivel, and the moment when the image starts to move on its own. He has learned some *new information* about his feeling ("fatherly-kind-of-love") and he has released deep *feeling* ("the tears were released").

Notice in these examples from therapy *how little interpreting is being done by the therapist.* The therapist does not supply intellectual answers or interpretations. He or she guides a process that facilitates the client's finding—unfolding—his/her own answers. The therapist does not do violence to the client's process.

Notice also the *attitude*[8] that the client takes towards his own experiencing process. The focusing method includes teaching a focusing attitude: *a reverence for bodily felt experiencing.* The client is invited to befriend his or her felt sense of the particular issue being worked on. The message is: welcome it; acknowledge it; open to it; embrace it; let it speak to you; listen to it—the 'it' being the body's current messages about the issue. Of course, one would not say **all** these words but would find the words that best express to **this** particular focuser the focusing attitude.

At this point I was originally ready to end this essay. Suddenly a skeptic appeared.[9] The skeptic has read the essay so far. Now he insists on butting in. He has questions. He wants answers.

Skeptic: Does focusing always proceed so smoothly as in your examples?
Me: No. See FOCUSING for tips on troubleshooting where focusing breaks down.
Skeptic: Is there always such a radical shift in content?
Me: No. I picked some specially juicy examples.
Skeptic: Does focusing always work?
Me: No. Nothing in psychology always works.
Skeptic: So when are you going to show some less-than-perfect-and-successful focusing?
Me: How about right now?

I am sorry to say that this last example comes from my own practice.

I am happy to say that it comes from 1977 when I was a novice therapist who had just 'learned' (i.e., been exposed to) focusing three years before.

The client is my first client on a day when I am not in such great emotional shape myself. Notice the clunky way that I introduce focusing into the session. Notice the surface level on which the excerpt stays. Especially notice the absence of sufficient listening responses. I will comment in parentheses on my mistakes and indicate what I wish I had done or said.

C: I'm not sure what to talk about today.
T: So let's try something new. (I am so eager to introduce focusing that I jump in without even checking that it is OK with him.) The first thing is to just close your eyes and get comfortable. Take a few deep breaths. Take your time and then signal me when you're ready to go on. (pause) OK, now just ask yourself inside, how am I right now? Don't answer, but turning your attention like a searchlight to your inside feeling place just greet whatever you find there. How am I inside right now? (long pause) Now, imagine that you're sitting on a park bench . . . (Again, I am forcing focusing on him. I do not inquire what is happening in the silence or ask him if he wants more time where he is. I am like a runaway focusing locomotive that is going to get his passenger to focus.) . . . and you're going to stack next to you everything that's in the way between you and feeling all fine right now. So, just say, what is in the way between me and feeling all fine right now? And as each thing comes, just imagine it coming out of you and stacking it a little bit of distance from you. Don't go into any one thing, just stack.
C: Books.
T: Ah, yes, put them over there.
C: Paper, pencils, tapes.
T: Um, mechanical things. (Why don't I just repeat his

list? Why do I have to provide a concept in which to sum them up? Does that influence his next comment?)
C: Mechanicals, drawing boards.
T: Don't go into it, just stack it over there and ask, other than that, am I all OK? And just wait.
C: (pause) Bank books, income tax, (pause) . . .
T: Just gently, to yourself, except for this, I'm all OK, right? (I do not say the things back to him. I wish I had.)
C: Feeling a warm tingle just on the inside of my skin. (pause)
T: The warm tingle isn't part of the stack. The warm tingle is the result of putting the stack out there, OK? (pause) Do you want to stay with the warm tingle or . . . ?
C: It changed.
T: It changed.
C: For a moment I dissolved.
T: Um. (I have no idea what he means here.)
C: I could feel the air flowing through me. (pause) Now my body is back.

(This may be the most important thing that has happened so far. But it is not part of my mind-set, not part of my "teaching focusing." I should have said, "For a moment you dissolved . . . and now your body is back." Instead, I let this piece go and stick to the script. I sacrifice the person to the script.)

T: See now whether you want to move toward that stack and feel yourself magnetically pulled toward that one thing in the stack that most needs your attention, the one thing you want to work on. See if you can let it pick you.
C: The drawing board.
T: So take the drawing board and ask, what's the whole feel of that, and that will be the drawing board and all it represents. Just say, what does the whole of that thing

feel like to me? Give your body a nice thirty seconds to get the feel of that thing.

C: (pause) Smooth surface, repetitive motion, glare, sometimes I feel like I can't see. The edge of the board presses into my chest . . .

T: These are sensations or things about it. Take the issue that the drawing board represents. Is it work or art or I don't know what it is but take whatever it is for you. Say, what does the whole of that feel like for me?

C: I feel tied to it.

(I seem insistent on summing up his details in my concepts. 'Sensations' is my word, not his: I could have repeated his words ["smooth surface, repetitive motions . . . "] or I could have said—"and what is the whole feel of the edge of the board pressing into your chest?")

T: So let's ask it some questions . . .

(This is bad focusing teaching. "I feel tied to it" is a direct statement of how he experiences the drawing board issue. I should have said slowly and with emphasis, "So you *feel tied to it* . . . " and then waited to see where he goes with this. Instead, the script again . . . and a missed opportunity.)

The session went nowhere. The best that can be said for it is I brought it to supervision and learned some of the points in the parentheses above. The example illustrates that the teaching of focusing in therapy has to be done with sensitivity to the client's process (see Gendlin, 1996).

VII

In sum, focusing can be done either in rounds or in mini-focusings. It can be used both for self-help and in therapy. A guide leads a focuser. In a whole round, focusing proceeds in steps. The focuser makes contact with a felt sense. As it is befriended and accurately symbolized, the felt sense shifts. Open-ended questions asked of it bring further insights and further felt shifts.

Focusing is about felt senses, a befriending attitude, accurate symbolization, and felt shifts. It is a Rogerian-like way to listen to one's own bodily sensed intuitive wisdom. It is a non-interfering way of being with one's own process. It is a friendly allowing-new-stuff-to-come way of sensing into one's inner flow of experiencing.

Honor the felt sense. It has intentionality and directionality. It wants a next step to happen. For the felt shift to occur the felt sense needs to be approached with an unhurried curiosity and receptivity. One does not try to make a felt shift happen. One simply treats the felt sense "nice."

Experiential focusing is a discipline. It is a skill that can be learned. It is a practice. When mastered it makes accessible to a person the intuitive resources that we all have inside. It provides the experience that the song lyric proclaims:

> It's in every one of us
>   to be wise,
> Find your heart,
> Open up both your eyes
> We can all know everything
>   without ever knowing why.
> It's in every one of us—
> You and I.

FUNDAMENTAL CONCEPTS OF FOCUSING

I have always been attracted to the economy of focusing. I do not refer to how much money it has made for me. I mean the economy of its basic concepts. 'Parsimony' may be a better ten-dollar word. Fewness. Focusing has few main concepts. Recently, I have boiled them down to six: (1) The felt sense; (2) The befriending attitude; (3) Accurate symbolization; (4) Resonating; (5) The felt shift; (6) Asking and receiving.

I will now elaborate upon each and their interconnections.

(1) The felt sense is that *bodily felt something* which starts out fuzzy and then comes into focus as I ask for the whole bodily feel of a problem, issue, situation, or something. For example, what is my felt sense right now? I put my pen down, close my eyes, and sense the feel of my body from the inside. There is a little tiredness in my chest area. There is some heaviness where I imagine my intestines to be. There is a pull downward in my shoulders. Taking these sensations as a whole—I feel weary and slumped. The things-that-are-happening-in-my-body to which the words 'weary' and 'slumped' directly refer (point) is my felt sense.

As Gendlin puts it, "A felt sense is the holistic, implicit bodily sense of a complex situation." Janet Klein calls it "the bodysense" (1996). The advantage of that term is that it has 'body' in it. A felt sense is first and foremost—bodily. It is that initially unclear something in the body that I sense as I focus my attention on a particular issue that I hold in front of me.

(2) In focusing, how shall I be towards this felt sense? I need to treat it as I would a very good friend who has come to visit with something important to tell me. I need to welcome it, acknowledge it, let it know it is OK for it to be here, be receptive to it, be patient with it, be curiously attentive to it—befriend it. The focusing attitude toward felt senses is very 'Southern': y'all come; y'all welcome. Elfie Hinterkopf says that focusing is "distinguished [from other processes] by the attitude of being friendly and compassionate towards all bodily experience" (1997, p. 27). Janet Klein talks of the importance of self-empathy and self-compassion: empathizing with and being compassionate to one's own experiencing. I sometimes talk in terms of 'embracing' one's felt sense.

The different terms are simply gradations of befriending—like the difference between a firm handshake and a hug.

It is important to note that in some sense one may not be positively thrilled to find a particular felt sense: e.g. "I feel hopeless; I feel despairing; I feel suicidal." (Or, conversely, I feel "almost too joyful.") Yet can one be welcoming that the felt sense has come to let you know that, e.g., despairing is there right now? Can one breathe, stand it, and be happy that at least one now knows what is with one? Can one take the attitude, "ah, suicidal. . . yes. . . what are you here to tell me?" If you can, you can focus on it.

(3) While keeping the befriending attitude, I am silently asking for a word, phrase, image, sound, or gesture to come which will accurately symbolize the felt sense. Words, phrases, images, sounds, and gestures are symbols. One kind of symbol is as good as another. There are no 'extra points' for, say, beautiful images or particularly sophisticated turns of phrase. The aim of focusing is accuracy. What is the accurate symbol for this felt sense? The felt sense is fussy and particular. It is looking for the right 'handle.' In my first example the symbols were 'tired' and 'slumped.' In the example in the previous paragraph a symbol is 'suicidal.' At this moment, when I stop writing and 'go inside' (i.e. put my attention into the feel of my body from the inside) the symbol is an image of a locomotive going full-steam straight ahead. If I were

feeling expressive (which I am not right now) I could chug around the room and make locomotive noises. The befriended felt sense is accurately symbolized.

(4) When I have a felt sense and what seems to be an accurate symbol, I resonate them. In his book on chanting, Robert Gass (1999) defines resonation as to "resound. . . " I am checking the body sensations with the symbol: Is there really a rightness of fit? Are the symbol and the felt sense a match? It is not sufficient for them to live in the same neighborhood or have a family likeness. I want the dart in the bull's eye. This does not mean I take a skeptical attitude towards the symbol. Quite the contrary. I simply hold symbol and felt sense up to each other and 'resound' them. I am looking for what Robert Gass calls 'entrainment'; i.e., the feeling that they go together.

(5) When I resonate an accurate symbolization with a befriended felt sense, I get a felt shift. The physical feeling in the body changes. In fact, this is how I know a handle is accurate. It gives a shift.[10]

There is a continuum of felt shifts from minimal to explosive. And there are three types of felt shift: release/relief (e.g. tears, laughter); sharpening (from 'sort of upset' to 'really pissed'); or a movement of the sensation to a different part of the body.

For example, when I now resonate "weary and slumped" with my felt sense, I get a shift. The feeling has moved to my throat. The symbol for it is 'sad.'

'Sad? Is this in my throat thing sad?' Yes. Sad now fits. Notice that with the felt shift there is now a new felt sense and handle—in the throat, sad. This is a new direct referent and I could go through the focusing cycle again.

(6) Or, I can ask the felt sense questions. Some it will answer. Some it won't. Don't be concerned when it doesn't answer. Simply receive with gratitude whatever comes. Don't argue with it. Protect it like a shy child on a stoop who needs to know he is safe.

I will illustrate this with my own list of favorite focusing questions. These are good ones—tried and true. And it is always okay to invent new questions.

What I am experiencing right now is a fluttering of my eyelids, some lights going on and off behind my eyes, some geometric patterns forming and reforming behind my eyes, and a pronounced *absence* of sensation in my torso, which feels smooth. The symbol for the felt sense is 'energized.' I say to myself, "energized. . . I feel energized. . . " My self says, "Yes, I do."

The energized gets a little sharper. Now I will ask it some questions. I will 'point' the questions right at the place(s) in the body where the 'energized' has taken up residence.

Q: What is the crux of it? What is the crux of this 'energized'?
A: The writing is moving along well. I have momentum.
Q: What is the worst of it?
A: Question does not apply.
Q: What is the best of it?
A: Some relief. . . whew. . . I was afraid I was stuck.
Q: What does the feeling need?
A: To keep writing this paper. To see it through to the end.
Q: What is a good *small* step in the right direction?
A: Keep doing what I am doing. Don't let that new idea that just whizzed past take me off into a tangent. Stay disciplined.
Q: What would it feel like in your body if this thing were all okay, all better?
A: It almost is. There is still that little place in my intestines. But I can live with it there.
Q: What is the exactly right focusing question for the felt sense right now?
A: "Can I use this example in the paper?"

Q: (I say the question silently to myself: 'Can I use this example in the paper?')
A: Yes. Definitely. It is a good example.
Q: Another question: 'Is this the end of the paper?'
A: No. Not quite. It needs some finishing touches. (I take thirty seconds to stretch and mark the end of the focusing session.)

This, then, is focusing. These are the irreducible concepts necessary to teach it and learn it. You get a felt sense. You befriend it. It gets accurately symbolized. You resonate the symbol and the felt sense. There is a felt shift. You ask the felt sense questions. You graciously receive its answers. The answers give you insights and physiological changes.

You have focused.

WHAT FOCUSING IS AND WHAT IT IS NOT

Focusing is a very special way of listening to oneself. It is listening to the body, not the mind. It is listening to the flow of felt experience in the body. It is listening to the way people, objects, situations are being carried in one's felt experiencing. Focusing is a special way of using concepts. It is a linking of concepts with felt experience. Let me elaborate and clarify what it is by talking about what it is not.

Stop reading for a moment. . .
Listen to yourself. . .
Go on, take a minute or so. I'll wait. . .
Now, what did you do? What happened?

If you don't already know focusing or naturally focus, probably you "heard" or "saw" or "heard and saw" words or images "in your head." The words could have been of several different kinds:

1. Alvin Adams is a professional basketball player who has just learned that his teammate, Walter Davis, has entered a drug rehabilitation center for the second time. Adams reports:

> I look at Walter Davis from many angles as I think about what's happening around me. My thoughts concerning Walter flow: "Man, he could hit the big basket when we needed it." "He sure made a stupid decision the first time he did coke." "It's fun playing on his team because Walter sure wants to win." "I wish I'd gotten to know him better." "I'm glad I didn't know him better." "I guess cocaine addiction is a disease with Walter." "Walter should be strong enough to

> say No to drugs." "Walter needs my support now." "Did Walter testify against his friends and teammates?" (*New York Times*, 4/26/87)

This is Alvin Adams listening to himself. His is an example of what I will call "mind-associating." In mind-associating one lets one's mind wander over a particular topic or over several. One free-associates. Alvin Adams is listening to his mind-associating.

Listening to mind-associating is mostly harmless. It can be distracting. It can be amusing. It can be creative. One can enjoy the play of concepts and ideas as mind joins and rejoins them. It is one kind of listening to the mind, to one's thoughts and ideas. It is not focusing—not listening to bodily felt experiencing.

2. Here is another example of the kinds of words that people sometimes hear and/or see "in their heads." This example comes from a time in my life when I was deeply troubled. I was at a workshop and I "heard" the following:

> My neck hurts; I've injured myself; maybe it's serious; my body won't survive this weekend; this will do no good; what do I have to go home to anyway, I'll never ever meet anyone again. . . what will I do when I leave. . . what will I do in San Francisco. . . if I feel like this I'll be miserable. . . I'll always feel like this. . . I was right, the vacation won't change anything. . . what else can I do? what should I try?. . . it's such a long ride home. . . I'm scared. . . I'll get sick out West. . . I'm spending too much money. . . and besides. . .

This is "mind-obsessing." The main characteristic of mind-obsessing is the repetition of words, ideas, and thoughts that make one feel bad. It is as if a needle is stuck in the groove of a record one does not like. One goes round and round and gets nowhere and feels down. One is listening too much to the blues.

Most of us know how to obsess. We do not need lessons. It is one of the characteristic things that mind does—almost like that is part of its job.

At times mind-obsessing gets way out of control. It becomes dangerous and unhealthy to listen to mind-obsessing. At its extreme, it can kill you. People commit suicide sometimes as a way of turning off mind-obsessing.

3. Here is another example of the kinds of words I sometimes hear and see when I listen to myself. This example comes from a Friday morning sitting in the Algiers Café in Harvard Square, getting prepared to lead a weekend Opening the Heart workshop:

> When I leave here I'll go to the bank, the photocopy place, and the post office. Then I have to plan the workshop. What do I need to do for the workshop? I need to talk with Rodney, buy some Kleenex, decide on the afternoon part of the design. Oops—don't forget to tell the church about the alarm.

This is an example of "mind-planning." Notice that the thoughts are very focused. They do not wander all over the map. In this example, the ordering principle is sequential. The thinking is a rehearsal for action and steps to follow.

Within limits, this kind of mind-planning is useful. It can help to think ahead. Making lists of things "to do" does help people. It is a useful use of mind—to a point. Mostly we overplan. We listen to ourselves in this way more than is really necessary. As theorists such as Fritz Perls, Claudio Naranjo, and Krishnamurti have pointed out, we're motivated by fear of the future. What we are doing is trying to control our experience.

What do these three examples have in common? They are examples of *listening to the mind*. As we have seen, the very special way of listening called focusing is *listening to the body*.

Here is one more example of a kind of listening to oneself that focusing is not.

Bob Beamon held the world record in the long jump in

track and field. Remembering his record-breaking jump, Beamon says:

> When I went to the top of the runway to begin the approach for my jump, my frame of mind was awesome. . . . I was positively motivated and disciplined; I was existing somewhere between time and space. I heard the cheering and the roars a while and then no outside sounds at all, *only an inner voice telling me to heighten that thing within myself that had been acquired from all the training and practice.* The effort had to be natural and perfect. (italics mine, *New York Times*, 5/26/89)

I will call this kind of self-listening, following Beamon and Robert Gass' nice phrase, "listening to the inner voice." It is listening to one's disembodied intuition.[11] Often what comes to one from this place seems deeper, more profound, and more surprising than what comes from listening to the mind. It is here that clairvoyance and other phenomena called "psychic" come in.

What attitude ought we take towards listening to intuition? The matter is complex. On the other hand, the experience of listening to the disembodied inner voice can be quite startling. A woman reports:

> At the end of our first date, when he left the house, I was in an interesting state. I found myself unaccountably humming a tune—out of nowhere. When I listened to the words I heard, "Oh, sweet mama treetop-tall, won't you kindly turn your damper down. . ." I was amused, and listening further very distinctly heard the lyric from that song, "I may not be the best in town. . . but let me be the best till the best comes around. . ." I noted this in my journal and did not think of it further.
>
> We entered a rather ambivalent relationship which ended suddenly one year later when, standing with him in a movie

line, another man in line introduced himself and soon proceeded to sweep me off my feet—and out of that other penultimate relationship. On our wedding day I re-read my journal and found the prophetic lyric. The best had come around.

In some circles nowadays, disembodied intuition is very "in." Much New Age literature champions it. Intuition is very useful. It also has its drawbacks. First, one has to know where to use it and where not to use it. It is probably best not to do one's income tax intuitively. Second, it is difficult to distinguish intuition from other phenomena—such as projection, wish-fulfillment, and fear. Paul Goodman once wrote, "Some of our intuitions about the world are true and some are not. It is important to learn to tell the difference" (1963, p. 21).

In particular, it can be very difficult to differentiate true intuition from fear or anger projection.

Listening to the disembodied inner voice is still not listening in the special way that focusing is. Here are some introductory focusing instructions:

> Close your eyes. . . sit comfortably. . . take a few deep breaths. . . now let your attention follow your breath down into your body and just see what is there. . . imagine your attention is like a searchlight, and turn that searchlight on and shine it down *into your body*—in your chest, belly, shoulders, wherever—and let it roam around, scan around, and just see what is there. . . And now see if there is a word, phrase, image, sound, or gesture that matches the sensations inside. . .

When I do this just now, I find a kind-of-heaviness in my chest and a tendency for my shoulders to droop and my chest to drop. The direction of the pull of my energy is down. I try the word "tired" and it does not quite fit the feeling. I discard it and try "weary." That feels more like it. The felt sense is weary. When I say "weary" back to myself I feel a little lighter, a little more lively. I straighten up a bit and my energy feels pulled upward. This is the felt shift. I feel a slight bit better. I simultaneously know that I was feeling weary *and* I feel less weary now that I know it.

I feel more grounded knowing what I feel and more attuned to myself. I could go further if I needed to, but instead, I stop and return to my writing.

In sum: why listen to the felt experiencing in the body rather than listen to the mind?

The problem with listening to mind is that mind does not always tell the truth. It tells stories. It lies. Mind can think anything. For example, right now my mind is telling me that I will live forever and inherit a great fortune. This sounds nice, but I don't think I ought to listen. It doesn't have the ring (or feel) of truth.

Conversely, the body tells the truth. When I listen to my felt sense of now, I find how I *really* feel about now. There is no question and no debate. Right now, I have a warm, light feeling in my chest. I'm feeling good. Yes, I am, and there's no doubt.

Listening to oneself in this way grounds a person. It harmonizes mind and body. Symbols match my felt experience. I know who and where I am and what the feeling is about. That's focusing: a special way of listening to oneself.

INNOVATIONS IN HOW I LEAD A ROUND OF FOCUSING

I make a distinction between a focusing round and mini-focusings.[12] A focusing round means either self-guiding or being guided through the entire eight steps in which I teach focusing. The very first example in "Experiential Focusing" is a round of focusing. In this essay I want to indicate what may be different, unique, or special about how I lead a round of focusing.

I now teach focusing as an eight step process:
(1) Saying hello. See how you are inside.
(2) Clearing a space. Put things out on a bench (optional).
(3) Picking a problem. Let an issue that wants to be worked on choose you.
(4) Getting a felt sense. Let the felt sense of that issue form in your body.
(5) Getting a handle. Let a word, phrase, image, sound, or gesture come that matches the felt sense.
(6) Resonating. Go back and forth between the handle and the felt sense and see if they match. If they do, there will be at least a tiny felt shift.
(7) Asking and Receiving: Let's ask the felt sense some questions. Some it will and some it won't answer. Just receive any answers that come. My questions are:
    (a) What is the crux of it?
    (b) What is the worst (or best) of it?

- (c) What's wrong?
- (d) What does it need?
- (e) What is a good small step in the right direction?
- (f) How would your body be right now if this thing were all better? What is in the way?
- (g) Ask the felt sense to send you a right question to ask it. Ask it. Receive.

(8) Saying good-bye. Now take a minute to use however you wish to mark the end of this round of focusing.

There are all kinds of 'fine print' qualifications. I will put some of them in the endnotes. Gene teaches focusing in six steps. What is the difference? As is typical of him, he has no ending step (although in practice he usually does provide something as an ending.) He does not make 'picking a problem' a step. Nor does he begin with 'checking-in.' Then he makes 'Asking' and 'Receiving' two steps.

Ann teaches focusing without steps. In her book, *The Power of Focusing*, she lists sixteen focusing phrases for the guide to make use of. I don't think this is optimal for teaching. There are too many phrases to remember. I prefer from a teaching standpoint clearly labeled steps of which the advanced student is advised to be able to let go.

It is like "We Shall Overcome." For learning purposes, it is best to learn the order of each verse:

We shall overcome. . .
We are not afraid. . .
Black and white together. . .
We shall live in peace. . .
We shall overcome. . .

However, at any particular sing, one can skip verses and make up new verses, improvising upon a given structure. More timely verses can be added. That is how I see focusing.

I see my contributions or relatively unique approaches to be as follows:

(1) The eight steps: Others may use different numbers of steps or no steps. I think my way is best. Otherwise I would not use it.

(2) Saying hello: For some people, clearing a space is the first step of focusing. Sometimes it is considered crucial.[13] I don't start with clearing a space. I start with checking-in: How am I from the inside right now? I do not want to skip over this step because it is, I think, the essential focusing question. So I start with it.

(3) Clearing a space is optional. I have been persuaded to this position by Ann's arguments. I would add that in my experience, 85% of all sessions do include clearing a space.

(4) "See whether there is a word, phrase, image, *sound* or *gesture* that feels like it comes from or will act as a handle on the felt sense inside."

This is part of how I instruct the person in the Finding a Handle step.

I have contributed the words "sound" and "gesture." I remember Gene sometimes referring to body movements as possible handles, but what is different for me is *always* including "sounds or gestures" as possible types of handles, the first time I teach a person focusing.

Sound and *gesture* are less content-oriented than the more familiar triumvirate of word, phrase, or image. Sound and gesture are better suited to leading to an intense feeling, a cathartic or expressive therapy "avenue"—which is a kind of therapy that I sometimes like to use after a focusing round.

For example, here is a male client who begins his focusing therapy sessions regularly with a 15-30 minute round of focusing. In the first step, today, he finds a scream inside. Notice how I combine *catharsis-invitations* with *focusing-invitations*:

T: If you shine the light down inside, just see what is there. . .
C: There is a scream. The scream is the felt sense.
T: So. . . scream.
C: (screams)
T: Louder!
C: (screams again)

T: Louder!
C: (screams probably as loud as he can)
T: Go inside again. What is there now?
   C's eyes have been closed the whole time. He now breaks into sobs, and then into paroxysms of rage. He pounds his fists on the pillows. I have no idea at this point what this is all about. It feels real, valuable, self-connected, a carrying-forward of previously uncompleted feelings. Shifts are happening. Energy is moving. I wait until the cathartic work seems done.
T: Now, *in the stillness*, can you see what is there now?
C: (after a minute of silent self-attending) I hate endings!
   The client then proceeded to trace the strands of meaning that ran through many of his endings (Gene calls this the "global application" step of change). The session ended with a lot of listening on my part.
(5) A recent change I've made is in my instructions for the "clearing a space" step, which I do in terms of "putting things out on a bench."

The way I learned this step was that *everything* that was between the person and feeling all fine in his body right now, even an 'always' background feeling, had to be put on the bench.

The way that I do it now with some people is "put the *main* things that are between you and all fine right now out there. You don't have to get them all, just the main ones."

This change came about after several experiences with a female client who habitually took fifteen minutes to a half hour putting *everything* on the bench. She would name, wipe out, rename, edit, drop, name again, etc., each minutiae of trouble for so long that her therapist (me) would feel like he was going crazy! She would have sometimes only ten minutes of therapy time left after this step.

I was exasperated. The instructions as I had learned them did not help her with her *agitated perfectionism*; they played right into this characteristic difficulty of hers.

The change in my instructions for clearing a space reduced the twenty-five packages she once put on the bench to ten. Now it is just "the main ones," and we have more time for focusing therapy.

(6) Finally, there is a question I have added to the asking step. It comes at the end of the focusing questions that are on my instructions sheet. The question is: "Ask the felt sense itself whether it has a question it would like to be asked and, if it does, ask it that question."

This is letting the felt sense do all the work. *It* generates the question—if one is there. It responds to the question. The focuser gets out of the way of the felt sense and receives the question *and* answer.

I came up with this step out of focusing therapy work on myself. I would sometimes find, near the end of a round of focusing, that my "inside place" had a burning question left that was not on the instruction sheet; e.g. "How long will this problem continue to bother me?", "What are the consequences if I don't?", "Are you sure?", "How shall I proceed?", "What is the best thing to do?"

I started spontaneously asking these (and other) questions of my own felt senses and then started to use the "felt sense asking" mini-step in every focusing round.

So these are my changes. I am aware of two final points:

1. I learned focusing from Gene Gendlin when he was in New York for three years in the mid-Seventies teaching at Richmond College and living at Waterside on 23rd Street. It was a transitional time in the history of phases of focusing teaching. It was after the step-less manual from Chicago, of which I have only heard, and before the emergence of 'clearing a space' as an especially important step.

   I learned and taught focusing as a step-wise process which I understood to be how Gene was teaching it.

When I am not being overly self-reflective, I tend to think of myself as someone who teaches focusing 'the old-fashioned way'—i.e., the way I learned it.

Writing this paper has helped show me that I have, indeed, made some changes from the way I learned focusing. I was not so aware of them before I wrote this.

(I should add that I LOVE guiding either an individual or a group in a round of focusing. That LOVE probably comes through my voice, my tone, my timing, and my ability to make up metaphors as I go along so as to keep bringing freshness into the guiding.)

2. Some of these changes are related to my being a focusing-oriented experiential psychotherapist who also teaches focusing. That is how I would describe myself. Changes four, five, and six all come from my focusing-oriented therapy experience. Change two may reflect this also. My using focusing rounds with therapy clients—and myself—has led to certain changes in how I teach focusing. This is an example of how the practice of focusing-oriented therapy can have feedback effects on how one teaches focusing. I am a better focusing teacher now for having been guided by this feedback from focusing-oriented therapy.

In sum, I would hate to see focusing no longer taught in terms of a step-wise process. I believe that it is easier to let go of the scaffolding of steps than it is to learn a step-less melange of possible suggestions.

A TYPOLOGY OF FELT SHIFTS

In the September 1989 issue of The Focusing Connection, I contributed an article on "Focusing, Catharsis, and Expressive Techniques." The paper dealt with my different experiences of focusing on sadness and anger. The article ended with questions rather than answers.

People responded. Phil Levy asked what was the difference between 'releases' and 'shifts.' It was a very good question. It led me to the following categorization of felt shifts.

I am happy and surprised that my article sparked so much response. It indicates to me that the issue of focusing and anger is a rich one and that *The Focusing Connection* is providing a real service to the network by inviting "participatory articles."

As to Phil Levy's question about shifts and releases: when I teach focusing these days I talk of three *kinds* of felt shifts and two *intensities* of felt shifts.

One kind of felt shift is release/relief. Tears are a good example. There was a tightness or a knot or a holding, and after crying there is a feeling of release or relief. Laughter is another good example.

Another kind of felt shift is sharpening. There is a confused, yucky, all-over-the-body upsetness, and when focused upon it shifts into a sense of anger. The felt sense sharpens up into a feeling of anger.

A third kind of felt shift comes when something felt moves from one location in the body to another. There was a "something" sitting here in my stomach, and after focusing I feel it now in my throat. It has moved.

There is also a continuum of intensities of felt shifts. At the "low" end, the felt shift may be very minimal, very subtle. One has to put a megaphone to it to really hear it. One has to put a magnifying glass to it to really see it. Yes, it is there, but one could skip over it if one did not know about it.

At the "high" end, the felt shift is intense, dramatic, obvious, explosive. No one would miss it. It is big. Usually it is this kind of *big* change that in the expressive therapy literature is cited as "release."

It is easy to get the distinctions among kinds of felt shifts when they happen in close proximity to each other. For example, he is talking about his mother's recent death. There is a felt sense in his stomach and "sad" fits it, and he sheds a quiet tear. There is a small sense of relief, following soon by a "something" now in his throat. It feels like something that was "behind" the sad in his belly has now moved to his throat. It had a "yucky-upset" quality and it sharpens into a very distinct feeling of anger as he recalls a specific aspect of the relationship. He sits with the anger for a while, and then, again, he looks more sad. I've been sitting with an impulse that has come and gone throughout the session. Now I say that I've been sitting with this impulse. . . didn't want to intrude. . . but if he'd like a shoulder to lean on, I'm here. "That would be good," he says. He leans his head on my shoulder and now paroxysms of sobs, waves of grief, are released. We sit like this for five minutes as wave after wave of tears breaks on my shoulder. There is a *big* release. It feels over. "Thanks," he says, "death sucks." We nod our heads together, I return to my seat, and the session moves on. The space between us feels now as fresh as the air after a strong thunderstorm has passed. The big release has left him lighter and clearer and with renewed energy and momentum for life.

BENEFITS OF FOCUSING

The "Benefits of Focusing" essay simply came to me one sunny day as I emerged from snorkeling off Coki Point. I had gone into the water with a different piece of writing on my mind. Apparently, the fishes or the current or something wanted me to switch my attention to focusing's benefits.

After publishing the initial draft of this article, a letter from Jan Stetson indicated that I had left something out (1988). Articles by Ann Weiser Cornell (1993) and Dorothy Fisch (1993) gave me something more to think about. These considerations have been incorporated into this revision.

Why focus? What are the benefits of focusing? What might you get out of it?

Focusing is so much a part of my daily routine that I tend to take its benefits for granted. It is my preferred method of self-therapy, preferred over, for example, affirmations, visualizations, yoga, tai-chi, and weightlifting.[14] I list here what I see as its benefits. I invite feedback on my list.

I begin with what I think of as the most basic of focusing's benefits and move towards the more advanced.

1. Focusing teaches that there is a realm called "inside."
2. Focusing brings one's energy out of the head and into the body.
3. Focusing helps overly emotionalized people get a handle on what they feel.
4. Focusing is physiologically good for a person. It is a means of stress reduction.

5. Focusing gives one new personal information. It is a source of insights.
6. Focusing strengthens the real self.
7. Focusing is self-empowering.
8. Focusing can lead to authentic action.
9. Focusing takes one to the doorway of altered states.
10. Over time, focusing can clear up disturbed places inside. It can lead to profound long-term personal change.

1. **Focusing teaches that there is a realm called "inside."**

The intent of the direction, "Close your eyes and put your attention inside," may be obvious to many of us, but there are those for whom "inside" is terra incognita. These are the people at the lowest end of the experiencing scale. Their attention is either externalized or in their heads. They describe events and situations and report thoughts. For such people, focusing opens up an entire new territory—the territory of experiencing. It opens up to such people a whole new realm of personal resources.

I was once such a person. Leida Berg, my therapist, interrupted my detailed war-stories with the question, "Yes, but what was the feeling?" I did not know what she meant. It was not that I had no feelings. I just did not know there were words for the inhabitants of the neighborhood called 'inside.' I did not know what the request or command 'look inside' meant. I am forever grateful to Leida for introducing me to a whole realm of existence of which I had been ignorant. (Friedman, 1983)

2. **Focusing brings one's energy out of the head and into the body.**

Some people walk around "in their heads." It is hard to feel contact with them. Often they are off somewhere on mental trips. They are not here and now.

Focusing is an antidote to being spacey. Focusing keeps one

grounded, centered, in one's body. A focusing person is moving in the direction of wholeness. His feet are on the ground. We know where he is. He inhabits his body and his feelings. His energy is centered in his center. It is not all up high. A focusing person gives off a realness and a sturdiness that come from having an embodied center of gravity.

This is a benefit of regular focusing. It brings one's energy down. It is especially good for overly intellectualized persons.

In this section, I am thinking about two diagnostic types. Schizoid people (Laing, 1965) have not quite landed on the planet yet. They are dreamy. They live in fantasy and in their imagination. They are ungrounded. They may be quite creative. They are quite imaginative.

Intellectualizers also live in their heads. They are interested in theories, ideologies, and philosophies. They can articulate these very well. They can always answer the question, "What are you thinking?" They are not dreamy. They may be very purposeful. But the purpose comes from the head. They think.

I was like this once. I was a political radical and intellectual. I read the *New York Review of Books*. I supported the Black Panthers. I read Franz Fanon. I thought about Imperialism. I was critical of Freudianism. I read and re-read THE SEEKER (1960), Alan Wheelis' wonderful novel about an intellectual seeking truth and meaning. I lived in the realm of "ism."

What I did not do is reliably consult the feltness of my experience. I did not hang out with my experiencing process.

Focusing brings such a person back to his body, to his experiencing process, to his felt internal universe. This is a revolution. The 'seeker' goes inside. The treasure is found.

3. **Focusing helps overly-emotional people get a handle on what they feel.**

Not everyone is overly intellectual. It is the major tendency in our society. There are also people who feel trapped in bodies that imprison them within overwhelming and unknown emotions. After she read the original article of which this is a revision, Jan Stetson wrote:

> Neil Friedman's article, 'Benefits of Focusing,' doesn't explicitly list the benefit I always mention first when I talk to people about focusing. He says that focusing 'brings one's energy out of the head and into the body.' That's very true, but for me, focusing does something a little different, maybe a little more than that.
>
> My experience of focusing isn't really about being more in my body and less in my head. It's more like having a stronger link, a broader, better-paved road between my mind and my body. Focusing is good for 'overly intellectualized persons.' But it's equally good for overly 'sensualized' persons. I know all too well that intellect alone does not solve emotional problems. All that mental wheel spinning, and I've done plenty, leaves the body's experience unchanged. But emotions alone doesn't really solve problems either. I can be so utterly caught up in emotion that my mind is blown completely out of the picture. In touch with my feelings? I am drowning in them. And when at last the tsunami drops me back on the shore, I am no closer to genuine change than when I started. There is a tremendous sensual rush to that kind of experience, but it's no more effective because again it's only half the story—only now the mind is left out.
>
> So I alternated between 'head trips' and 'body trips'— until I discovered focusing. Focusing sets up a conversation between my mind and my body. Seen in this light, the focusing steps go something like this: My mind asks my body, 'What's going on?' An answer comes from my body in the vague wordless sensory language the body knows. Then I wait for the 'handle.' Something my mind can get hold of. In a sense my mind asks, 'Can you say that in my language?' And some word or image comes to mind from my body.

> Then my mind asks, 'Is that it?', and offers back that word or image. My body answers, again in its language—sensation. And so they can talk, these two aspects of myself that may seem so alienated. They can talk, discuss the situation, reach agreements, make changes. I can find my heart without losing my head.
>
> So yes, focusing is 'about the descent of the mind into the heart.' But it is equally about the ascent of the heart into the mind. (Stetson, 1998)

In focusing jargon we talk of people who are "too close to their feelings" and people who are "too distant from their feelings." People who are too distant are too far away from their experiencing process. They can think, have sensations, and imagine, but they have trouble feeling.

Conversely, "too close" people get overwhelmed by their feelings. Their feelings are all over them at times and can run their lives.

I have known both states myself, but when I first thought about the benefits of focusing I thought about them for "too distant" people. Jan's letter brings "too close" people (or, process) back into the picture.

4. **Focusing is physiologically healthy for the person. It is a means of stress reduction.**

Focusing is relaxing. It feels good in the body.

When I begin focusing, my body often feels either cramped or tight or tense somewhere, or there is an all-over-the-body upset or discomfort. The focusing experience usually releases something and leaves me feeling more calm, whole, serene, at peace.

It is as if in the focusing experience the "offness" that my body has been experiencing first gets concentrated into one place—one knot, one constriction—and the rest of my body can take a breath and relax.

Then, focusing on that one spot—that felt sense—helps it to shift, too.

The body no longer has to carry either a diffuse or a pin-pointed tension.

The simple act of slowing down—which focusing makes happen—is part of this. To simply close one's eyes and tune into one's body requires a break from the usually frenetic pace of life. The body goes slower than the mind, and so to focus is to slow down.

Feeling better is a product of the act rather than the content of focusing. Focusing improves the day. A focusing break helps one feel better regardless of the particular content being focused upon.

Andras Angyal has written that we need techniques for inducing a state of "tonic relaxation" in which the person is relaxed and alert and in which "the grip of neurosis is temporarily loosened." This is a good description of the state to which focusing leads. (Angyal, 1965)

It feels better in the body to have focused. A dis-ease is released.

5. **Focusing gives one new personal information. It is a source of insights.**

In the quote referred to above, Angyal goes on to say that in the state of "tonic relaxation," new insights come to a person. The insights are a by-product of the state.

Such is the case with focusing.

One learns new things about oneself through focusing. No, Peggy, it is not the broken china. It is the feeling of being left behind. Focusing helps one know what is really going on.

These insights usually have a new, fresh, aha! quality to them. They are experienced as a reliving.

Karen Horney said that a "*real*ization" is not a *real*ization unless it feels real, unless it comes with affect.

Focusing insights come with affect.

Focusing leads to increased self-knowledge as a by-product of the focusing state. One does not try to gain the insights. From the focusing state, if questions are asked, the insights come.

Putting 4 and 5 together I sometimes say that focusing feeds both heart and mind, or focusing is about the descent of the mind into the heart.

6. Focusing strengthens the real self.

In considering human nature, some duality seems useful. Horney contrasts the real self and the idealized self. Winnicott and Laing contrast the real and the false self. Angyal talks of the healthy and the neurotic system. Jung distinguishes the persona and the self.

Whatever the duality, focusing strengthens the real, the healthy, the authentic self.

This is because the "healthy system" or "the real self" is not just a concept. *In fact, a conceptual something is exactly what it is not!* The real self is lived experience as it is presently felt. When I put my attention inside and access a felt sense, I am strengthening the real self because I am contacting it. I am having direct access to my existence. I am getting away from merely conceptual living.

7. Focusing is self-empowering.

Focusing gives me direct access to my own inner resources and inner wisdom. When I am focusing I am knowing myself from the inside. I am not inclined to give power over to another who interprets myself to a dumb me.

I once noted in my journal, "I don't know how people get along without focusing. She comes into therapy, wants to know *how* she feels, asks me to tell her! How should I know? I'm not her."

There is a meta-learning to focusing as there is to all therapies.

In most therapies, the therapist functions as the specialist who initiates interventions and interpretations. The Gestaltist says, "Be

your sadness." The analyst says, "Are you really saying that. . ."
The psychodramatist is the director.

There is an implicit lesson, a meta-learning in all this. "I know what you need to do. . . I expert, you patient."

Sometimes this is needed. Sometimes the therapist is the expert. But a steady diet of ingenious therapist-initiated interventions can have the unfortunate effect of unduly increasing one's dependence on the outside expert as the source of wisdom.

Focusing is more self-directed than any other therapy I have experienced. Focusing respects the focuser. The focuser is in charge. The focuser is arbiter of his/her own experience. There is no giving over of power, authority, and control. The message clearly is: the message lies within.

8. Focusing can lead to authentic action.

Alperson refers to authentic movement. By that she means movement that is connected with—that comes from—one's feeling process. It is the movement implicit in one's experiencing. It is the movement that carries the experiencing further.

By analogy, authentic action is action that is implied by, that rolls out of, one's experiencing process. It is action from the self.

Ann Weiser Cornell emphasizes how focusing can dissolve blocks to action. (1993) Dorothy Fisch portrays "The Dance of Freedom": "Focus and act, focus and act, let action arise from the momentary turning in. I think of these steps as the dance of my process. In the waltz, it's 'one, two, three; one, two, three.' In my life, it's focus and act, focus and act." (1993)

Should one act? One can focus on that question. Is it a 'should'? Or, is it genuine, from me, really me? Focusing is seldom the action itself (except when the action is to focus). But focusing can lead one to see and take right action. Gene once wrote that "brave choices" are also needed; that is, the brave choice to a) act upon one's focusing and b) don't act upon anything else.

Let me give you two examples. I was to move into a new house. I visited it once. I focused after: "Don't do it." Loud and clear. I did it anyway—for other reasons. The results were disastrous.

I was interested in a woman I had just met. It would have been daring to approach her. I focused. The handle on the felt sense was "To dare is the only wisdom." I dared. Ten good years together followed.

Focusing can lead to "bodywisdominformedaction." It is a gestalt. Choosing to listen to it and to do it is no absolute guarantee of success. But it sure helps one's chances!

I would encourage focusing-guided action over action that is guided exclusively by, say: the tarot, astrology, a guru; 'shoulds' from any number of different authorities; channeled beings; a list of pros and cons; cosmic illumination. All of these other ways may have a place in one's decision-making. I would just give focusing a central place. Focusing can verify or deny cosmic illumination, etc. Focusing is grounded. It grounds action in Being. One's Doing is not cut off from one's Being. Focusing-informed action is wisdom-guided action. Focusing-informed action allows one to say: "I gave it my best."

9. **Focusing takes one to the doorway of altered states.**

10. **Over time, focusing can clear up "disturbed places" inside. It can lead to profound, long-term personal change.**

I combine these two only because my report speaks of both together:

> Several years ago just about every time I focused I 'saw' a female mannequin's head and bust coming at me. The image was preceded by a sense of swaying inside; sometimes I would feel as if my chair were like an old barber's chair that would swivel up to the ceiling and then return to the ground; I would 'see' and 'feel' myself moving. The mannequin im-

age was accompanied by a feeling of fear—I would visibly wince as it got close.

This image kept happening for about a year. It was a spontaneously recurring image that felt like it came from very deep inside me. Slowly, changes happened. First, I got less fearful of the image. I became friendly to it. I didn't wince. Then the mannequin began to give way to a mundane family scene: the female relatives of my extended family seated in our living room. There was no fear with this image.

Finally, slowly, my father appeared, coming down the steps from the second floor to join the picture. All this happened over the course of a year of regular focusing, which seemed to open 'deeper' places inside. At times I experienced automatic writing inside me, other spontaneous images with no personal meaning to me, and sensations of rising, falling, swaying, and other positional changes (while, of course, I was all the time sitting still) all occurred.

Finally, the whole series of images disappeared (as did the sensations)—never to return.

A little later my sense of my own maleness increased dramatically and I married. It seems to me that a troubled 'place' inside got fixed over the course of the focusing and then my 'real' life changed accordingly.

This report shows both focusing leading into a "deeper" state—technically, the theta state—and the long-term change related to weekly focusing work. I do not mean to imply that the two have to go together. Simply put: some focusers report profound personal change over time. Some focusers report various kinds of "altered state" experiences. Sometimes these go with each other and sometimes they don't.

I want to conclude with one reader's feedback on a draft of this article:

Yes, yes, but don't leave out that focusing is/can be fun! Don't make it sound too lifeless, too bloodless, still another 'technique.' Focusing is a way of life, a Western yoga. It is good for the organism. It 'tastes' good—like a sauce that one savors. One can do much, much worse than make it one's daily practice. Let me get closer to my own experiencing: How delicious!"

PART THREE

FOCUSING &

PSYCHOTHERAPY

PROLOGUE

Parts two and three are the meat and potatoes—the tofu, steamed vegetables, and brown rice—of this book. They are the main course. They are the heart of the book. I do both focusing and therapy. I am a focusing teacher. I am a focusing-oriented experiential therapist. I have had this dual identity since I first met focusing. I enjoy doing both.

This part is about focusing and therapy. We start with terminology.

II

By what name shall we call Gendlinian psychotherapy? This is an area of possible confusion. The name has changed over time. First I will try to clear up the confusion. Then I may add to it.

When I first met him and for quite some time after, Gene called his work Experiential Psychotherapy. I did the same. It was a good 'in the neighborhood' name. But it neglected to mention the most singular aspect of the therapy—focusing. At this point, Experiential Psychotherapy was what Gene called a 'meta-orientation' to therapy rather than a special kind of therapy.

All this changed with the publication of his therapy book. He named it *Focusing-Oriented Psychotherapy* (1996). I do not know exactly when he started using this name. It named a new kind of therapy—his kind. The book's subtitle, "A Manual of the Experiential Method," kept that 'Experiential' in the picture.

Meanwhile I had titled an article simply "Focusing Therapy" (1993). I believe I got this name from Kathy McGuire. I knew it was not exactly right. I knew it left some stuff out. I hoped it was short enough to encourage usage. When Gene introduced the name, "Focusing-Oriented," I agreed that it was more precise. I switched to it.

But I was not completely comfortable. It was like my toes were still being pinched by my shoes. The name was too tight. I wanted to get that 'Experiential' back in there more prominently.

Why? Because there is a tradition in the mental health field to speak of an Experiential family of therapies. These are therapies which work via the affective realm. Gestalt, co-counseling, bioenergetics, psychodrama, primal, Reichian, hakomi, psychomotor—these are some experiential therapies. They are also some of my favorite sources of interventions to combine with focusing.

Hence: Focusing-Oriented Experiential Therapy. That is, I do a therapy in the experiential family which uses focusing as its main method.

Most therapists use more than one method. There are many kinds of experiential therapists. There are gestalt-oriented experiential therapists and hakomi-oriented experiential therapists and co-counseling-oriented experiential therapists and so on.

I am a focusing-oriented experiential therapist. I combine many different interventions, often drawn from the experiential therapies. Focusing is my main method. It is the touchstone to which my work keeps returning. You will see this in the following essays.

III

The first essay presents four criteria for calling something a Focusing-Oriented Experiential Therapy. The criteria are: (1) Focusing is used as a major method; (2) A focusing attitude is taken towards experiencing; (3) The therapist uses focusing on his/her self; (4) Focusing is combined with other methods that the therapist knows. When these four criteria are met, Focusing-Oriented Experiential Therapy is happening.

"The Man Who Never Said What It Was About" reports a one-session focusing-only therapy experience. It is a reminder of how valuable focusing all by itself and without any words from the client can be. Other articles will emphasize combining focusing with other methods. This article is a good counter-balance: just one session, just focusing, no words from the client.

"Experiential Listening" is a very important piece. Focusing is my main method. Listening is next. Focusing and listening go together naturally. In this lengthy essay I do a step-by-step breakdown of how I do listening. I feel specially good about this piece. I am seldom so precise and so exhaustive in defining, describing, and illustrating what I do. Later essays show how I integrate listening into my therapy. This essay is basic to ones that follow, especially the next.

"How I Do Focusing-Oriented Experiential Therapy" is a very early (1982) attempt to categorize what I do in therapy. I am surprised how well it stands up with time. It needs to be read in conjunction with the last two pieces in this section. They are more recent (1996) attempts to do the same. The three pieces together come as close as I have come to describing how I do this kind of therapy.

The 'secret' reason for the inclusion of the next piece—"Gendlin and Angyal: Focusing and Holistic Insight"—is so that I can include in this book at least a brief summary of Andras Angyal's masterpiece, *Neurosis and Treatment* (1965).

If I had to go to a desert island—or a psychotherapy training program—with just one psychology book, it would be Angyal's. It is the best single overview that I know of human nature, personality, development, neurosis, and the therapy process.

The essay also gives me the opportunity to relate one aspect of Gene's work to Angyal's. Gene has not written much on the relation between his own work and that of others. This is a start.

"The Use of Focusing for Self-Therapy" just managed to get into this section. Originally, I referred to it as being about "focusing for self-help." But then I got to thinking about the implied dichotomy between professional therapy and any other kind of helping relationship. It did not stand up to scrutiny. Hence, the thoughts with which I start the article. The word 'therapy' names a process. It ought not refer exclusively to a situation in which one person is called 'the therapist' and the other 'the client.' Working with a focusing partner can be therapeutic. So can working with one's journal. Working with a therapist is not *necessarily* therapeutic. It depends upon what is going on. This essay describes the two ways in which I use focusing and my journal for self-therapy.

The next piece, "Hemingway-Influenced Focusing-Oriented Therapy," just happened. I was immersed in Michael Reynolds' five volume biography of Hemingway. The whole paper came to me, and I wrote it in thirty minutes. Deciding on the title took longer.

"Body Therapies: A Review" is a warm-up for the last piece in the section. It introduces body-oriented therapies. It leads toward talk of focusing as a body-oriented therapy.

The last two essays are my most recent attempt to describe and illustrate how I do therapy. They need to be read together and in conjunction with the piece from 1982. All three together give a picture of what I do in doing Focusing-Oriented Experiential Therapy.

IV

What do I do? After re-reading all the pieces in this section I put together this list of things-that-I-do-in-therapy.
(1) I do focusing.
(2) I do listening.
(3) I self-disclose.
(4) I do 'empathic imagining.'
(5) I make content-less statements designed to keep a person at a feeling place.
(6) I make content-less statements designed to bring a person back to a feeling place.
(7) I make interpretations.
(8) I ask questions.

(9) I combine verbal methods with focusing.
(10) I combine 'soft,' 'hard,' and 'expressive' body-centered interventions with focusing.
(11) I use methods that are not experientially-oriented per se.
(12) I talk as I would in an ordinary conversation.

The list is not exhaustive. It could not be. I keep evolving. Perhaps today I will do something I have never done before. Perhaps it will work. It may very well be added to my repertoire.

V

There is so much more to be said about therapy. I have not explicitly touched upon the therapeutic relationship. I consider it as important as focusing to good therapy. You will have to read between the lines of these essays to get that. This prologue is long enough as it is. Let's move on.

FOCUSING-ORIENTED EXPERIENTIAL PSYCHOTHERAPY

Focusing is not and was not meant to be yet another complete school of psychotherapy. In his 1969 article "Focusing," Gene wrote: "Experiential focusing is a therapeutic procedure... It is not alone sufficient for psychotherapy. Rather, I view it as an essential sub-process" (p. 4). "In presenting focusing I would not like to give rise to its being practiced exclusively..." (p. 10).

In his 1991 article "On Emotion in Therapy," Gene reiterates this point: "I have never proposed focusing as a method of therapy by itself... In a real sense focusing misses every other useful avenue of therapy. It needs to be combined with them all" (p. 264).

I agree. Yet, having endorsed this viewpoint, can we, as Kathy McGuire has suggested (*TFC*, March 1990), still speak of what I will call a "Focusing-Oriented Experiential Therapy"? I believe we can.

Focusing-Oriented Experiential Therapy is a therapy in which: (a) focusing is used as a major method; (b) a "focusing attitude" is taken toward experiencing; (c) the therapist uses focusing on his/her self; and (d) focusing is combined with other methods that the therapist knows.

When these four criteria are met, Focusing-Oriented Experiential Therapy is happening. Let me elaborate on each of these points.

Focusing is used as a major method. At some point or points in the session, the client is either asked to or spontaneously checks in with his/her felt sense of a "something" and stays with this with the help of the therapist to achieve one or more felt shifts.

At some point or points in the session the person is focusing on inner data in inner space.

In "How I Use Focusing for Self-Therapy," I introduce a distinction between *focusing rounds* and *mini-focusings*. A focusing round consists of guided movement through the eight steps of focusing. Mini-focusings result from one, two, or more focusing questions; for example, "How are you from the inside right now?" "What's the crux of it?" "What's a good small step in the right direction?"

Both focusing rounds and mini-focusings may go on in a focusing-oriented experiential therapy. For example, a person may spend 15-30 minutes of a session with me leading him/her through a whole round of focusing. In my own practice, one of twenty sessions a week looks like this.

Much more frequently I tuck focusing questions inside other kinds of verbal exchanges. In my sessions it is clearing a space, finding and resonating the felt sense, and/or some asking questions that I use most frequently.

For how much of the session is focusing going on? The amount varies. It is not the amount of focusing that makes it a focusing-oriented experiential therapy. A therapy is a focusing-oriented experiential therapy when focusing provides the flavor, the atmosphere, the vibration of the therapy.

But it is not sufficient for focusing to be a minor method. For example, in Al Mahrer's *Experiential Therapy* every session goes through the same exact steps, of which focusing is the first. Yet for me the relegation of focusing to just the first step—setting the stage for the real action—is not sufficient for us to speak of it as a focusing-oriented experiential therapy.

Similarly, Steven Jacobsen in his book *Characterological Transformation* devotes several pages to a description of focusing which he will use as one technique among many with a schizoid person. But the relegation of focusing to one diagnostic category makes it not sufficient for us to speak of it as a focusing-oriented experiential psychotherapy.

A focusing attitude is taken toward experiencing. The focusing attitude is a respect for, a reverence toward, concrete bodily felt experiencing. The therapist communicates. "Can you be friendly toward what is happening right now in your body as felt? Open to it. Embrace it. Everything felt is welcome. Felt senses—y'all come." There is a direction away from the mind and into the body. This is an attitude that pervades the session—though not necessarily every minute of it. There may be times when, for example, feelings or thoughts rather than felt senses are being worked with. *Therapy is more than just the digestion of felt experience.* Yet the focusing attitude—the respect for bodily felt experience—is a touchstone to which client and therapist return over and over again.

The therapist uses focusing on his/her self. The therapist works upon himself in many ways. But right before and during the session, the therapist is in what might be called a focusing relation to himself.

In preparation for a client I check in with myself: How am I from the inside right now? What is my felt sense in anticipation of this person and this session?

During the session I'm not closing my eyes, but I am checking in. How do 'we' feel right now? What is happening in me as he/she talks/doesn't talk right now? How does *this* silence feel? I am doing 'eyes open' focusing.

Sometimes my next response will be a report based on my focusing—a personal sharing. Sometimes my next response will come from, roll out of, my whole present felt sense. I'll hear inside "more focusing instructions" or "introduce a gestalt experiment" or something. Sometimes I will check in and note my felt sense but not use it to guide my next response.

In any event, the therapist is in a focusing relationship with himself in an ongoing manner during the session and this grounds him *vis à vis* the client.

Focusing is combined with other methods that the therapist

knows. This is crucial. It builds "combining" into the very definition of focusing-oriented experiential therapy. This may be what is unique in my definition. I have always known that more than bioenergetics goes on in bioenergetic therapy, more than analysis in psychoanalytic therapy, more than cognitions in cognitive therapy. Yet the "more than" is usually not built into the very definition of the therapy. In focusing-oriented experiential therapy it is.

Observing myself during a recent week of doing focusing-oriented experiential therapy, I noticed myself using: focusing, listening, self-disclosure, giving feedback, asking exploratory questions, making interpretations, having a person talk to an empty chair (gestalt), using hakomi probes, arm-wrestling with someone, having someone hit a pillow with a bataka, meditating with someone, a laying on of hands, having someone repeat a key phrase over and over, louder and louder (gestalt), having someone do Nathaniel Branden's sentence completion exercise.

The list is not exhaustive and is only of "techniques." There was also time for chit-chat and time for just saying whatever words I heard inside myself in response to the client. Not all of therapy is methods and techniques. But focusing-oriented experiential therapy explicitly includes methods and techniques other than focusing. And some but not all of these methods are drawn from other experiential therapies.

In conclusion, consider these words of Claudio Naranjo from *The Techniques of Gestalt Therapy.* They are very close to what I am saying about focusing-oriented experiential therapy: "The techniques of Gestalt Therapy are many and cover a whole spectrum. . . some of these techniques are not unique to Gestalt. Yet a session of Gestalt Therapy could not be confused with any other, for the approach, we might say, constitutes a new and unique Gestalt" (p. 3).

Similarly focusing-oriented experiential therapy may combine focusing with many and various other techniques and embed focusing in many different personal styles. No two focusing-oriented experiential therapies will look exactly alike. Yet there will be a family likeness, enough so that we may say, "Ah, this is focusing-oriented experiential therapy."

THE MAN WHO NEVER SAID WHAT IT WAS ABOUT

He called, gave his name, which I recognized as a colleague's, and asked if he could come for one focusing session. Matters of fee and logistics were handled easily and he arrived Tuesday, September 21st at 10:00AM. This was seventeen years ago.

He came in and said that he wanted me to lead him through the focusing steps. He said he would signal me when to go on to the next one, and that he did not want to say anything else.

I led him through the steps. He went relatively slowly and the whole process took about forty minutes. At one point I thought I saw a tear. Otherwise, there was little motion on his part and not a single word.

At the end of the session he paid and thanked me and left.

I saw him ten years later at a conference. He was very friendly and thanked me profusely for the session, which seemed still as vivid to him as it was to me. He told me that he was then working on something that he could not share with anyone, and that had it not been for me and focusing he would not have known where to turn. He said that the one session had gotten him unstuck. He had been stuck for a *long* time.

He did not volunteer and I did not ask anything about the content. The words I heard in my head were, "It's none of my business."

The experience brought home to me one value of focusing. There need to be places where we can go and work in the company of others but in the privacy of our selves. Why should therapists have to know their clients' content? What a presumption!

Our meeting at the conference was brief but rich. It gave me closure. I had had faith in focusing and that had sustained me in the absence of any verbal feedback through the session. Now and then I had had some fear—Was I doing it right? Was this a waste of time? I quieted my fears and did my job and our meeting at the conference confirmed what most of me knew: Trust the process!

EXPERIENTIAL LISTENING

Vasudeva listened with great attention. It was one of the ferryman's greatest virtues that, like few people, he knew how to listen . . . the speaker felt that Vasudeva took in every word, quietly, expectantly, that he missed nothing . . . He did not await anything with impatience and gave neither praise nor blame—he only listened . . . Siddhartha felt how wonderful it was to have such a listener who could be absorbed in another's life . . .

—Herman Hesse, *SIDDHARTHA*

Besides focusing, the most important method I use is listening. This essay defines, describes, and illustrates listening.

Experiential listening is an empathic, supportive, non-interfering way of saying back to a person the felt essence of his or her message and checking with the person to make sure it has been said back correctly. Experiential listening helps people clarify and articulate their inner processes, explore issues, get past stuck places, and carry their experiencing forward. It is useful both for non-professional help and professional therapy. *Listening helps people focus.*

Put simply: The person being listened to says something. The listener takes the person's whole expression inside, listens to its resonance, and then says back words that point towards the felt sense that has been communicated. Then the listener checks with the listenee; did I get that right? If yes, the listenee goes on to whatever he has next to say. If no, the listenee corrects the listener, who then tries again to say it just right.

The entire process—"saying back" and "checking in"—is listening.

To illustrate: consider the following listening I did with the very practiced 45-year-old male client, whom you met in the essay on focusing. In parentheses I will point out the felt sense and felt shift as they occur.

C: (Matter-of-factly) Let me state the problem as I see it. I have a raging need for autonomy, coming from my mother's having been too close to me. And I have difficulty asserting that need with women . . . for fear of displeasing them.

T: Let me see if I get that.

C: OK.

T: (More slowly than C has been speaking) You sense in yourself a need for autonomy, a need that is like a fire, raging out of control . . .

C: (Interrupting) Yes, but not out of control.

T: (Correcting himself) The need for autonomy is not out of control.

C: Right.

T: (Continuing, slowly) And you sense that that need—stemming from mother having been too close to you—is blocked by an equal or stronger need—coming from the same source—to please or at least not displease women . . .

C: (Quickly) Yes, exactly . . . (Pause) When I hear that back, I feel sad and slumped inside. (This is the felt sense.)

T: Sad and slumped come from hearing it back.

C: (More slowly now) Yes . . . it feels heavy . . . a heavy burden to carry around.

T: The whole issue feels heavy to you . . .

C: Right.

T: As if, like some heavy weight you carry inside?

C: (After some consideration) On me . . . on my chest.
T: You feel as if it sits on you, on your chest.
C: No. Sitting in me, not on me . . . Pushing down from inside.
T: It feels like a heavy weight inside your chest depressing you.
C: (Quickly) Yes. The image is of a black square.
T: A black square sits in your chest pressing down deep.
C: I sense anger there.
T: The square has anger . . . ?
C: No. UNDERNEATH it.
T: Oh . . . BENEATH the sad and slumped, ANGER lives.
C: (Voice picks up speed and expression from here on) Yes, exactly. When you said that . . . it moved! I feel it now in my jaw . . . I'm pissed. Pissed! (This is the felt shift.)
T: The rage beneath the slumped has risen.
C: It's spreading through my body. Wow. Through my arms, legs. My head wants to shake from side to side. I hear the words, "Let me be." "Leave me alone." "Let me be." (felt shift)
T: (With expression rising to match C's) Your whole being is angry . . .
C: No—ENRAGED.
T: ENRAGED!
C: Yes.
T: And just wants to be left alone, let be . . .
C: The words come in a torrent now . . .
T: Something has been heard and released in you.
C: (Tears flow) Yes. (Another felt shift.)
T: Like the rivers raging after a thaw . . .
C: Yes (Cries), thank you.

As the example shows, listening is a close and careful being with whatever is "inside" a person ("Beneath the sad and slumped, anger lives"), letting oneself be corrected ("No. Sitting in me, not on me"), and thus allowing the "inside" to shift ("The words come in a torrent now. . . "). Listening is a way of helping a person contact a **felt sense**, a way of keeping a **felt sense** company, and a way of saying it back in such a way that one's words have an **experiential effect**; they permit a **felt shift** to happen (Gendlin, 1981).

Listening is useful both in therapy and in non-professional helping (e.g., between friends, spouses, parents and children). Receiving good listening is a powerful, effective, and, for most people, **unusual** experience. People seldom get to hear back what it is they are groping to express. It is a rare treat to be listened to by someone such as Siddhartha's ferryman who wants you to have the experience of really feeling understood. Everyone ought to learn how to listen. Everyone deserves the experience of really being listened to. If you have not had it, you don't know what you are missing!

In this essay I first trace the historical development of listening. Then I present a listening manual: how I listen and why I listen. A conclusion brings us back to matters of the heart—the place where listening is most appreciated.

II

Listening is an offspring of the union between Carl Rogers' "reflection of feeling" therapeutic response and Eugene Gendlin's "experiential method." It can be called "an experiential reformulation of active listening." It deserves to be recognized as one of the latest steps in the evolution of client-centered therapy into the person-centered approach (Levant and Shlein, 1984)

"Saying back" is the quintessential helping response in the client-centered tradition of therapy. It has been called variously "reflection of feelings," "clarification of feelings" (Snyder, 1947), "active listening" (Gordon, 1970) and, simply, "listening" (Gendlin, 1981).

Carl Rogers describes its origin:

> Very early in my work as a therapist I discovered that simply listening to my client very attentively [and saying nothing] was an important way of being helpful. So when I was in doubt as to what I should do, in some active way, I listened. It seemed surprising to me that such a passive kind of interaction could be so useful.
>
> A little later a social worker, who had a background of Rankian training, helped me to learn that the most effective approach was to listen for the feelings, the emotions whose patterns could be discerned through the client's words. I believe she was the one who suggested that the best response was to 'reflect' these feelings back to the client . . .
>
> (Rogers, 1980, p. 137).

Rogers was a remarkable listener.[1] An excellent sample of his listening style is this excerpt from his work with "Mrs. Oak." In her thirty-first therapy session Mrs. Oak is trying to describe a feeling as it wells up in her:

> C: I have the feeling it isn't guilt (Pause. She weeps.) Of course, I mean, I can't verbalize it yet. (Then with a rush of emotion) it's just being terribly hurt!

Rogers: M-hm. It isn't guilt except in the sense of being very much wounded somehow.

> C: (Weeping) It's—you know, often I've been guilty of it myself but in later years when I've heard parents say to their children "stop crying," I've had a feeling, a hurt as though, well, why should they tell them to stop crying? They feel sorry for themselves. I thought that they could let him cry. And—feel sorry for him too, maybe.

> Well, that's something of the kind of thing I've been experiencing. I mean, now—just right now.

Rogers: That catches a little more the flavor of the feeling that it's almost as if you're really weeping for yourself.

> C: Yeah. And again you see there's conflict. Our culture is such that one doesn't indulge in self-pity. But this isn't—I mean, I feel it doesn't quite have that connotation.

Rogers: Sort of think that there is a cultural objection to feeling sorry for yourself. And yet you feel that the feeling you're experiencing isn't quite what the culture objected to either.

> C: And then of course, I've come to—to see and to feel that over this—see, I've covered it up. (Weeps) But I've covered it up with so much bitterness, which in turn I had to cover up. (Weeping) That's what I want to get rid of! I almost don't care if I hurt.

Rogers: (Softly, and with an empathic tenderness toward the hurt she is experiencing) You feel that here at the basis of it as you experience it is a feeling of real tears for yourself. But that you can't show, mustn't show, so that's been covered by bitterness that you don't like, that you'd like to be rid of. You almost feel you'd rather absorb the hurt than to—than to feel the bitterness. (Pause) And what you seem to be saying quite strongly is, I do hurt, and I've tried to cover it up.

> C: I didn't know it.

Rogers: M-hm. Like a new discovery really.

> C: (Speaking at the same time) I never really did know. But it's—you know, it's almost as though I were looking

within myself at all kinds of—nerve endings and bits of things that have been sort of mashed. (Weeping)

Rogers: As though some of the most delicate aspects of you physically almost have been crushed or hurt.

C: Yes. And you know, I do get the feeling, "Oh, you poor thing." (Pause)

Rogers: Just can't help but feel deeply sorry for the person that is you.

(Rogers, 1961, p. 93)

It would be difficult to overstate Rogers' role in the history of psychotherapy. His client-centered listening and the philosophy of relationship in which it is embedded changed the course of counseling and therapy. There is almost a "before Rogers" and an "after Rogers" psychotherapy.

But Rogers' listening is better than his theory of listening. He did it better than he describes it. There has always been a gap in his writings about listening. It has been mostly unclear just exactly what a "reflection" is supposed to reflect.

This is where Gendlin and his theory of experiencing come in. Gendlin says:

> I came to Rogers' group in Chicago in 1952 from my work in philosophy and my interest in the question: How does raw experience become symbolized? I thought that this happens in psychotherapy. A person struggles with and finds words and expressions for unclear—but lived—experience. I found that Rogers and his group were not very clear in their own minds just what in the client they were responding to. It was the client's 'message' or 'feelings' . . .
>
> (Gendlin, personal communication)

Gendlin's point is that the words 'message' and 'feelings' are but an imprecise and sometimes misleading shorthand. What they stand for is "unclear but sensed experience." This is the true referent of the reflection of feelings response.

The concept of "experiencing" and the experiential method specifies the referent of the reflection of feelings response more exactly.[2] Gendlin says that there is an ongoing flow of experiencing in the human being. He refers to this as a bodily felt but conceptually vague flow of felt meanings (Gendlin, 1961, 1964, 1973, 1981). The listening response is an attempt to make contact with and carry forward this experiential flow. It is not enough for the therapist to just say back the client's words. **Words are not feelings.** The listener is trying to point his words at the concrete experiential flow for which the listenee is making symbols (words). The listenee checks the listener's words against this ongoing flow. When the listening response is just right, it has an experiential effect—the flow of experiencing is carried forward.

In his last writing on empathy, Rogers acknowledges his debt to Gendlin and makes Gendlin's sometimes abstruse philosophical writing more accessible via clinical example:

> An example may clarify both the concept [experiencing] and its relation to empathy. A man in an encounter group has been making vaguely negative statements about his father. The facilitator says, 'It sounds as though you might be angry at your father.' The man replies, 'No, I don't think so.' 'Possibly dissatisfied with him?' 'Well, yes, perhaps' (said rather doubtfully). 'Maybe you're disappointed in him.' Quickly the man responds, 'That's it! I am disappointed that he's not a strong person. I think I've always been disappointed in him ever since I was a boy.'
>
> Against what is the man checking these terms for their correctness? Gendlin's view, with which I concur, is that he is checking them against the ongoing psychophysiological flow within himself to see if they fit. This flow is a very real

> thing, and people are able to use it as a referent. In this case, 'angry' doesn't match the felt meaning at all; 'dissatisfied' comes closer, but is not really correct; 'disappointed' matches it exactly, and encourages a further flow of the experiencing, as often happens.
>
> (Rogers, 1980, p. 141)

In other words, listening responses are offered in such a way that they point the listenee in the direction of checking the response (anger? . . . dissatisfaction? . . . disappointment!) in a focusing way against his/her experiential flow.

In sum, client-centered listening was a method developed by Carl Rogers in response to clinical exigencies. It has produced an abundance of practice and research. It has lacked a grounding in a philosophy of experiencing. Gendlin provides that philosophy. The listener points his response at the felt sense of the listenee. The listenee checks that response against his ongoing experiential flow. If it is accurate, the flow moves forward to a next step. If it is not, the listenee corrects the listener, who then tries again.

This is experiential listening.

III

How does one do it?

Using the imprecise language of "feelings," Rogers warns that—"listening to 'feelings' and 'reflecting' them is a vastly complex process." (1980, p. 138) To this I can only add—Amen.[3]

What follows is my attempt at describing how I do listening. I was at first tempted to call this section "How to Listen" but discarded that for the less grandiose "How I Listen". It is as far as I can tell a specification of what I do when I am listening. Others' descriptions exist (McGuire, 1981; Gendlin, 1974, 1981; Cornell, 1993). The reader is invited to compare and contrast.

HOW I LISTEN

(1) I begin by quieting my mind and turning my full loving attention towards the person to whom I am listening.

There are two steps: quieting the mind; intending towards the speaker.

First I note whether my mind needs quieting. I do this usually by practicing the first step of focusing. Before my client arrives I close my eyes. I sit comfortably, breathe, and ask myself, "How am I from the inside right now?" I let my attention come down into my body and, in a friendly way, roam or scan around and see what is there. I ask if there is a word, phrase, or image that matches the feeling inside. About 75% of the time nowadays I get a word like "clear," "calm," "meditative," "open," "ready." I sit with that feeling for a moment and then go to the waiting room to get my client.

The other 25% of the time I get: I need to do the "clearing a space" step of focusing. I usually put out on the imaginary bench an inventory of what is in the way for me, what is between me and feeling "ready to listen." Most often there will be one or more recent disturbances and perhaps a chronic nagging place in the way: For example, right now I have a pain in my back, left-over anger from this morning, and some weariness inside.

By identifying the trouble spots, giving them a moment's quiet attention, and then promising them I will come back and work on them if need be—they agree to mostly clear.

I only listen when I'm mostly clear.

Notice that **mostly**. Don't make these guidelines into absolutes. I have done good listening while a background upset was not completely resolved. I have done good listening while images from basketball and soccer games danced in the back of my head. There can be background noise in the receiver while one is listening: There cannot be foreground noise.

A further word about clearing a space before listening: When we begin to develop the habit of consciously clearing a space, we start to recognize how unclear we tend to be. Many of us much of the time and all of us some of the time are distracted, scattered, not truly attentive, formulating our next point while the other is speaking, drifting off, preoccupied, anxious, angry, defensive, rebutting, interpreting, judging, etc. We are not truly present. We have internal chatter going on. We are not one-pointed (Schuster, 1979). The receiver is partly jammed. There is static. We have anxiety, fear, guilt, worry, anger, self-protection, interfering with good contact.

When any of these are happening for you, get listened to yourself. Get listened to about your own barriers and obstacles to good contact with people in general and with each particular person (client) in your life.

Know what it feels like inside when you are clear. Know what it feels like when you are unclear. Know the difference and ways to get from the one state to the other.

A quiet mind helps one listen. Keep working on quieting your mind.

Getting mostly clear is only the first step. From that same space of clarity I can write articles, make decisions in my life, make love, etc.

Step two is to bend myself toward the speaker lovingly.

I have emptied my mind. I have become receptive—an open channel. Now I 'turn' towards the speaker.

I let my whole body express this 'turning towards.' I make eye contact. I turn my posture in the direction of the person I am to listen to. I lean a little forward. I look inviting and non-intrusive. My body expresses, 'I am here to listen to you.'

(2) I take in the whole of the person to whom I am listening.

This is a global or holistic 'grokking' of the person. I let my 'presence' hear his or her 'presence.' My whole 'being' is listening to his or her whole 'being.'

> She comes in. I see her very clearly. Somehow as she sits down I 'hear' inside me the word 'fear.' She starts talking rather vaguely about her job, her week, her relationship. Her posture is a little laid back; her gaze a little glassy; her

words a little vague. The whole effect is very subtle. It is more a vibration I am getting from her than her words. I say back, 'So there is something there about your job, your relationship, and your week, and am I getting that that something is fear?' She is startled for a moment. She hasn't mentioned fear. Tears overtake her and they begin to flow. 'Yes,' she says, 'I didn't know. That is exactly what I am feeling. I'm scared . . . of it all.'

Gendlin states:

"The therapist must attend not only to the client's words, but to how they are said, and to how the client is living right in this moment, in saying this. This means observing the person's face, body, voice, gestures, and taking the person in much more broadly than verbally" (in Corsini, 1973, p. 338).

Narrowness of listening is avoided by this step. When I fail to attend to this step, I may miss the larger message being lived by the person at this moment.

Sometimes I just do this step naturally. Some days I am very tuned in to this level with people. When I am not, it is good to silently remind myself by asking inside, "What is this person's being expressing right now? What is the background feeling from which he or she is speaking? What is the general feeling I have inside as he/she walks in?"

It is worthwhile to remember that people always speak from within feeling states. There is an implicit richness behind every statement one makes. Not everything is or can be made explicit. Often the person is unaware of this background state.

So I step back, figuratively speaking, and take in a mural sense of the person, attending to the whole feel of his being.

I do this even if I don't make explicit use of the information right away. It is part of tuning in to the person being listened to:

I am doing a therapy demonstration for a class. She volunteers. She sits down across from me. I observe her eyes: large, open, clear. I take in her erect posture, her bearing, a certain grace in her manner. I hear inside myself the words: 'She is very open and vulnerable, undefended. Just listen to her words very exactly.' I do. She quickly opens up, goes deep, cries, resolves a problem and feels better.

(3) I reflect back to the person the whole felt essence of what I 'hear' him saying.

I would not say all of this, of course, but the experience inside me might be: Sitting here and emptying myself, I turn my full loving attention toward you. I take in your posture—sitting on the edge of the chair, 'bug-eyed,' a tic in your cheek, a haltingness in your speech. I hear you say you have a final exam tomorrow and feel unprepared. I say back: "So is there some fear, or worry, or concern in you about the final you don't feel prepared for?"

Let me elaborate upon this "saying back" step:

(3A) For every 'unit of meaning' I make words that reflect back to the person my best understanding of what he/she is experiencing.

"People need to hear you speak. They need to hear that you got each step. Make a sentence or two for every main point they make, for each thing they are trying to get across . . . . Don't just 'let them talk,' but relate to each thing that they feel . . . . Try to get the crux of it exactly the way they mean it and feel it."

"Say back bit by bit what the person tells you. Don't let the person say more than you can take in and say back. Interrupt, say back, and then let the person go on." (Gendlin, 1981, pp. 119-120)

Reflection ought to be fairly frequent. There is no absolute rule. In learning listening, it is best to do reflections more frequently; as your listening becomes more naturally a part of you, you may want to do it less frequently.

It is important to take in only as much as you can 'hold' before reflecting. This amount will vary with your experience level, memory span, and the way your listenee speaks: Scattered speech is harder to hold than connected speech.

(3B) My reflections point toward the felt sense.

There are three different possibilities concerning the relationship between words and felt sense.

Sometimes the listenee's words exactly reflect the felt sense. We have seen this in some of the focusing examples. When this happens, the listener says these words back pretty exactly:

> C: I feel hurt, wounded, pained inside.
> T: Hurt . . . wounded . . . pained . . .
> C: Yes. Those words are exactly right. When I said them, they felt right inside and when you repeated them I felt them more strongly and clearly . . . and now I feel a bit stronger.
> T: A bit stronger inside now.
> C: Yes . . . it was really fear.
> T: The feeling was really fear.

Notice that this is not how people usually talk. More often, the listenee's words only **hint at, suggest, partially express,** or **approximate** the felt sense. They are around or near it.

When this is so the listener augments these words by making use of whatever else he is picking up from the listenee's nonverbal expressions and whatever else he may guess about the felt sense:

> It is not enough [in this case] to simply say back the content being said. It is also essential to reflect back any unsaid feelings from the person's tone of voice . . . her body posture, facial expressions, and gestures . . . and your own guesses at what a person in her situation might be feeling . . . .
>
> Reflections of unsaid feelings are . . . offered . . . as guesses—the person then can check your guess against her inside feelings and come up with a more accurate word . . . .

Guesses needn't be right—the important thing is that they lead the person to look at . . . her feelings, to ask herself, 'Well, if it's not that, what am I feeling about this?' (McGuire, 1981, p. 56)

In the following example, notice how the therapist makes use of non-verbal cues and her own imagination of the situation described and thus helps the client into the felt sense:

> C: (Her voice is shaky, quivery, with long pauses) My mother died when I was seven . . . . My sisters were four and two . . . . I had to take over then . . . . I did the washing . . . the cleaning . . . got them dressed and all . . . . Then I walked off to school by myself . . . and a neighbor lady took care of them.
> T: (Softly, slowly, with care) I'm imagining you felt very lonely . . . and sad that you didn't have her anymore . . . and burdened that you had your sisters to care for.
> C: (Tears start to form in her eyes; her words come faster now) Yes, all of that, and now I see that the worst was how **guilty** I felt about leaving them (cries). I didn't do a good enough job.
> T: Oh . . . Like you had loved your mother very much (C: Yes) and what really hurt was your feeling **guilty** . . . like, you'd let her down.
> C: Yes. Exactly. She'd left them to me.

The felt sense comes into sharper focus ("now I see . . . how guilty I felt . . . ") after the listener reflects back unsaid feelings.

Finally, sometimes the listenee's words ignore or obscure the felt sense. Words and felt sense may be like two trains traveling on parallel and non-intersecting tracks. The listenee may know nothing about words coming from felt senses.

The listener then imagines the felt sense that might be there and points at it. More use is made of the non-verbal and the holistic 'grokking' than of the verbal productions:

> C: (Sprawls into chair, arms akimbo, like a marionette whose strings are being tugged in several directions at once) Well . . . there's so much to tell you. My week was . . . I really have to pay my rent . . . and there was the thing with Charles, oh Lord (a herky-jerky motion; suddenly he sits bolt upright). What was I saying? Oh yes, work was so . . . Did I tell you about Dorothy? (maniacal giggle)
> T: So . . . does it feel all jumbled inside? Like confused . . . and maybe all rushing past like an express train?
> C: Next stop Greenwich Village! . . . Yeah (smile) something like that . . . How did you know? (Friedman, 1982a, p. 103)

It is important for the listener to recognize where on this continuum a person's verbalization is coming from. "Is this particular word or phrase coming from a felt sense?" The listener needs to develop the kind of sensitivity which can answer that question.

Remember that what the listener is attempting to do is make contact with the experiential flow 'in' the client. When words are 'coming from' this flow, saying them back pretty exactly and with intonation, rhythm, etc. that reflect the client's will help make contact with that flow. Words that don't 'come from' this flow are not treated in the same way as words that do 'come from' this flow. Words and the way they are said are clues to the person's felt process. Some clues are better than others. A good listener comes to know which words best 'point' to the felt sense.

Noting where an expression comes from helps guide one as to whether to say something back exactly or paraphrase it—one of the important decisions to be made in listening. A good rule of thumb: say back pretty exactly those words that either match or come from very close to the felt sense; paraphrase the rest.[4]

Clients often say many words that tell the story of external events and few words that describe the felt sense of these events. This is especially so in the early part of therapy. It is the therapist's task to briefly summarize the story of the external events and then highlight the felt sense words.

For example:

> C: My father had some medical tests done yesterday. We drove him to Beth Israel and waited there. They gave him the upper and lower GI series. He had to fast all morning and only had some milk all day. We made arrangements for his room and then hung out watching TV. The tests were all negative. Was I ever relieved!
>
> T: The tests were all negative and you felt relieved.

Similarly, a long account of an unhappy vacation was paraphrased, "The trip was unpleasant, and you were disappointed." A detailed description of an argument between two brothers became, "You two fought and it makes you sad and angry."

The same principle applies when the felt sense is not so clearly articulated. The therapist pays special attention here. By pointing his reflection at the unclear felt sense, he helps the client grapple with it and become more clear:

> C: We went to see The Purple Rose of Cairo. I felt something funny between us during the show. I couldn't really identify it. Afterwards, we had a bit to eat. When I took her home I kissed her goodnight. It was sort of a nice evening, I think . . . .
>
> T: You think you had a nice evening . . . (more slowly) and there was that something funny you felt during the show . . . something you felt there . . .
>
> C: It was like we were and weren't together. I can't explain it. . . I felt confused by her . . . and TWISTED by the confusion. . . I guess it wasn't so great an evening!

T: The main thing there was—TWISTED by the confusion...

Notice that the story-line is downplayed and the client's emphasized feeling word (TWISTED) is reflected exactly. As Gendlin says, "Therapists can paraphrase most of what a client says, but are wise to keep crucially charged words the same. We might paraphrase a long story... But if the client uses the word 'apprehensive,' we would not change it to 'scared' or 'worried' because then the client might lose hold of the connotation that word right now holds. Such a word can be a 'handle' that helps us hold onto a whole suitcase." (Gendlin, 1984, p. 86)

(3C) I vary the way I say things back.

Good listening has variety to it. It is creative. It holds the listenee's attention.

A steady diet of "it sounds like you are saying" becomes repetitive, tinny, parrot-like and artificial, and may induce anger and resistance.

Therefore:

Sometimes I affirm my reflection declaratively; sometimes I offer it as a question tentatively.

Sometimes I 'become the other' as in psychodramatic doubling and say my reflection as though I were he.

Sometimes I use a 'sounds like you are saying' lead-in.

Sometimes I embellish a reflection by saying the feeling words that had not been said; sometimes I pare down and sum up an over-stuffed statement.

Sometimes I rearrange the words in a reflection so as to highlight the felt sense.

Sometimes I add emphasis to sharpen up the feeling tone of a statement.

In the following excerpt I identify in parentheses the several different ways I say things back:

C: I've had enough of going along with other people's cock-eyed opinions!
T: I'm sick and tired of other people's crap! (becoming the other; adding emphasis)
C: Damn right . . . I've lost myself too often. It makes me so mad!
T: You're pissed about having lost yourself so often. (Paraphrasing and sharpening the language in the feeling words.)
C: More than that—what I've missed in life by being so damn good.
T: Worse than the anger is the missing. (words rearranged)
C: Yeah . . . I put my own needs on the shelf.
T: You aren't at your center. (Paraphrase; rearranged)
C: It feels awful! I'm wasting my life. I can only live as a hermit. I can't form a relationship. I can only take care of me if there is no one else around. I can't be 'twoed.'
T: Sounds like you are saying that the problem doesn't happen when you're all alone (uh-huh) . . . but it does keep you from having a relationship (yup) . . . and since you are really wanting to be 'twoed' (yesiree) . . . you really feel the need to get this fixed up. ("sounds like" formulation)
C: You got it! Life is with people. I need to learn how to be with people and take care of myself.
T: You are determined to be able to do both. (paraphrase)
C: Yes.

(3D) I use imagery, metaphor, and analogy in my listening responses.

A listening response aims to be evocative (Rice, 1974). It wants to be vivid. Connotative language (imagery, metaphor, analogy) helps 'spark' the felt sense; it resonates with the ongoing experiencing process.

Consider these examples:
First, from Rogers:

> C: Well, now I wonder if I've been going around doing that, getting smatterings of things, and not getting hold, not really getting down to things....
>
> T: Maybe you've been getting just SPOONFULS here and there rather than really DIGGING IN somewhere rather deeply... (Rogers, in Snyder, 1947, p. 171)
>
> ****
>
> C: I'm gonna take off... I just want to run away and die.
>
> T: I guess as I let that soak in... I guess the image that comes to my mind is sort of a—a wounded animal that wants to crawl away and die. (Rogers in Corsini, 1979, p. 158)

Imagery should be tailored to the vocabulary and interests of the client. Metaphors are personal worlds. Seldom would I quote baseball to a ballerina. The image is fit to the person, not vice versa.

For example, in working with an ardent Zionist I did the following reflection:

> C: I want the job at the university. It's special to me. I'm tired of volunteering... and I don't want to teach at the high school level or the state college. I want the university to be my home!
>
> T: "I want Israel. Don't try to sell me Madagascar!"

(Whereas with a baseball enthusiast I might have said, "I'm ready for the Big Leagues. Don't send me back to the minors!")

It helps considerably when therapist and client share a metaphorical realm in which they can communicate vividly and as if in shorthand:

> He is a sports fan. So am I. Early on in therapy I get in the habit of sprinkling football, baseball, and basketball images

into my reflections: "Sounds like it's the fourth quarter, the score is tied, and you're feeling like the wind is against you" . . . "You're finally in the batter's box—and there's their ace reliever on the mound." In his focusing, sports images come frequently. One day, for the first time, an ice hockey image appears: "Hey, I just got the winning goal in a Stanley Cup seventh game!" We note both the winning and the new sport in the image. The next week he reports significant breakthrough activity—in a new realm of life.

Metaphors and analogies related to the client's spheres of interest (sometimes not yet mentioned in therapy) will come spontaneously to the therapist when he is especially well-tuned in to the client:

C: What's the use? Why bother? Life is a drag and a half.
T: You really feel like giving up!
C: Yeah—really!
T: Sounds like you're at your lowest depths . . . The underground man.
C: More Dostoevski than Gorki.
T: Raskalnikov?
C: Yes! Exactly! (He brightens up) Murder not suicide!
T: War or peace?
C: War! No question about it! Too much peace at any price.

(4) After I offer a reflection, I watch and listen to the listenee's reaction, and I am guided by it.

(4A) I am explicitly or implicitly asking the listenee to check my reflection against his or her felt sense.

I will discuss three possibilities here: (1) The client doesn't check the reflection against the felt sense. (2) The client checks it, and it is correct. (3) The client checks it, and it is incorrect.

My invitation to the client to check my reflection may be either verbal or non-verbal. If I don't sense that the listenee is doing such checking, I explicitly ask that he or she do so. I sense "not-checking" from the client's continuing to talk rapidly, lack of change of expression on her face, a sense in me that I have not been taken inside, that I have been ignored. When this happens I want to slow up the interaction and explicitly invite her to check my reflection against her felt sense:

> C: (Talking rapidly) I'm depressed, down, hassled . . .
> T: You're feeling depressed, down, hassled.
> C: (Going on over my last word) I don't know what to do . . .
> T: Wait . . . I'm not sure that you are feeling all that. Would you check?
> C: (Confused) What do you mean—check?
> T: (Explaining and teaching focusing) Does 'depressed, down, hassled' match what you are feeling in your body?

When I sense that my client is checking my reflection inside, I watch and listen for tell-tale signs of whether or not she feels understood.

I watch her face, her breathing. I listen to the quality of her next statement.

Being accurately heard leads to a relaxation. I look to see whether there are signs of that relaxation.

Being accurately heard leads to a something new, a sense of further exploration. I listen to whether the next thing said indicates a going further.

Conversely, being inaccurately heard leads to signs of annoyance: a grimace, a squeezing up of the face, a raised eyebrow. Being inaccurately heard leads to the person saying the same thing over again or changing the subject abruptly and staying at a superficial level.

(4B) When my client does not feel understood, I drop my previous reflection, let myself be corrected, and try again:
For example:

> C: I don't feel understood by Mr. X. He doesn't really see me.
> T: You are angry that Mr. X doesn't understand you.
> C: No. Not angry. I just don't feel understood.
> T: It's not anger. It's being NOT UNDERSTOOD. (emphasis)
> C: Right. He does what you just did—putting his own interpretation on me. But at least I can correct you!
> T: I do it wrong like he does, but at least I can learn.
> C: No! At least *I* can correct you!
> T: There . . . I did it again. (Both laugh) The important thing is that YOU can correct me.
> C: Right.

"Checking-in" is as crucial to experiential listening as is "reflecting." Without checking-in, therapy can go off-track:

> She is consulting to the Board of a Corporation. The members can't get along with each other. She intuits a sentence for each to say. It is supposed to sum up each's position. She puts them in dyads and has them say the sentences back and forth to each other. She never has them check the accuracy of her intuition. If she is wrong, there is no correction. They interact around **her** sentence, not **their** own experiencing. Some members leave feeling frustrated, annoyed, not understood. Had she known listening, her intuitive hunches could have been powerfully used; without listening they tend to be wasted or harmful.

Checking-in allows even wrong reflections to be useful, helpful, not destructive. The therapist's 'off-ness' is quickly and easily corrected. The therapist does not lead the client into blind alleys—often, the therapist's blind alleys.[5]

There are two guidelines here: (1) intend to be accurate, and (2) be correctable.

Checking-in takes a burden off the therapist. It is not necessary that your listening always be 'right.' It is necessary that you try to make it 'right,' sometimes succeed, and that you are not ego-attached to your reflections.

This last point is important.

Sometimes I demonstrate this by saying a reflection in such a way that it **requires** correction.

> There is a lot of feeling in her voice, though few feeling words come through. She is talking about her mother's drug addiction. With long pauses and a sense of heaviness in her throat she says, 'There wasn't . . . much . . . I . . . could do.' Then, she is silent, as she often is. I say, 'I probably won't get all this right, and so you'll have to correct me . . . but is it like you're hurt, and disappointed, and, maybe, real mad, or possibly even guilty, that you just couldn't do much for her?' The form of my reflection shows that it is simply designed to stimulate her to say it the way it was. She responds, 'more guilty . . . less angry . . . my responsibility.'

I am happy to be corrected. My ego isn't hung-up on being 'right.' I readily drop my reflection and follow your correction.

Being listened to drives this home to me over and over again. A 'wrong' reflection can help me clarify what it was I was trying to say. It can help my self-exploration process. Feeling its 'wrongness' leads me to find words that would be more right. It will only get in my way if you insist on it. If you are willing—nay, eager—to drop it, then I can move on.

I find this one of the most difficult things to teach about listening. Especially to therapists. Many therapists feel that they have to get it right. And many feel that they are always right. I remember telling a therapist that when I was four I was cutting a string on my teddy bear, and the knife went into my eye, leading to a traumatic hospitalization and operation. He said, "That was masochism." I stared at him. He was shaking his head affirmatively, agreeing with himself. I said, "How can you be so sure?" He said, dismissively, "I'm sure." His own certainty meant more to him than my hint at doubt. After a few examples of such kinds of intervention on his part, I went elsewhere.

It helps to remember: listening shows the therapist's **intent** is to understand. Unconditional positive regard is carried by that intent. The energy exchange goes something like this: The client sees the therapist leaning toward him. The client feels hopeful: "Oh boy. It **may** happen here, I **may** be understood." When the therapist is wrong, the client starts to fade, to withdraw, to be deflated. Hope may be dashed. But then the therapist notices the withdrawal. He asks, "Did I get that wrong?" "May I try again?" The client feels hope returning. He may have been too shy, too used to being misunderstood to initiate the correction. But now he responds to the therapist's recognition that he has misunderstood. The client tries again. He tries harder to be understandable in response to the therapist's well-intentioned effort to understand and his willingness to be corrected. Hope returns—so long as listening is successful part of the time, and the therapist/listener improves after being corrected.

Hence, the crucial guideline: don't be attached to your reflection. In sum, here are my basic guidelines for listening:

> (1) I begin by quieting my own mind and turning my full loving attention towards the person to whom I am listening.
>
> (2) I take in the whole of the person to whom I am listening.
>
> (3) I reflect back to the person the whole felt essence of what I 'hear' him saying.
>
> (3A) For every 'unit of meaning' I make words that

reflect back to the person my best understanding of what he is experiencing.
- (3B) My reflections point toward the felt sense.
- (3C) I vary the way I say things back.
- (3D) I use imagery, metaphor, and analogy in my listening responses.
(4) After I give a reflection, I watch and listen to the listenee's reaction, and I am guided by it.
- (4A) I implicitly ask the listenee to check my reflection against his felt sense.
- (4B) I am correctable. When my client does not feel understood, I drop my previous reflection and try again.

IV

Thus far I have outlined a brief history of listening, a theory of listening, and how I listen.

Now I turn to the questions: Why do listening? What are the aims, goals, and purposes of listening?

I will answer these questions by reference to **empathy, community, relationship, self-exploration, focusing,** and **catharsis**. All contribute to change.

1. I listen in order to develop and demonstrate empathy.

When therapists are asked to describe the ideal therapist, empathy is the outstanding quality mentioned (Raskin, 1974). Yet, this ideal is realized far less than it is promoted (Rogers, 1980).

Listening is a way to develop and demonstrate one's sensitivity and empathy.[6]

Rogers defines empathy as follows:

> [Empathy] means entering the private perceptual world of the other and becoming thoroughly at home in it. It in-

volves being sensitive, moment to moment, to the changing felt meanings which flow in this other person, to the fear or rage or tenderness or confusion or whatever that he/she is experiencing. It means temporarily living in his/her life, moving about in it delicately without making judgements, sensing meanings of which he/she is scarcely aware . . . It includes communicating your sensing of his/her world as you look with fresh and unfrightened eyes at elements of which the individual is fearful. It means frequently checking with him/her as to the accuracy of your sensings and being guided by the responses you receive. You are a confident companion to the person in his/her inner world. By pointing to the possible meanings in the flow of his/her experience you help the person to focus on this useful type of referent, to experience the meanings more fully, and to move forward in the experiencing. (1980, p. 142)

This, of course, is a description of the listening response.

I listen in order to become empathic and to demonstrate empathy.

I use listening to help warm myself up to my client. By saying back her words, taking in her gestures, her rhythms, her tone, I am attuning myself to her. I am trying to get into her shoes. At times this may be a quite deliberate action on my part. I am walking in her footprints so as to begin feeling like her inside. I am quite exactly tracing her steps in order to create an empathic space inside myself.

At first this may be 'as if.' I'm trying-on her ways from the outside in. This is a planned, conscious, deliberate trying to get with the person. I am using a method self-consciously to transcend our separateness.

Sooner or later, the situation changes. I feel a little 'click' inside, a 'something' will come to me that is no longer coming from my conscious mind.

Often when this happens in me there will be a 'click' in her too.

At this point I am being empathic. (Up to this point I am becoming empathic.)

Now I use listening to demonstrate my empathy.

I use it to give the person the experience of really feeling understood.

2. I listen in order to dissolve alienation and create community.

More than one theory of emotional distress relates it to 'a state of isolation' (Angyal, 1965). Sullivan theorized about the pernicious effects of isolation on mental health (1953). Freida Fromm-Reichmann wrote, "real loneliness . . . leads ultimately to the development of psychotic states" (1959, p. 326)

My own translation of this is that we all spend too much time in our own little closets. We see the world out of our own little windows. We feel separate, alienated, cut-off, alone. Disconnected from others, we experience a 'shut-up-ness' of the self. When we lack the experience of being real with people, we start to lose a sense of our own realness. Our tin roofs keep others from 'dropping in.'

Listening relates us. It dissolves alienation and promotes communion: "For the moment, at least, the recipient finds himself or herself a connected part of the human race." (Rogers, 1980, p. 6) As Jung is reported to have said, a schizophrenic ceases to be schizophrenic when he feels understood. (cited in Rogers, 1980, p. 152)

3. I listen to create the kind of relationship listening engenders.

Listening reduces the authoritarian potentials in the therapeutic relationship. (So does focusing.)

When I am listening, I, the guide, am in fact a follower, being led by the real expert in the situation, the client, who leads me on a journey into the nooks and crannies of his/her experience.

Compare the gestalt or bioenergetic therapist: "Talk to your inner saboteur"; "Speak in gibberish"; "Hit the pillow"; "Put your sadness in the chair." These are directive responses from an expert who has authoritatively taken over the interaction, leading the client into the next step.[7]

Listening promotes a more nearly egalitarian relationship. It empowers the client. "I hear you saying . . . " is a following rather than a leading response. It says "the ball is in your court." It doesn't impose. It is like stepping into the other's footprint in the snow. It deepens the impression while leaving it up to the other to choose the next step.

4. I listen to encourage self-exploration.
Listening is an unusual response to give someone. Mostly in life we interrupt each other too soon. We give advice, interpret, judge, jump in. We act as if the other is speaking final copy—not a rough draft—and as if we are to respond with final copy of our own.

A listening response works partly due to its unconventionality, its differentness from this 'final copy' mentality.

Mostly people speak in rough drafts. We need the space to do our own editing aloud—to develop an idea, to follow it as it unfolds, to listen to ourselves fumble and struggle towards clarity. We need help in finding out from our own innermost places what it is we really have to say.

Listening provides the supportive space for such self-exploration.

> Listening is based on a philosophy which says that, when a person is being unclear in what to do next, or needing help, the best possible thing you can do is to help her find words for the feelings she is having—that being able to symbolize this whole inner experience of confusion or trouble leads to change in that trouble and the possibility for new actions and decisions. Once the person has been able to symbolize in words what is going on inside, solutions and next steps will come from within the person herself. So listening is used to help the person find words . . .
>
> (McGuire, 1981, p. 53)

I use listening to help a person roam around in a 'something.' This may be an issue, a problem, a situation, a decision to be made, a feeling. This roaming around is allowed to be unhurried, tentative groping. My reflections encourage the groping ("Is it something like. . . ?"). They are designed to help the person find the words (symbols) that reflect the experiential truth that he/she is searching to express.

5. Listening promotes focusing.
As we have seen, listening responses promote the very helpful kind of self-exploration called focusing.

When a therapist empathically listens to a client within a helping relationship characterized by therapist realness, acceptance, unconditional positive regard, and faith in the client, the client will focus. She will be able to tune into and hear from her own inner spaces. When a therapist listens, a client "can check [the therapist's] words against the feeling inside and try talking again, trying to find words [that better fit] those feelings. Again, you help just by saying back what you have heard her say." (McGuire, 1981, p. 53)

Listening helps a person focus. It gently lowers a person into the experiencing from which she is trying to speak. It helps ground the person. We saw this in the very first example presented in this essay. When I reflected back to my client that his needs for autonomy and approval counter each other, he responded, "Yes, exactly . . . (pause) when I hear that back, I feel sad and slumped inside . . . " Thus, focusing has begun. Then, when I reflected back his statement that underneath the sad and slumped place there was anger, he experienced a felt shift: ". . . it moved! I feel it now in my jaw." I reflect this, "The rage beneath the slumped has risen," and he responds with more of a shift: "It's spreading through my body. Wow . . . "

This example is somewhat dramatic. The person knew focusing and listening. He came in primed for the session. Such is not always the case. People don't always 'go inside' and get movement so quickly. Sometimes one must listen carefully for some time. There may be a circling round the felt sense for a while. But with persistence, patience, and sensitivity to nuance, the listener will sooner or later promote focusing.

6. Listening promotes catharsis.
Many theorists have pointed towards what is variously called catharsis, discharge, or abreaction of feelings as a source of therapeutic progress (e.g., Jackins, 1965, Janov, 1970, Hart, 1975).

It has not generally been stressed enough in the literature on catharsis that accurate experiential listening promotes discharge.

For example, consider Gendlin's experience with Miss L:

> Miss L found exact client-centered listening enormously powerful. Every little while it would make her cry to have her exact feeling restated out loud. The crying went with a feeling of inward movement. Once she experienced this powerful effect, nothing else would do. She would get unhappy and frustrated with any other response from me. 'Why don't you reflect my feeling?' was a constant reminder. . . . The words had to be exact, all the main words had to be the ones she's used. Then only would she have the sense of powerful impact, and only through these moments would she get to a further step. There were times when she would tell me exactly what to say, and then, when I said it exactly, it would make her cry. (Gendlin, 1974, p. 223)

Emotional release is a common phenomenon when listening is working. Something opens inside. Tears well up. Anger is felt more sharply. Laughter occurs. There is a deep sigh. Feelings are felt more deeply, find expression, and shift. Other methods can then be added on in order to increase the volume or intensity of the discharge. But by itself good, careful listening can do the opening.

In sum:

> I listen to develop and demonstrate empathy.
> I listen to dissolve alienation and create community.

I listen to create the kind of relationship listening engenders.
I listen to encourage self-exploration.
I listen to promote focusing.
I listen to promote discharge.

V

Thus far in this essay I have endeavored to be specific, precise, and analytical about where listening comes from, how I do it, and what it does.

Now I want to shift gears.

Having engaged your head I ultimately want to speak about the heart.

That is where listening is most appreciated.

Listening helps open the heart.

Let me share with you the occasion for this realization:
Listen, listen, listen
To my heart's song.
Listen, listen, listen
To my heart's song.
I will never forget you.
I will never forsake you.
I will never forget you.
I will never forsake you.
Listen, listen, listen
To my heart's song.

The Opening The Heart Workshop begins with the group singing these words.[8] I've heard them hundreds of times now. But one day I heard them a little differently. I was working on this essay and I was stuck for a conclusion. I kept hearing the words, "Listen, listen, listen/To my heart's song" over and over. Then my conclusion came to me:

Someplace inside, someplace deep inside, we all want someone to listen to our heart's song.

We want to sing an aria of our pain, a ballad of our love, a medley of our anger, hurt, sadness, joy.

We want to give voice to what is inside each and every one of us: the particular ways we have been blessed and hurt by life.

We all long to be heard.

But mostly our songs stay inside, shut up.

We move our lips, but we don't sing our songs.

We each peek out from our own cubby hole.

We have walls, masks, moats, gates, fogs, secret chambers, secret police to protect our innermost places.

Why?

Because we have all been hurt by life.

They weren't there. They were wrapped up in themselves. They told us not to be so sensitive. They told us to act appropriately. They didn't see. They didn't hear. They didn't listen. They yelled at us. They abused us.

Listening is the antidote.

Listening is an invitation to me to sing my song.

Being heard helps undo the hurt.

When I feel listened to I feel better. I feel heard, seen, kept company, understood. I feel less alone. I feel supported. I feel like I have an ally. I feel the way a team feels when it has a good cheerleading section. I feel more clear. I feel calm, peaceful, meditative, energized.

My battery has been charged.

The problem may be no different—for now.

But I am different.

My heart is more open.

So remember this about listening: it is a way for one person to really get with and be with another person. The particular specifics of technique are not as important as is this overall effect.

How do I know whether I'm doing it right? I know it by your having the experience of really feeling understood.

That is the essence of experiential listening.

HOW I DO FOCUSING-ORIENTED EXPERIENTIAL THERAPY (1982)

In this essay, I describe what I do in a Focusing-Oriented Experiential Therapy.

In my essay on the experiential in the history of therapy I have said that one of the goals of my sessions is to get my clients in touch with the concrete bodily felt experiencing process that is ongoing in them; to help them to be open and friendly towards it; to invite them to embrace and surrender to their organismic stirrings. I defined as experiential any therapy which encourages clients to stay with this affective process, to keep it company, to help it move forward. I showed that various theorists of therapy have pointed toward this experiencing process as central to therapeutic change. My review led me to endorse Gene's claim that the experiential meta-orientation is compatible with various vocabularies and techniques of therapy (Gendlin, 1969).

How I help clients make contact with and stay with their process is the main focus of this essay. But to sharpen the contrast, let us take a glimpse first at three examples of therapeutic work that is *not* experiential.

> I go to a demonstration by Harold Searles. He is very quick, very active, very directive. He picks up on words the patient uses and interprets their possible hidden meanings. He never asks the patient what he is feeling. The patient talks. Searles asks him questions that seem to come from left field. The

patient is constantly off-balance, responding thoughtfully to Searles' curve balls. They joust. The patient leaves the stage looking befuddled. In the question period after the session Searles confesses that he often gets feedback that he doesn't allow patients time to get into their feelings.

I go to a therapist for a first session. I feel lousy. I start right in the midst of it. "I feel miserable. I feel trapped. I'm feeling torn apart inside." The therapist asks me to give him some background information about myself. I'm dismayed. He doesn't want my process. He wants data. I decide to persevere: "It feels like I'm all boxed in." He asks what would be a way out. I'm jolted again. He isn't with me. I start to think my way to an answer but instead say, "If I could answer that I wouldn't be here." He says, "You sound angry." "I am." "Tell me about your anger." Now I'm angry that he wants me to tell him *about* a feeling, a feeling that I'm having in response to his derailment of my process. I feel frustrated with him. I recognize this interaction as a mirror of interactions that have *led* me to this place. "I'm feeling frustrated with you." "Do you feel frustrated often in life?" I groan. I smile and think—yes, because people like you don't listen to me. He takes my smile as a sign of his therapeutic acumen. The session is about to end. He asks me how many siblings I have. I don't return.

A colleague sends me a paper to read (Scheff, n.d.). Mostly I like it. One example though disturbs me: "The patient was describing an incident to the therapist in which his father had attacked him with a knife. In the midst of this recollection, the patient becomes visibly distraught. He wrings his hands, stutters, and seems unable to continue. The expression on his face becomes quite sad. He seems to be choking with emotion. The therapist asks: 'Were there any good times with your father?'"

I am horrified reading this. I want someone at some point (and what point is better than right when he is in it?)

to keep this person company in his distraught sadness, to help him feel it further, to stay with the rage that may come up next, to let the feelings speak, to ask them friendly questions. I want the therapist to simply witness and encourage the unfolding of the client's experiencing. Help him get deeper into it; don't help him avoid it!

What do these examples have in common? *The therapist is not breathing along with the client.* He is intrusive. He takes the client away from his/her experiencing process. The client's experiencing is left lonely and isolated. The engagement is at best head-to-head rather than person-to-person.

Persons *are* experiencing processes. There is in each and every one of us at all times an inward ongoing flow of experiencing which we can at any moment dip into in order to have direct access to our here and now bodily felt existence. Authentic personality change comes from a carrying forward of this experiencing process (Gendlin, 1964). In our three examples the therapist interrupts the flow, deflects the person from it. He is like a fat boulder in the midst of a thin stream. The stream's own movement is obstructed.

In contrast, my focusing-oriented experiential therapy is guided by Eugene Gendlin's theory of the experiencing process. Specific techniques do not make a therapy experiential. What makes therapy experiential is a certain attitude: an attitude of respectful attentiveness to, and attunement with, a person's experiencing process.

What I Do

How do I embody this attitude? What do I do? What are the typical interventions that I make in my particular way of being a focusing-oriented experiential therapist?

(1) I do focusing. This is absolutely basic to my therapy and perhaps the most novel thing about it. I help clients make direct reference to their experiencing.

(2) I do listening. I reflect back the felt meaning in my clients' messages so as to gently lower them more deeply into their feelings.
(3) I self-disclose. I respond from my own experiencing process. I share myself in a way that engages my clients in a feelingful interaction.
(4) I do empathic imagining. I feel my way into my clients' worlds to sense where they are at this very minute. I utilize the person's non-verbal behaviors as cues to his present feeling state.
(5) I make content-less statements designed to keep a person at a feeling place.
(6) I make content-less statements to bring a person back to a feeling place.
(7) I make interpretations in an experiential way so as to keep a feeling process moving.
(8) I combine gestalt methods with focusing.
(9) I combine bioenergetic methods with focusing.
(10) I do things which are not experientially-oriented per se.

I will now elaborate upon and illustrate each of these things-that-I-do.

(1) **I do focusing.**

Focusing is a quiet, gentle, quasi-meditative way to get a client in touch with the whole *felt sense* of a problem, issue, or situation, and, through specific steps, to help the person achieve a *felt shift*, a piece of bodily resolution of the issue (Gendlin, 1981).

Focusing is a skill. It proceeds in steps. The focuser is invited to turn her attention like a searchlight into her body and just scan or roam around in it sensing, "How do I feel from the inside right now?" She is invited to do this in a friendly way. She is asked to at first let the procedure be wordless. Then she is asked to see if there is a word, phrase, image, or other kind of symbol that feels like it matches, comes from, or will act as a handle on the visceral sensations inside. When the focuser finds such a symbol, she then checks it against her organismic stirrings to see if it is "just right." If in this resonating she finds an inward "yeah," a nod, a "whew," a sense of either some relief or some sharpening of the feeling, then the handle is right and she is ready for the next step. If instead there is just a lukewarm "almost-ness" to the possible handle or a definite internally sensed "no," then she is instructed to go back to the body and await a more exactly right handle.

When she finds a just right handle she has symbolized her *felt sense* and achieved a beginning *felt shift*. Now she is invited to "hang out" with the felt sense, to keep it company, to tap it, to nudge up against it, to ask it friendly open-ended questions. The therapist may say something like "let words, images, memories, poetry, music come from the felt sense," or "keep your attention right on the feeling and ask it, 'What's the crux of this?'"

What comes to the focuser next may be words, phrases or images (symbols), or it may be other bodily sensations. If it is a symbol the next instruction is to take this symbol back to the body and get "the whole feel of *that*." If it is body stuff, the next instruction is to find a symbol (handle) for it.

Thus, there is a zig-zag back and forth between felt sense, symbol, felt shift, new felt sense, symbol, felt shift, etc., in a "self-propelled feeling process," (Gendlin, 1964) which spirals ever downward toward a state of deep relaxation and profound self-discovery. Focusing is a process of finding felt senses and then interacting with them in a friendly way so as to feel movement.

Focusing allows clients to make direct reference to their bodily felt experience. Sometimes I lead (or follow) them through a whole round of focusing. Sometimes we do only the first step of focusing. "What are you feeling?" "What are you aware of in your body?" These are the basic questions.

      These questions are designed to center the client—to get the client to make contact with "what is" right now.

T: What's in you?

C: I guess I feel. . . lonely. . . (cries). . . it wouldn't be an exaggeration to say I feel like this all the time.

T: What's now?
C: I don't know (pause). . . A feeling, uh. . . I want some affection!

T: Where are you?
C: I'm angry! At Helen! (goes into details)

T: What is?
C: I don't want to say much. . . just sit quiet. . . I feel quiet. . . (cries) I feel like I could cry more and more.

The centering questions are designed to either start a feeling process going or deepen it. My own tone and specific wording varies. I can ask them tenderly, in a friendly way, and I can ask them more sharply.[9]

I use these questions practically from the very start of therapy. Sometimes they work. Sometimes they don't. When the questions work, we are right where we want to be—in touch with the client's immediate experiencing. But often, especially in the early hours of therapy—and sometimes for months—the client does not *meet* the question. Instead, the client is flabbergasted, flustered, comes up with ideas rather than feelings, tries to pawn ideas off as feelings, questions the therapist's meaning, intention, sanity. Such responses come from several places. The client may have a preconceived agenda of what should go on in therapy. The question interrupts this plan. The client may be so concerned with the question "why" that he or she never pays attention to the "what." The client may be invested in the impression he *wants* to make or the feelings he *should* have. The client may operate from a set of beliefs that denigrates feelings or considers them dangerous. Thought is to be master. The client may be so enamored of an ideology that he loses touch with what is. The client may be so preoccupied with the past or the future that a question pointing at the now takes him by surprise.

The variety, intensity, and persistence of such alienation from one's present ongoing feeling process differs from person to person. The therapist keeps asking the centering questions now gently, now insistently. At the same time the therapist also uses the other ways to help clients open themselves to their feelings, and teaches clients the focusing process so that they can learn to make direct reference.

Sometimes I slip focusing in between steps of talk therapy. In the example below, I italicize the focusing questions.

C: I'm feeling tired and heavy and not really pleased with what I'm doing.
T: Hmm. Tired, heavy, and not really pleased. *What's the quality of that whole feeling?*
C: (crinkling up his nose) Sort of blah, flat, unenthusiastic.
T: Blah, flat, unenthusiastic. Kind of plodding?
C: Yeah.
T: Plodding... *Can you just tap up against that?*
C: It's teary and envious. I see my friend Bob's face and I'm jealous that he is so inspired.
T: Some tears there for you, for yourself, and envy of him. "He has it and I don't!"
C: Yes!
T: Unhappy with you and jealous at his inspiration... *Go see what that is.*
C: I feel deprived! No one feeds me! At least, not enough. I don't have enough inside and not enough is coming from the outside. He is more fortunate than I.

Notice that here we have gone in thirty seconds from a possibly unpromising tired heaviness to an exciting exploration of feelings of deprivation. Mostly I was doing listening (see below) and tacking focusing questions onto the end of listening responses.

Thus I use focusing in at least three different ways: (a) I take a person through a whole round of focusing steps; (b) I take a person through the first step of focusing to be followed (see below) by another method; (c) I intersperse focusing questions between listening or other kinds of responses.

Focusing is a powerful tool. When a person begins to use it successfully a whole new realm of experience opens up for him. A look of surprise and often pleasure comes over his face. When it happens early in therapy with an otherwise dejected hopeless person, a new breath of hope may come in as well as the specific information conveyed in the focusing, as in this example:

> I have been seeing him for just five months. He has been complaining for several sessions about his job in the telephone company. He doesn't know, he says, what he wants to do with his life. He talks on—angry, frustrated, stuck, going round and round. He has had one focusing workshop with me. I invite him to focus on what he wants to do with his life. He feels energy and "wanting-to-do" in his hands. I ask him to ask the felt sense in his hands what it wants to do. He smiles. It responds. He gets some answers. He is pleased that he has gotten these responses. But they don't seem final. He asks himself what kind of career he *really* wants to have. He is calm and relaxed. The answer comes: "I want to help people, to work in human services!" He smiles with surprise and contentment. He knows the answer he didn't know at the start of the session. Putting the answer into practice will require further work. But after just five months of therapy he has consulted his experience and found he knows more than he knew he knows. This gives him some hope.

(2) **I do listening.**

I try to reflect back to the client the exact *inwardness* of what he/she has just said, checking with the client as to whether I've gotten it right, and—when I haven't—trying again. I'm not worried when I get it wrong. My client will appreciate my effort and correct me. He will experience wanting-to-be-heard.

My listening response is directed at both the *expressed* and the *inchoate* feeling in the welter of words that has just come. It is a gentle lowering of the person into that from which his words have emerged. Listening is helping a person sense and "get into" rather than merely "talk about" feelings. Gene describes this as finding the trap-door, the deepening response which helps a feeling open. If what is still implicit, preconceptual, forming in the client's message, is empathically responded to, then the person moves forward one step further beyond what he/she has already symbolized.

Examples from early therapy sessions show how I experientialize client-centered listening (See also Gendlin, 1974; and McGuire, 1982).

The first example is from the third individual session with a man whom I had previously seen eight times in a group. His lover has just left him. They had made a date to meet on the corner of 45th and Madison. The lover didn't show up, any my client never saw him again.

We will follow this client through several sessions. He begins therapy tending to deny his feelings:

> C: (flatly) In general I feel pretty good. . . (with more feeling) but I'm more in touch with a. . . sadness. (For a second he looks sad; then he lifts himself in the chair and out of the sadness) I mean I'm just as happy as ever; everything's going well; that hasn't changed; I'm not in pain. . . (his voice trails off).
>
> T: So, everything is going nicely and you're not in pain. . . but, you're more in touch with (slight pause, said deliberately) a sadness. . .
>
> C: Yeah. You bet I am. . . (reflectively) I came to one realization that is hard to talk about. . . when I do feel sexual. . . (shifts in the chair; starts over) When I *did*

> get a feeling of sexuality. . . sometimes it is somebody I even *despise* or is contemptuous of me that I choose.
>
> T: (reflecting the feeling) "I feel uncomfortable saying this to you but I like. . . no. . . I'm *attracted* to someone. . . *contemptuous* of me. . ."
>
> C: Yes. Definitely. (He goes on to feel his way into his attraction to the other's contempt for him)

The same client, the next session. He talks about how he has helped a fellow worker to go on a diet even though he doesn't really like the person. The description is monotone. Then:

> C: I'm jealous! (Firmly) I don't want him to lose weight. He looks at me as someone liberated, free, and I won't let him know I'm really unhappy. I'm putting on something of an act. I'm *happy* seeing him not making progress. . . I guess part of it is I feel *I'm* not making all that much progress and so why should I encourage him to jump ahead?
>
> T: So there's a feeling there—*I'm* not making all that much progress—
>
> C: (cutting me off, more emotionally involved) No, I'm not! I guess *that's* what bothers me. If *I'm* happy and content I don't care what others do.
>
> T: (reflecting the feeling that sounds strongest) Why help him when *I'm* not happy with my progress!
>
> C: Yes, that's the anger. Why doesn't someone ever encourage *me*—
>
> T: Yeah—
>
> C: I'm helping all these people. (with more feeling) It *annoys* the hell out of me. . . (He goes further into his anger and annoyance with all the people who don't inspire him)

A third example captures more of the "trap door" phenomenon. The next interview. He is talking about his ended love affair. My response is to the feeling just below his words:

C: I really wanted him. It was like his body was on fire. I went home and rubbed an urn... like a prayer... (he is embarrassed)
T: (gently) You were really hot for him, so hot you prayed he'd come back... Was there a feeling there... I really wanted him... but I didn't... *deserve* him?
C: (sadly) Yes... (pause... tears)
T: (repeating—slowly) I didn't *deserve* him...
C: How could *I* have been so lucky!
T: (expressing the feeling that may be there) I feel so... unworthy.
C: No... more like... grateful to the gods...
T: Oh, so it's not *unworthy* so much as *grateful* for outside forces sending him to you.
C: Yes. I couldn't have gotten him on my own... I guess you're right. I don't feel I was worthy of him. He was in another league... I'm an understudy. He was the star of the show. God, I wanted him... Like the shoreline wants the sea...
T: It was like a natural craving, two pieces that need each other to be complete, to make a whole... maybe like an inferior being needs a superior being to raise him up, to make him more, to fill him?
C: Yes... He filled me. Literally. (blushes) I felt stronger when he was inside me. (tears) I hear Roberta Flack singing, "That's just the way life changes/like the shoreline and the sea..."
T: (finishing the song; I know it well) "Hey... that's no way... to say good-bye..."
C: (deep, heavy sobs)
T: "I yearn for him so..."
C: (nods his head and cries more)

In these three excerpts we see a progression. The client entrusts me with increasingly deeper material. At first he denies feelings. He cuts me off lest I get too close to him. Then as I carefully empathize he opens himself up more both to himself and to me. He ventures into deeper waters. When I can, I respond to the feeling one or two steps below what he has expressed. He gets closer to his feelings, stays with them longer, finds deeper feelings in himself. A therapeutic process is begun.

(3) I self-disclose.

People change through direct emotional experience. Clients can have such an experience with a therapist who is *there, present, real, responsive*. My expressions of my experiencing process facilitate mutual, spontaneous feelingful encounter (Kempler, 1981).

I am a very human therapist. I express my feelings when my client is stuck—going nowhere, externalizing, intellectualizing, making small talk, not engaging me and therapy. I do so also when clients are with their feelings, I have feelings related to theirs, and expressing mine will probably move us forward.

Sometimes it doesn't. But so long as I quickly check in with my client after an expression of my feeling, no harm is done. If I'm off the track, we get back on it. And if my client doesn't want to hear from me, he tells me, and I respect his choice.

It is important that I carefully delineate my own feelings, express them as my own, and then wait, patiently and eagerly, for what comes next from the client. I want my clients *present*, wholly engaged in our interaction. I don't want them partialled out, divided, neither here nor there. So it is important that *I* am fully present, responding from *my* center, not drifting off, analyzing, staying aloof. Only then can we meet each other.

I say:

— I feel sad. I can't find you.
— I feel pushed away by you, and I don't like it.

— When you said that, I felt very moved. . . very deeply connected with you.
— I feel frustrated with you now![10]
I grimace.
I laugh.
I frown.
I grunt.
And, I cry.

G. never shares his feelings with anyone. He comes in looking sad and fearful. He says he wants to share his feelings with me. For my own reasons, unconnected to him, I'm feeling very teary myself. I sigh deeply in response to his saying he wants to share his feelings. Tears come to my eyes. He looks afraid.

C: I get unfocused when I hear you sigh. . .
T: And see the tears in my eyes.
C: Yeah.
T: What does it do to you?
C: (looking at the floor) It gets me scared. . . (pause; he looks up and at me) I don't feel so scared now, but I feel odd. It feels *weird* that you react like that. . . I guess it's because when I cry I feel weak. . . and bad.
T: When I cry I sometimes feel strong and good. (He starts to weep; I start to weep. Despite weeping, I keep my attention focused on him.)

After a long pause he gets into how he is sharing his feelings in his new relationship with M. He cries freely off and on during the rest of the hour. He has never done so in therapy before nor has he talked of a loving relationship before. Near the end he says, "I'm growing. It seems hard to believe sometimes." We both laugh.

I do two different kinds of self-disclosing. I tell things about myself. These are not here-and-now things. They are personal sharings in the way that a good friend may tell another good friend about his life. I do this to make myself more real to the client, to share things we have in common, or to emphasize my unique difference from him, or to teach something by example. I do this unobtrusively and briefly. I don't hog the session. In a sentence or two I say something about myself that helps build our relationship. Then I go right back to listening.

The second kind of self-disclosure, the one being exemplified here, is here-and-now sharings of my present experiencing. A couple of instances from the therapy with my abandoned client show how these brief personal sharings often propel therapy forward:

> C: We had made a date for Friday night. It was December 22, 1976. We had been together for seven months. I was waiting on the corner of 45th and Madison. He never showed up. He never called. When I got home there was a note saying he didn't want to see me anymore.
>
> T: How heartless!
>
> C: You sound angry.
>
> T: You're damned right I'm angry! I'm angry for you. . . and I'm also angry for when something like that happened to me.
>
> C: I wasn't angry. . . I never told anyone this. . . (sobs) All night I pretended he was still with me. I made dinner for us. We sat and ate together. I slept next to him. . . In the morning I admitted he was gone.

***

> C: My father died two years ago. I was remembering how I spent the last day of his life with him. (cries) He was so courageous to the end. He left us instructions about his funeral. (sobs, sees my tears) It affects you too, huh?
>
> T: (tears) I'm remembering my father's death, how he did the same thing, and also how uninvolved in it I was. I'm envying you that precious experience.

C: (cries more deeply) I appreciate your sharing that. . . He was a beautiful man. . . (we cry together) He died suddenly. . . Men always leave without warning.

(4) I do empathic imagining.

Listening is a good way to get into another's world. It encourages a person to say more. It gives the person the space that few friends give each other: the space to explore further without having to react to my reaction to what you've said so far. Leaving oneself outside the door, so to speak, can help a person really feel seen and understood.

But it is not the only way to tune in to a client. And it can get too artificial if done too much.

By "empathic imagining" I mean a process whereby I imagine what the person may be feeling at this particular moment. I say or express what I imagine to be there. One place I do this is when a silence is happening.

(C. has been quiet for about four minutes.)
T: I'm looking into your eyes and imagining an infinite sadness there, a pool of grief, and I'm wanting to say—let it out; let me share it with you.
C: (cries) I was remembering my uncle's death.

***

(C. has told me he is an uptight person. He has been quiet a couple of minutes.)
T: I'm sensing that you're trying to relax.
C: Yes.
T: The silence suddenly felt tense to me.
C: Yes. I had been relaxing and then I became aware I was relaxing and tensed up. I'm going to sit quietly and relax some more (silence for 5 minutes).
T: I was just starting to feel like Martha, like I was supposed to reprimand you or something.

C: She never let me have a moment's peace and quiet!... I wanted you to break in and I didn't want you to.
T: I was picking up half the message.
C: People tell me I do that.
T: Do what?
C: Invite them to interrupt my solitude.
T: Ah... they tell you that, do they?
C: Yes. I have to look at how I send out those signals.

Gene has written about three categories of in-therapy client behavior which he labels (a) silent and unresponsive; (b) silent but responsive; and (c) verbal but externalized (Gendlin, 1967).

As we have seen, I do empathic imagining especially though not only in response to the first two of these types of behavior. I sit through a silence imagining what this quiet person with me may be feeling and, after a silent time, I check out my impression:

T: (The client mumbles something about loneliness. Then he sits silently for a few minutes. I don't want him to be lonely here too. I say softly) I imagine you are feeling quite sad... maybe, cut-off... (no response) maybe, isolated—
C: Yeah. (He starts to cry and goes on to bring up vivid experiences of first loneliness, then sadness, then anger. He becomes quiet again, but it feels like a different kind of quiet. Five minutes or so pass.)
T: I imagine it feels... *good* to share all that with someone—
C: Finally...
T: Finally...
C: Yes, it does. I've held it back a long time. I do feel better now.

I do empathic imagining in other circumstances too. The person may be talking and suddenly a picture, tune, memory, or physical sensation goes through me. I have learned that this is my empathic response to what is in the other person pre-conceptually—just behind, beyond, or below the words being said. I tend to express these imaginings less tentatively. They happen when I'm especially tuned into the client and very clear inside. I am talking from inside the client at these points.[11]

She is talking about an unhappy love affair with an unemployed, alcoholic Sicilian whom she says she wants to leave. I suddenly "see" the Statue of Liberty.

> C: (angrily) Why do I care so much for him *still*?
> T: "Give me your tired, your poor."
> C: (she looks startled and annoyed) What did you say?
> T: While you were talking, I saw the Statue of Liberty. . . the torch. . . providing shelter for the homeless. . .
> C: (she starts to sob; pause) Is that what I'm doing?
> T: Is it?
> C: (pause, reflectively, with a slight smile) Strays and waifs. . . (she nods her head, sighs, and then laughs)

These experiences can be uncanny.

> C: (First session) I don't feel like myself. . . like I'm together. . . I feel younger than twenty-seven. . . I don't feel whole. . .
> T: I don't know what this means, but I just saw the outline of another person's shape as if connected to you on your right-hand side.
> C: (His mouth falls open; his face takes on an impish, sheepish, young-looking grin.) How did you know I had a twin brother?
> T: I didn't!
> C: I had a twin brother. We did everything together. When I was fifteen we were suddenly separated. . . hey, hey, he always walked on my right-hand side. (We both sit there dumbfounded.)

And sometimes I'm wrong:

C: (This is the end of a five-minute, very moving soliloquy. I'm very tuned into him.)... I want to be able to sail on the sea, not be stuck on land. I want to be like Bulkington in Moby Dick and leave the slavish shore. The deeper waters call...

T: (explicating an image that has popped into my consciousness) Is there something about your mother in all this?... I say that because I suddenly saw the scene from Interiors (C: I've seen it.) where the mother drowns and the step-mother saves Jodi's life.

C: It doesn't connect for me. I think it's your stuff.

T: Could be. Just ignore it then... You were saying that deeper waters call...

C: Yeah... I need to take some new steps (continues in same vein)

(5) I make content-less statements designed to keep a person at a feeling place.

We therapists have the idea we always have to be doing something. We have to be saying something smart. We have to be devising a brilliant experiment for the client to do. We have to be formulating a right diagnosis that sums up all the material the client has given us. We have to give a brilliant depth interpretation of what the client is saying.

Sometimes all that is wrong. We have to be doing something, in fact, quite simple: keeping the client company.

I have said that the immediate goal of my sessions is to get a feeling process going and then to stay with it, allowing it to deepen. Some clients most of the time ("externalizers") and most clients some of the time start to touch a feeling and then whoosh off—out of the feeling, on to the next story. I want them to stay where they are when they are "at" or "into" something. I want them to let it register, to resonate with it, to savor it. So now and then when I sense that they are about to desert their experiencing I will simply *underline* with a content-less statement that, at this moment, they are in touch with something in themselves, something that deserves our attention. I'll say:

— *That's* heavy.
— Let's make some space for *that*.
— You sure have a strong feeling *there*.
— Wait a minute! Let's take *that* in...
— Aha! *That's* new... Let's be with that...
— Whoa! Tread water there. Let's just hang out with that feeling and listen to it.

(6) I make content-less statements designed to bring a client back to a feeling place.

Despite such efforts clients often flee the feeling, get away from their process. If they move on to another felt place, that is fine. But if they start intellectualizing, externalizing, telling stories, making chit-chat, then I will try to bring them back to that felt edge, the feeling place they had scooted away from. As soon as I get a chance I'll say:

— I'm still sitting with the feeling, "He won't respect *my* space." Could you go back and sense the flavor of that?
— I'm still back where you said, "I'm so *mad* at her!" Could you go touch that "mad"?

I often follow up (5) and (6) with process-furthering focusing instructions. I may say,

Let's let that feeling you just expressed register... "I want more out of my life"... go see where you *feel* that, where in your body (pause)... Be friendly towards the feeling (pause)... Nudge up against it and just ask it to tell you more... Listen to it.

(7) **I make interpretations.**

I do the previous things (treading water, "I'm still sitting with the feeling," client instruction) mainly when a therapeutic feeling process has not yet taken hold. On the whole, interpreting comes later.

That is, I do not look to interpretations—by and large—to get a feeling process started. I find they too often reinforce my clients' tendencies to alienated intellectualizing. I start to make interpretative remarks more frequently when my clients have gotten in touch with their feelings. And I make them in such a way as not to interfere with the process.

When I do make interpretations, I do not do so in the classical sense. I am not a Freudian therapist. Nor a Jungian. Nor a Horneyian. Nor a Gestalt therapist. I do not use just one school's interpretative armamentarium. My interpretations do not come from any one total theory of human growth, development, behavior, and symbolism. My interpretations are directed towards the preconceptual richness of the clients' experiencing, now pointing at it from this angle, now from that, now from still another.

Similarly, I do not think in terms of resistance or defenses. If one response of mine doesn't work, I try another. Or, I try the same one again a little differently or more persistently. For me, the challenge is always to find the response which reaches my clients *now*, which helps open them to their feelings *now*.

How then do I use interpretations? I give expression to whatever has come to me in response to *this* statement, gesture, or silence of the client. Drawing upon my own reading and therapy experience this may be a Horneyian interpretation, a Sullivanian, or Angyalian, or a T.A. interpretation ("*who* is talking now?"), or a Gestalt interpretation ("be the razor in the dream") or an interpretation from Existential thinking, or in terms of socio-cultural factors.

What do I do after making an interpretation? If it is clear that my response has "struck home"—if my client expresses the equivalent of a deep sigh, a "yes," and then something fresh and feelingful comes from him—if that happens, we go with what has come. But if not, if my client is silent, or changes the subject, or looks peeved, I want to check in with him. I want to know what my client is experiencing and whether and how it relates to my intervention.

So as soon as I have a chance, I'll say, "Did *that* comment of mine *say* anything to you?" or "What was that for *you*?" or "What came up in you when I said that?" or "OK, that was my trip; now where are *you*?"

In this way, even a "wrong" interpretation—poorly timed, off the mark, more true of me than of my client—can be useful. *The checking-in is all-important.* It keeps me from going on my merry speculative way. I am not invested in the correctness of my interpretation but in finding where my client now is and now wants to go. What will move the process forward now—that remains the basic question.

The following example illustrates interpretation and other things that I do. I especially like the example because it also shows how I deal with "chronic wrongness." Orthodox Rogerians sound as if they *always* side with the client.[12] I do so a lot but I don't buy "The client is always right" as an absolute viewpoint.

I was always being corrected by this client. I couldn't listen to her just exactly right. And she demanded exact rightness. The following interaction followed several months of my untiring efforts to hear her to her satisfaction, efforts that she at times appreciated but which, more often than I am used to, fell short of the mark.

C: You just don't listen well.
T: You're mad at me about that.
C: Yes, mad and disgusted.
T: Mad and disgusted... You know, I'm pretty mad and disgusted with you too. (she looks up) It doesn't feel good to me to be criticized and corrected so much (self-disclosure).
C: I didn't know you felt this way.
T: Well, I do... I've been wondering... Is there anything about you-and-your-father in all this? Something about how he didn't listen to you? (interpretation)
C: (checking this) No... It's more like me-and-my-mother... And it isn't that she didn't listen. (T: Oh) More that she *demanded* I listen exactly to her!

> T: Oh! So I had it wrong... again. (We both laugh.) It's more like you are sometimes doing to me what she did to you. (interpretation)
>
> C: Yes! *That's* it. Hey, you got that one right!

(8) I combine gestalt methods and focusing.

By "gestalt methods" I mean the action experiments developed by Fritz Perls and other gestaltists (Naranjo, n.d.). These are designed to heighten awareness and intensify feeling.

Focusing has been called, jokingly, gestalt for introverts. It emphasizes the inwardness of experiencing. It teaches the client to explore the nuances of his feeling life, to track in loving detail the meandering meanings of inner experiencing. The focuser becomes a virtuoso of felt meanings.

The two approaches complement each other. Focusing is a more subtle, assimilative, passive, introverted process. The gestalt experience is more explosive, active, cathartic, extroverted. Zigzagging back and forth gives the client a full and varied experiencing of himself.

Focusing also stresses the self-directedness of the client more than gestalt does. Thus it makes more person-centered and less abrasive what can be a too directive therapy.

The intra-self dialogue is one of the best known gestalt methods. Here is how I combined it with focusing in the treatment of the spurned lover we have been following in this chapter:

> T: Go see how you are inside right now. (focusing directive)
>
> C: I feel torn apart inside. Part of me says, "Forget him." The other part says, "Go after him."
>
> T: Let those two parts talk to each other. Write a skit. (gestalt directive; I set up two chairs for him to switch between. We have used this method before and I know he takes to it.)
>
> C1: I still want him and I'm going to get him! I'll wait

outside his office! (switches chairs)
C2: Oh, come off it. Face the facts. He doesn't want you and he's not good for you. You were his slave, remember? Let him go. (switches)
C1: I want to be his slave! Still! Yes! (switches)
C2: Oh, come on. I thought you'd given that crap up. You're still so hung up on winning your father's love? Pshaw! (looks toward me for direction)
T: Now, switch to a third seat, the seat that is yours, place it wherever between these two feels right, and see what's there now. (focusing again)
C: (puts third chair closer to C1 than C2) Longing. . . Father's face. . . Father beating me. . . I still *need* that. (shaking his head ruefully)
T: Be friendly to what still needs that and go see what's the crux of that. (focusing)
C: (teary) That was all I *had* with him. . . It was our *only* contact. . . (cries harder). . . I know it's crazy but it meant to me—he loves me! (deep sigh)
T: Yeah. . . so the meaning for you of the beating was—"he loves me" (C: Yeah). . . so there's a healthy human longing for love which is coming in this way. . . (An Angyalian interpretation, reframing and stressing the healthy trend inside the neurotic symptom)
C: I can see it but I can't feel it. (He is telling me the interpretation makes intellectual but not emotional sense.)
T: You don't feel it the way I said it. (listening)
C: Nah. . .
T: What's the feeling now?
C: Some sadness. . . regret! Regret for the wasted years. . . barking up the wrong tree.

Similarly, when I use other gestalt methods I let them emerge from a focusing experience and tuck focusing questions inside them:

C: (A very intellectual person... gives me a five-minute analysis of his job situation)
T: Continue in the same tone of vice but speak in gibberish. (Again, we have used this method before and it has worked.)
C: "la-la-la-la-la-la-la."
T: What do you feel inside now? (focusing directive)
C: Distant... uninvolved... I don't really care about what I'm talking about.
T: What *do* you care about?
C: Nothing! At least I *live* as if I care about nothing.
T: Go see what *that* is.

***

T: What are you feeling now?
C: Discouraged. (shrugs his shoulders)
T: Exaggerate those movements (I shrug my shoulders to model this. He shrugs his.) Do it more. (He does. After a while—) What do you feel inside now? (focusing directive)
C: Angry!
T: Go see what that anger's quality is.
C: No, that doesn't feel right to me.
T: OK, what would feel right? *My* direction doesn't feel right. Go inside and see what would be right for you now. (This is a use of focusing to help the client direct his own therapy.)
C: I really need to beat some pillows.
T: Go to is. (self-directed gestalt)

There is one particular place where gestalt does something that focusing cannot do. It is in what gestaltists call "undoing retroflections" (Perls, Hefferline, Goodman, 1951). It is not helpful to let a client sink ever deeper in a focusing way into feelings of being the victim. This is a place where continued focusing is counter-productive.

(He has identified himself as feeling victimized, weak, oppressed. We have previously explored these feelings. I invite him to be the victimizer, the strong one, the oppressor.)

C: The Great Boyg has me in his clutches.
T: Be The Great Boyg. Let me be you. Do to me what it does to you. (gestalt experiment—undoing retroflections.)
C: (Hovers over me menacingly. I cringe. He starts saying at me all the critical things the Great Boyg says at him.) You aren't enough! You are a wimp! You can't get things right!
T: What is it doing to you non-verbally? Do to me non-verbally what it does to you.
C: (spies a child's pirate knife on the table, goes and gets it, jabs at the air right above me. I cower. With each stab he gets stronger, less oppressed.)
T: Is there a sound or words with it?
C: Take that! And that! And that! (punctuating each phrase with the knife thrust; after a while—) It's my father stabbing me with his criticism.
T: Ah!. . . Stab some more. (His expression starts to change after some time. He looks more teary.) Now go focus; see what's there.
C: (He sits down, tired. He starts to sob. . .) Images of my relationship with my father are coming to me. . . (sigh of recognition) And there's something else there now too. . . I have an image of Oedipus catching up with Laius, his father.
T: Be the image (Gestalt again. Notice the back and forth.)
C: (suddenly cries harder) I don't know where this comes

from. I want to say to him, "Forgive me, father, I know not what I do."

T: Say it to him. Stand on the road, blocking his way, and say it to him.

C: (gets up and talks to a piece of sculpture—a Rastafarian head I have in my office) Forgive me, father. . . I didn't know how to talk to you, and you didn't know how to talk to me. You were so *self*-critical, and you took it out on me. Now I do the same to me and to those I love. Forgive me, father, I have to move beyond you. I have to kill the you in me. Not all of you (tears). . . not all of you. Just this big part. I have to move beyond you. You, this, it—you are blocking my way. The road is impassable. . .

T: See how you are inside. . .

C: (sits down) More teary and less angry. My heart is open. I don't feel critical of either him or me right now. *The* road feels clear. *My* road feels clear.

(9) I combine bioenergetic methods and focusing.

Gene writes that focusing is a sub-process of therapy. It is not a new school of therapy. It can be integrated with whatever else the therapist uses. In these two sections I am showing how I integrate focusing with gestalt and bioenergetic exercises.

Bioenergetic methods are very bodily. They are cathartic. They increase energy levels. They help people discharge feelings. Focusing is more reflective. It is a meditative-like observing of inner process. Bioenergetics changes inner process, achieves the felt shift, through large physical movements. It is important, again, to zig-zag. Bioenergetics without focusing can be merely physical exercise. Focusing without bioenergetics can be too mild.

A later session with the client whose lover left him on the corner of 45th and Madison illustrates the way I move between focusing and bioenergetics:

C: I want him back!
T: Reach for him. Put him in the chair across from you. Just beyond your reach. (We set the scene up. I get behind him, put my arms around his mid-section, restraining him.) Go on, reach for him, call to him. . .
C: Bobby! Bobby!
T: Reach your hands all the way out!
C: Bobby! Bobby!
T: He doesn't hear you! He isn't there! He doesn't care!
C: (straining to reach him; I hold him back) Bobby!. . . (screaming) You fuck!
T: Yeah, let it out. Say the worst words!
C: You fuck! You motherfucker! (He is straining to get out of the chair and reach Bobby. I am struggling to hold him back.) God damn you! God damn you!

This continues for a few minutes. He is screaming and I'm encouraging him to let it all out. Suddenly, he collapses in tears. I let go and sit in my chair and wait. When the tears have stopped I ask him:

T: What's inside now? (focusing direction)
C: I feel cleared out, calmer, deep inside myself. Reflective.
T: See what the reflectiveness in you has to say. (focusing)
C: "I won't abuse myself any more!" There is a lump in my throat and I'm thinking/feeling, "I want to live on. . . and differently."
T: (listening) So, like, I'm not going to do that to myself again (C: hm-hm). . . I'm not going to make someone into a god. . . It really hurts. . . but I'm not despairing (C: Yes). . . In fact, I feel determined to move forward *and* to learn from this.
C: Yeah, you've got it (deep sigh). I'm not done with him

> yet though... I'm not sure whether I want to choke or caress him.
>
> T: (offering my wrist) Try both out. Alternate. This is Bobby's neck. Choke it... Caress it. See which feels connected (this is an invitation to him to focus while he is doing the bioenergetic exercise).
>
> C: (He squeezes my wrist a few times. Then he strokes it lovingly a few times. Then he squeezes it menacingly again.) *That* feels more like it.
>
> T: Go with it.
>
> C: You prick... You fuck... You bastard... (squeezing hard)
>
> T: (as Bobby) I don't want you anymore. I'm leaving you!...
>
> C: (squeezing harder) Then go. Go! Go! Go! Go! Go! Go! Go! Go! Go! (With each "go," he squeezes my wrist. After a few minutes he feels finished.)
>
> T: Now, in a friendly way, go see what's there... (focusing)
>
> C: I see my father's grave. (sobs)... He's gone and I can't have him back... "You can't always get what you want"...
>
> T: What's the feeling now?
>
> C: Acceptance... What's done is done... I can't reclaim what is over... I expect the rage and the hurt and the longing will all return at some point—
>
> T: I expect they will—
>
> C: But right now I feel done with it and ready to move on.
>
> T: Yeah!

Bioenergetic experiments concretely mirror troublesome life situations and lead to felt shifts through physical exertion and activity that connect with deep internal states.

> He feels weighed down. I ask him to focus.

He feels as if his despair is like a weight on his back holding him down. I ask him to stand up. I get behind him and lean on his back. I become the weight holding him down. "You won't get rid of me," I shout at him. I give him a bear hug and lean my weight on him. He starts to give up, to crumble. "I'm stronger than you," I shout in his ear. I feel him strengthen. He starts to struggle. "Bastard," he yells. "You can't get rid of me," I retort. "Yes, I can." We are now struggling. I am his despair, holding on, leaning on him, weighing him down, sapping his strength. There is a shift inside him. He starts to get stronger. He is pulling me around the room, "Get off my back!" "No!" We are acting out his issue. With a burst of strength he is free. We are both exhausted from the tussle. I invite him to sit and focus. He sees a portrait of his depressed father. "I've been carrying him on my back." In the next week he feels lighter.

Conclusion

I have named and illustrated nine kinds of experiential interventions I make in therapy: (1) I do focusing; (2) listening; (3) self-expressing; (4) empathic imagining; (5) keeping a client at a feeling place; (6) bringing a client back to a feeling place; (7) making interpretations; (8) combining gestalt and focusing; (9) combining bioenergetics and focusing. I have saved for last (10) doing things which are not experientially oriented per se.

There are a whole slew of interchanges in my therapy that I would call "ordinary interactions." A. gives me advice on how to get my avocado to grow. I suggest to M. that she read Maya Angelou's autobiography. H. and I share a joke. I make D. a cup of coffee. R. recommends I see *Swept Away*. B. and I discuss the financing of condominiums. L. shows me his sleeping bag. R. and I gossip. The emphasis on experiencing exists within the framework of a human relationship in which humor, small talk, simple acts of kindness and shared moments of ordinary interactions also have a place.

As do interventions that come from one of the other families of therapy. For example, sometimes I help clients devise behavioral strategies for change.

I purposely end this essay on How I Do Focusing-Oriented Experiential Therapy with these non-experiential moments so as to renounce any claims to purist fanaticism which may otherwise have crept into this presentation:

> I am feeling tired as she comes in. I have a virus and am at low energy. Most of the session is spent rather constructively with us reviewing together what she has been learning about herself. A lot of cognitive-intellectual understanding happens. I give her Angyal's chapter to read for next week (homework) and suggest she underline the passages that speak directly to her. She has no strong emotional experience in the whole session, yet the session feels to me like "connected thinking" (as opposed to "alienated, truncated, disconnected thinking") is going on.

> He brings into the session his time-management notebook. Most of the session is spent helping him to strategize how to better allot his time between his job, his relationship, his kids, his thesis. I sneak a little focusing into this basically behavioral session; I suggest he focus to see what exactly would be a good reinforcer either after or before he does his writing.

> He has come in very focused and clear. He misses "fellowship." He has been a loner all his life. He misses being touched. We decide on action for the next two weeks until I see him again. He will join a therapy group, a men's group, come to a focusing workshop, and get a massage once a week. The session has been used to plan activities which meet his needs.

> She is very depressed. I give her Burns' book, *Feeling Good: The New Mood Therapy*, to read. It is a popular version of

Beck's cognitive therapy. I assign her to read the first few chapters and carry out the exercises that *feel* useful to her (note the focusing emphasis in this otherwise cognitive-behavioral intervention).

We end on the note that more happens in experiential therapy than the experiential. Gene writes that an effective therapeutic response is one that carries forward the client's experiencing process (1961, p. 241). This formulation is too theoretical. An effective therapeutic response is one that works. My goal is not to 'prove' or exemplify Gene's theory. My goal is to help my client. When I have to let go of theory in order to be of help, I let go of theory and be of help. That is my job, my vocation, my calling. That is what I do.

GENDLIN AND ANGYAL: FOCUSING AND HOLISTIC INSIGHT

Focusing is basic to my therapy. Gene Gendlin has written little about its relationship to other theorists' conceptions of therapy. In this essay I will explore some interconnections between focusing and the work of Andras Angyal.

I want to introduce you to the work of Andras Angyal and make an important connection between it and the focusing process.

Angyal is a neglected genius. His major book, *Neurosis and Treatment* (1965), is very hard to find.[13] In it he put forth a holistic theory of human nature, personality, development, health, neurosis, and therapy. The book foreshadows gestalt and existential therapies while remaining within the tradition of interpretative and insight-oriented therapies.

In this essay I will show that focusing is an excellent way to facilitate the "holistic insight" Angyal considered basic to therapeutic change. I will set the stage by first summarizing Angyal's conceptualization of human nature, personality, development, and the generalized course of treatment.

Angyal saw personality as an "ambiguous gestalt." He likened it to the visual illusions one finds in texts on perception. In the most popular, looked at in one way it is two profiles; in the other way, it is an urn or vase. Similarly, Angyal argued, two systems—the healthy and the neurotic—vie for dominance in the personality. Each organizes the based human needs for *autonomy* (self-determination) and *homonomy* (belonging) according to its own system principal. The system principal of the healthy orientation is loving confidence. The system principal of the neurotic orientation is fearful diffidence. The basic "data" remains the same. No life is all trauma. No life is all free of trauma. We are *both* the profile *and* the urn. But which we appear as depends upon which organizing system is dominant at any particular moment. I find this an enormously rich and rewarding way to conceptualize the human condition.

At the start of therapy the neurotic system is dominant. Angyal saw neurosis as a "sweeping condition... a way of life" (p. 71). It is not a localized blemish on an otherwise clear skin. Neurosis is a set of generalized implicit attitudes which organize every nook and cranny of the neurotic person's existence: "The self is felt to be small, weak, and inadequate... The world... immense, alien, unmanageable, overwhelming, unapproachable." "Safety first" becomes the implicit motif of life (p. 77).

The initial period of therapy should be marked by the twin processes that Angyal calls "demolition of the neurosis" and "reconstruction of the [dormant] system of health." Through the therapist's interpretations, the patient achieves *holistic insight* into the basic neurotic attitudes, his own unique patterning of them, and into the health inside the neurosis. (It is this phase of treatment and its relation to focusing which the next sections zoom in on.)

But insight alone will not conquer a neurosis. Rather, Angyal sees it as merely ushering in the next stage of therapy—"The Struggle for Decision." The neurosis has been weakened, the health strengthened. The two systems have reached nearly equal strength. The person is now in civil war—"half slave, half free." This is a stormy and long period. There are rapid shifts in dominance from one system to the other. The person is now the profiles, now the urn. Parts of each day may be experienced from within the neurotic system, other parts of the same day from within the system of health. "Mood" swings are common and extreme.

I have sometimes summarized my own therapy experience using Angyal's scheme. When I began therapy my neurotic system was running the show. It was as lush as a rain forest. I was obsessing on the past and future and being anxious and resentful. What I wasn't doing was feeling—my grief, my anger, my power, my real self. Through the relationship with Leida Berg, the intensity of affect, and her interpretations, my healthy system was strengthened and my neurotic system weakened. I became present. I got out of my head and into my experiencing. Acres of unexamined feeling started to emerge. The struggle for decision seemed at times to be a permanent state.

Angyal writes that, if the therapist handles this phase correctly, the neurosis is "defeated" in the fire of an intense emotional experience. The person experiences the utter bankruptcy of the neurotic way of being. The healthy system gets the upper hand. The person's allegiance is thrown to the health. Angyal divides this final stage of therapy into two tasks: "getting well" and "staying well." He portrays its vicissitudes and appraises its outcome soberly. Neuroses are never excommunicated. Angyal concludes his gripping overview of the course of treatment with heartfelt words that deserve quoting:

> To remain well, the patient must recognize that his neurosis has not been erased once and for all when health got the upper hand. Though it is a bitter pill to swallow for a patient who has hoped for a golden era, he has to learn that recovery means no more than this: The strength of the neurotic pattern has been reduced, and he has learned how to live in a wholesome fashion. But the potentiality for his special way of malfunctioning always remains with him. It is immediately activated when the patient succumbs to conceit, pride, or self-centeredness and retreats into his agony, anxious isolation. . . Horney, in her last book, called the totality of neurotic attitudes 'the pride system'; one could rightly call the healthy organization 'the humility system'. . . (p. 260).

Holistic Insight

Now let's backtrack.

Angyal wrote that people change in their roots, not their branches (p. 205). In order to change they first need to reach *holistic insight* into the basic, implicit generalized attitudes which underpin their neurosis.

But at the start of therapy the patient is mostly living *inside* the neurosis. He does not see the forest for the trees. If at all, he takes only glancing note of his basic neurotic attitudes. More often he may speak week after week of one specific troubling area: his relationship with his lover, his bodily aches, his horrendous childhood. Or he may jump back and forth among seemingly unconnected topics: Today he may tell a dream. Next week he may review this week's events. The next hour he may shift from a fight at work, to his attachment to a favorite aunt, to his theory of society. To the therapist any session may feel like buckshot—as if bits and pieces of life have been strewn around him. The therapist may feel as if he were drowning in the material, or the therapist may feel anxious or assaulted by the outpouring. The patient values equally the wheat and the chaff. Indeed, he does not know the one from the other. He does not know what he needs to talk about. He does now know *how* he needs to talk.

What is the therapist to do?

Angyal counsels: The therapist's first task is to help the client discover the *syndromes*—the larger dynamic units which connect the data. If the patient speaks of only one area of life, the therapist needs to extend the field of discussion. "Starting from the problems initially presented, the field must be broadened to include other areas of the patient's present life, his past history, childhood, and those mental states that are not given serious attentions in everyday life, such as dreams, fantasies, seemingly random or inconsequential thoughts" (p. 214). If the patient speaks of various areas, the therapist's interpretations should be directed at the interconnections and relevance to the patient's present life. In Angyal's words, "The first step toward discovering the idiosyncratic variants of neurotic attitudes is to reduce the vast array of symptoms, peculiarities, and other manifestations of neurosis by grouping them into larger units or syndromes" (p. 208). *Holistic interpretation* leads then from "specific items" to "syndromic units" and "through them to personal attitudes of wider scope." In this way the initial exploratory phase of treatment brings home to the client on at least an intellectual level the generalized neurotic assumptions common to all neurosis *and* the specific patterns of his own.

Angyal is adamant. A single symptom can be interpreted only as part of a syndrome. Consider premature ejaculation. "On the face of it, this phenomenon is a shortcut, an abbreviation of the normal process" (p. 208). The therapist is alert to evidence of the same syndrome in other contexts. The person cannot tolerate hunger, cannot bear to wait in lines at movies, gets ideas but cannot carry them through to completion. The evidence points to the existence of a syndrome of "generalized impatience" and it is *this* to which attention must be directed.

But in any particular person this symptom may *not* be part of *that* syndrome. Or, it may be part of *that* syndrome and *others*. The symptom may be homologous with other fears concerning intercourse itself. "Here the person's situation is comparable to that of a soldier who, to reach safety, must cross a strip of land under enemy fire. The strategy is 'get through as fast as you can'" (p. 210). Angyal goes on to list five categories of such fears, how each can lead to premature ejaculation, and how the therapist induces from the evidence which syndromes the symptom is part of.

In sum, the patient begins therapy by talking. The therapist makes *holistic interpretations* to increase the patient's *holistic insight*. The broader the attitude into which insight is gained, the greater the potential for real change. But the intellectual insight will not of itself induce change. The painstaking process of interpretation serves merely to pave the way for what Angyal calls "the more dynamic processes" to come later.

Perhaps there is a better way.

Focusing

It is unclear in Angyal exactly how intellectual insights lead later to the emotional experience that produces change. This is a gap in his theory. Focusing fills this gap. *Angyal's interpretations bring home to the patient the intellectual interconnectedness of his syndromes. Gendlin's focusing procedure enables the client to experience this interconnectedness in a concrete bodily way.* The "broader attitudes" are *felt* and are felt *as a whole*. When they are felt and *accurately symbolized*, what Gendlin calls a "felt shift" occurs. This is not merely intellectual insight. *The client is directly experiencing the syndrome in the process of change.*

What happens when a person comes for focusing-oriented experiential therapy?

He doesn't talk in his usual way. Instead, he sits down, closes his eyes, relaxes, and is invited to ask his body for the whole feel of how he is right now. He listens to his organismic stirrings. He is encouraged to take a friendly attitude to his bodily felt insides and simply inquire—"what's there?"

Then he is invited to see what's wrong or what needs work today. The therapist may say something like:

> See what's between you and feeling *all fine* right now. . . Imagine yourself sitting on a park bench. . . you are going to stack at a comfortable distance from you everything between you and being all fine right now. . . Just let each thing come up. . . Don't go into anything yet. . .

The person puts on the bench the stack of troubles his body is carrying at this particular moment. They may include a particular symptom, a trouble from the previous week, a transitory feeling from the morning, a continuing work or relationship difficulty, a usual background tenseness or bitterness or "poor me" attitude which he habitually carries.

Now the therapist asks the person to feel magnetically pulled toward the one thing in the stack that most needs his attention today. He is asked to let form in his body "*the feel of the whole of it.*"

Let us stop for a moment right here where the person needs thirty seconds to a minute to let this felt sense form. Notice that focusing is a *holistic* process and a *bodily* process. The question is how am *I* right now—not how is my arm, leg, stomach, or some other part of me. Placing all the items on the bench sometimes already suggests to the person possible interconnections. And the *holistic felt sense* of an issue is on the way to Angyal's *syndrome*. But it is not just intellectually pieced together. It is *felt* and it is felt *as a whole.*

I hope an example will make this point clear. The client is a 45-year-old teacher about to go into business for himself.[14] He is a practiced focuser. His eyes are closed. He has put a hefty stack of troubles on the bench and picked one to work on—starting his business. I ask him to attend to the whole of it.

> He says, "I feel some sort of calm yet urgent and anxious 'want-to-have-this-thing-done' feeling."
> I repeat: "A 'wanting-to-have-this-thing-done' feeling?"
> He nods yes and sighs.
> I say: "Let words, images, or memories come from that feeling."
> C: "I see myself at the start of a class. . . aha. . . it is the same feeling that I have whenever I start a class. . ."
> He wrinkles his brow like that isn't quite right.
> C: "No, it's more like whenever I start a *new* class. . . I feel a deeper calm now. . . I just got the sentence: 'Will I be able to do it?'"
> He chuckles.
> C: "Oh yeah, that's the same feeling I often have before I go to bed with a woman for the first time."
> He is quiet again. He tells me what is happening in his body process.
> C: "I feel alive and vibrating. . . on the track. . ."

He is telling me he is tracking a feeling. I say: "Ask the place where you feel it all—'what's the crux of this? What is the main thing about it?. . .'"
A minute passes.

C: "I'm quiet, listening closely to myself. . . I want to try out a few possible sentences that feel close to right. . . 'Will I succeed?'"
He shakes his head no.

C: "'Am I enough?'"
Again, apparently, this is not it. He shakes his head.

C: "Ah. . . 'Can I sustain it?'"
He is quiet, no head nodding. He has been "hearing" these sentences emerge from his feeling place and then checking them against the feeling place.

C: "Not quite right, but close. . . More sentences are coming. . . 'Do I have persistence?'. . . 'Can I overcome the obstacles?'. . . None feels exactly right, but all feel near the core. . ."
I take my cue from his words. "Ask it, 'what's the *core* of this?'"
His response tells me I'm on target.

C: "When you said that I felt energy swirling right between my eyes. . . And the sentence, 'I'm not sure that I'm enough. . .' came to me. . . 'I'm not sure that I'm enough. . .'"
He is saying it over to check that just *this* is the right sentence, the *name* for the *syndrome*.

C: "When I said that over I got very still and then real quickly other instances flashed by. . . the first appointment with a new customer. . . the way I feel when I wake up in the morning. . . how I feel each time before focusing. . ."

We are now in the phase of focusing Gendlin calls "global application": "The individual is flooded by many different associations, memories, situations, and circumstances, all in relation to the [same] felt referent" (1964, p. 121). I let him go on citing each instance and then, when the tide subsides, remind him of the key sentence, "I'm not sure that I'm enough!" I invite him to begin another round of this feeling process by asking again, "And what's the *whole* feel of *that*. . ."

The process continues, widens, deepens. Without interpretation, without a lot of talk, we are working on a bodily level with the syndrome called "I'm not sure that I'm enough!" This general attitude is one root of various difficulties. *All* of them are being worked on at once. In subsequent sessions the person will *feel* more about it, will *feel* scenes from his past, will *feel* changes in it. He'll be able to check in with himself and see if that "whole business" about "being enough" is there in any particular situation, and he will be able to feel when that "place" in him has changed. All of this comes from work at the level of the *bodily felt roots*.

Conclusion

In this essay I have experientialized via focusing Angyal's method of holistic interpretation. Psychotherapy is no longer as dependent upon using interpretation as it once was. Indeed, there is evidence that Angyal was not satisfied with relying on it. In his chapter "Reviving the Pattern of Health," he wrote, "we should be able to develop some practices that would *temporarily relax the grip of neurosis* and create a frame of mind *permitting the unexpected to come up* or enabling the patient to see in a clearer light what happens to come up." He goes on to describe a state he calls "tonic relaxation," "in which the whole body is [felt] as one piece, energized, without strain, poised." Angyal says of this state that it "corresponds to the emergence of the real self. It is characterized by a feeling of ease, by the disappearance of obstacles to thought, perception, feeling, will, and by awareness of the availability of resources." Angyal laments that "we are not equipped with techniques that could. . . [induce] tonic relaxation" (p. 293).

Focusing is one such technique. The person is instructed how to take a friendly attitude toward his own process, to "clear a space," to lay down if only for a moment the burden of neurosis, and to listen to himself with what I will call a Rogerian attitude. When he does this, the grip of neurosis is temporarily relaxed. New things can come up. *The healthy pattern is strengthened by this very way of being with oneself.* Holistic insights are felt. Syndromes are discovered. Focusing helps the person *change* the syndromes in the very process of feeling them further.

I like to think Angyal would have loved it.[15]

HOW I USE FOCUSING FOR SELF-THERAPY

Psychology has made too much of the distinction between *self-help* and *psychotherapy*. The distinction often assumes that psychotherapy is going on only and always when one person called 'therapist' and one person called 'client' are in a room together. This is nonsense. As I wrote once in a flyer, "A lot that goes on in talk therapy is just that—a lot of talk. Therapy is not a function of the labels or roles that people assume. Therapy is happening whenever and wherever a therapeutic process is happening. That may or may not happen in 'therapy.' And it may or may not happen outside of 'therapy.' We should call 'therapeutic' any situation in which a therapeutic process is happening."

I mean by self-therapy any arrangement where a person is either with his/her self therapeutically or is with a person who is not in the role of therapist but who is being helpful. It is demeaning to call it self-help.[16] During the time that I put this volume together, I had a focusing partnership and a focusing plus catharsis partnership. I was actively self-guiding with my journal, and I was in psychotherapy. On any given week, one or the other of these activities was the most therapeutic for me. I did not experience 'being in therapy' as qualitatively different from or consistently more helpful than the other activities. The name 'therapy' has a mystique to it. Whether that mystique is a stigma ("Oh, him, you know—he's in therapy") or a badge of honor, 'therapy' ought not be segregated off in our minds from other sometimes helpful processes. Hence, I call this essay about my work on myself 'self-therapy.'

In this essay I define and illustrate the two basic ways that I use focusing for self-therapy. I call these two ways "mini-focusings" and "focusing rounds."

Mini-Focusings

"Mini-focusings" are brief experiences of just one, two, or maybe three of the focusing steps. Usually, though not always, they begin with the first step of focusing. I stop what I am doing, close my eyes, breathe, allow my attention to come down into my body, and ask, "How am I from the inside right now?" I "send" the question down to my bodily felt experiencing process, hang out with calm and friendly expectancy, and eventually let a word, phrase, image, sound, or gesture come that seems to match whatever visceral stirrings I sense inside. I say the word, phrase, image, sound, or gesture back to myself, check to see that it feels right, that it matches the sensation inside, and then I may go on to another focusing step or two that feels called for.

Typically, mini-focusings take from 30 seconds to a few minutes. I may do them in a coffee shop, while awaiting a client, during a bathroom trip, or in line at the supermarket. Mini-focusings are brief focusing breaks—times to check in and see what is going on inside.

I recorded in my journal a series of mini-focusings I did once in the course of writing a paper. I present them here as examples of mini-focusings:

1. 1/12/87: The writing is going well right now. I stop, close my eyes, go inside: There is an absence of sensation in my chest/stomach area. The image of a placid pond of water comes to me along with the word "mellow." I check that: Yes, I'm feeling mellow right now.
2. The next day: The writing is going well. When I close my eyes, I "see" a three-ring circus, and I "hear" the lyric, "Life is a carnival." I see mokojombie people (stilt-walkers at St. Thomas carnival). The feeling in my chest

is light and buoyant. I ask it, "What's the crux of this?" I see peoples' fingers snapping to an upbeat rhythm: **I'm** upbeat, flowing.

3. Another day. The writing is stuck. I close my eyes. I "see" a dark storm cloud filling up the sky, needing to burst. The feeling is in my chest; it is heavy. I try out the sentence, "I need to burst." "Yes," I hear inside, "You sure do, buster." I am on the beach. Bursting doesn't seem to make sense here and now. I check inside. It says it would be fine to wait until I get home. For now, go swimming.

4. Several weeks later: I have not worked on the paper in weeks and just today came back to it. When I close my eyes there is the immediate image of a locomotive, very powerful, something like a Lionel O-gauge train. The feeling in my chest and behind my eyes and in my arms is forceful, forward-moving, and powerful. The words come: "I'm on track and moving full steam ahead." I smile. Those words fit.

5: 3/19/87: Finally, the paper is now finished. Or is it? I sit back and close my eyes and turn my attention inside. "Is the paper done?" I ask my own insides. At first the feeling is in my chest area, a kind of constriction, a tightness, a not-quite-breathing-freely. "What is that?" "What is the crux of it?" I "see" a question mark right there in my chest area. I'm not **certain** the paper is done. Is that true? Yes. When I say that again ("I'm not **certain** the paper is done"), my head involuntarily nods in agreement, my chest area loosens. "What does it need?" I ask the question wordlessly, hang out and wait, and a final paragraph to the paper appears to me—whole and complete! **That** is what was needed; and now I feel complete and satisfied, and I breathe more fully and deeply.

These are mini-focusings. Notice that in examples 1 and 4 I use only the first step of focusing (How am I from the inside right now?). The other examples follow-up the first step with an open-ended question: What is the crux of it? What does it need? The particular question used is suggested by the felt sense itself; it "wanted" to be asked the question used. The other steps are skipped.

Mini-focusings are brief focusing breaks. They short-circuit the usual steps of a round of focusing. Only the steps immediately called for are utilized. Mini-focusings do not take very long. Thus, they easily become, as Laury Rappaport once put it, "part of the daily routine: washing, dressing, brushing my teeth, and focusing." (personal communication)

Again, mini-focusings are brief centering and grounding experiences which, when done regularly, keep a person "in touch" during the day. Then, "therapy" and "life" cease to feel so much like separate categories.

When do I do mini-focusings? I tend to do them several times a day. I do them (1) when I have become upset; (2) when I have a decision to make; (3) before I see a client; (4) when I am feeling particularly good; and (5) when I remember to do so. Here are some examples:

1. When I am upset I want to know what has triggered my upset and what kind of upset it is. I want to understand it, and I want it to shift. Therefore I focus:

   (a) It is Sunday evening and suddenly I feel somewhat sad. I feel the sensations around my eyes, in the relaxed falling of my face, and in an undefended slumping of my chest. When I say back to myself, "I feel sad," I sense a hint of tears behind my eyes. "I feel sad." "Yes, I do." A tear is shed and I feel some relief—less sad. I then ask the felt sense, "What made for the sad?" I get an image from several years ago of my older daughter waving good-bye to me. "Oh, the sad is about being left." I say that to myself and hear inside, "No—it is about being left **behind**." Oh, that makes sense. Several friends left our house just a few moments ago; I was left behind. . . Now, knowing this, it shifts; it doesn't hurt as much. I feel better.

(b) I'm feeling a pent-up, hemmed-in, yuck inside my chest. I notice that my teeth are gritted and my face grimacing. I'm walking along Brattle Street on a sunny day, and, as I walk, I ask myself silently, "What is that? What is the crux of it?" I "hear" the words inside, "I'm mad," and I "see" the image of an acquaintance who has recently been berating me. I did not react—outwardly—to his ire, and now I see that I am carrying my anger around inside. But I want to know more. "Yes, of course, I don't like being yelled at. Who does? But why did it bother me **so** much?" I say all this to myself, to the felt sense, and I get an image from childhood of losing daily in stickball to the only other boy on the block I grew up on. He was four years older and beat me (in both senses of the word). I sense old anger there, triggered off by the recent "beating" from this other bigger male person. I feel better, calmer, for knowing what my feeling is and where it comes from.

2. Focusing is basic to decision-making. However large or small the decision to be made is, the question is—how is my body carrying this decision? How would it feel about different possible choices? Whether the issue is what to choose from the menu at Joyce Chen's or where to live, the process is the same: Focus!

> For example: I am faced with two possible overall lifestyles. I could carry on my therapy practice in two locations, shuttling back and forth. Or, I could try to find a paying job in one area and return to the other just to be with my daughter.

How do I work on this issue on my own?

First, I imagine myself standing at a crossroads. Down the left fork is being self-employed in two locations, shuttling back and forth. How does it feel—what is the felt sense—of going down that road? I see my 1987 Jeep on the road, and I feel both excitement and trepidation. I am curious about the trepidation. "What is the crux of it?" It is about the traveling. "What about the traveling?" There is a felt sense of weariness and homelessness. "What is the worst of it?" "Winter." That comes quick and clear as day. I don't like and fear all the winter travel. "What is the crux of that?" "I am afraid I can't take care of myself." That for now seems to be the bottom line. (The coldness of winter symbolizes for me having to take care of myself and not feeling like I can.)

I come back to the crossroads. Now I'll look down the right fork. There, I am trying to get a paying job in one place and returning to the other just to see my daughter.

"What is the whole feel of that?" I feel really split. The having a job part feels—like a relief! Whew! That will help take care of me. The coming back to see my child feels—heavy. "What is the crux of that heavy?" It feels like a lot of work for a very short time. "Given that the feeling is split, how does it feel to encompass both sides of the split?" I hear the sentence, "It's a mixed bag."

Do I feel ready to decide? No, not yet. I have to live with this one somewhat longer. What do I need to look at?

I go back to the crossroads. This time I ask: "What do I have to look at further down both forks?"

I start to feel overwhelmed. There are too many questions. It feels better to stop where I am: excitement and trepidation down one road; relief and heaviness down the other!

No decision. But greater clarity about the issues. I'll check in with them again next week, starting from where I have left off. My decision is not yet made, but I have a greater clarity about what is at stake for me, and I can start, so to speak, somewhat further down the road when I return to this issue again later.

3. Before I see a client I want to be sure that I am ready, that I am "psychologically fit" to see this person. If there is anything in the way, I want to do a little work on it so that I can put it aside and give good attention to this person.

> He is my first client of the day. I check in to see if I am ready for him. "How am I from the inside right now?" I "see" a person making a "Bronx cheer" and I feel a "setness" in my jaw. I'm feeling hostile. "OK, that is not the best way to feel before doing therapy," I say to myself with a tinge of humor. "Let's see what that is. What is the crux of it?" "I don't think he heard me last week, and I'm mad about that." "What does that feeling need?" "I need to see where he is today, and I may need to share my upset with him if the situation recurs." That feels better.
> Now I am ready to listen to him!

4. I focus when I am feeling particularly good. Why? As I have said before and want to emphasize, focusing is not just remedial. It is not just to "work on" troubled places inside. It is just as useful for pleasant and, indeed, transcendent states. These states deserve attention, too! Otherwise, our passion for self-therapy may leave us biased in the direction of feeling bad!

> I have just concluded a very important negotiation to purchase a piece of property sacred to me. I stop and focus. I feel as if I am blended into my surroundings. It is as if there are energy currents moving inside and through me—and similar currents around me. It is a bodily feeling of no boundaries. I "see" an image of a painting by a French impressionist—the people and the environment are pained with the same kind of strokes. They blend into each other. That fits.

I try the handle "no boundaries" and feel another surge, another rush of good feeling. I feel exuberant, joyous. The good feeling is heightened by being correctly labeled and focused upon. I hear song lyrics: "My love keeps taking me higher. . ."

5. Finally, I do mini-focusings when I remember to do so. I don't focus every time I feel upset, and I focus sometimes when I just feel like doing so. I am not mechanical in my application of focusing for self-therapy. Notice that my samples of mini-focusings (about my paper) do not fit the first four categories of when I focus! People are not machines, and I see these notes more as guidelines than policies. Focusing should never feel like a chore. I keep my guidelines in mind and focus when I feel the need, feel disciplined, and remember to do so.

Focusing Rounds

"Focusing Rounds" are longer and more complete than mini-focusings. They may take anywhere from ten minutes to a half-hour. Typically, I lead myself through all the movements of the focusing process. I have my journal in front of me. After each step, I jot down in the journal a shorthand of what has happened. (I also do focusing rounds in my focusing partnership.)

I used to do a focusing round at least once a week on my mid-afternoon break. I would go to a coffee shop, order an iced mocha, take out my journal, sip the drink, and lead myself through a focusing round. It was a weekly routine, a kind of "exercise" that I disciplined myself to do.

In what follows, I illustrate focusing rounds with experiences I had the week before and the week after the birth of my younger daughter. I am copying these from my journal.

I use a shorthand in the journal. "**How now?**" is the way I ask myself the first focusing question ("How am I feeling inside right now?"). "**On bench**" is "Put on the bench whatever is between me and feeling all fine in my life right now." "**Pick**" is shorthand for the "Choose one thing to work on" step. "**Whole feel?**" is the step of letting the felt sense of the issue form, finding a symbol/handle for it, and resonating the handle. After that step, whatever particular questions I asked the felt sense are indicated.

It should be noted that these focusing rounds came after about eight years of pretty regularly using focusing in my life. For the first five years, I focused only with another person as guide. The guide would lead me through the steps. It never worked when I focused alone. It is only in the last ten years that I have begun to focus successfully by myself. These entries come from a generally good period in my life.

11/10/87 (four days before Zoe was born)
How now?

The words "slightly down. . . less than happy," come along with a touch of heaviness in my chest.

On Bench
Boredom
A particular client
Not doing exercise
Awaiting the baby
A feeling of "lack of. . ."

Pick?
"Lack of. . ."

Whole feel?
I get the image of my hands being slapped and the words "I'm being good." Let me resonate those words: "I'm being good." Yep, that's it. I'm being good; I'm not checking in to see what I want to do, and so I'm bored. When I say that, there is a shift; I feel lighter.
What's the worst?

The feeling that it could go on and on till the baby comes.
What is a step?
Just accept today. Don't try to make today something that it is not: "This too shall pass." There are days like this, and they just need acceptance. I feel lighter about the day after this. It does not weigh me down so much.

11/18/87 (four days after Zoe was born)

How now?
The word "up" comes to me along with a sense of lightness in my chest, a bouncyness. I try other words—"no stress," "no build-up," "flowing," and all are right, but "up" says it best: "I'm up."

On Bench
Slight irritation at someone's neurosis
Inconclusiveness re: writing
Sense of "not enough time for me"
Today
Health worries

Pick?
Health worries

Whole feel?
I get a dim picture of death, represented by a skull and crossbones, on the far horizon. The image comes with the word "grim." The body sensation is heavy. What feels right is the sentence, "Death is grim, but distant on the horizon." Yes, I say it twice to myself, and there is a sigh and less heaviness.
What right question?
I am asking myself what is the right question to ask the felt sense. I get: "Why 'grim' and 'distant'?" When I ask myself that, I get a line from Hemingway's *For Whom the Bell Tolls*.

As I remember the line, what bothers the hero about his imminent death is "the missing of it all." **That** is the grimness, but there is also the sense that I do have a long time till that comes. **That** sense is new-ish. I don't feel death close. No, I don't. Why not? I "see" some lights jumping behind my eyes and hear the words, "Zoe means life." Oh, I see, literally. (In Greek, Zoe means life.)

What's the crux of all this?

Zoe's birth has shed some heavy not-good-health energy from me. Zoe is life, and I feel more healthy and desirous of taking care of my health.

These realizations come with a rush of good feeling energy and a sense of "rightness" inside. At the end of the focusing round I'm feeling bouncy and peppy and with renewed energy for the day. The shift is strong and unmistakable.

When do I do a focusing round? For several years I used to do one at least once a week. I liked to do the round at the same time in the same place each week. It became my focusing time and place. This regularity is good, and I also do focusing rounds at other times as the need arises.

When I am working in this way, it means that at least once a week I am taking stock of the felt state of my life. I am taking inventory of where I am, and I am working on at least one issue a week. I feel that this helps me stay current. Too much gunk does not pile up. I record my weekly focusing rounds in my journal and review them periodically. These reviews give me a longer term perspective on the felt course of my life. I can trace the emergence, passing through, and passing on of issues as well as their chronicity.

It is important to recognize what self-therapy can accomplish and what it cannot accomplish. Self-therapy is very useful if it is not misused. What do these mini-focusings and focusing rounds accomplish, and what do they not accomplish?

First and foremost, they keep me grounded. Most of the time

I know what I feel, moment to moment, and I experience myself as knowing as much as I need to know about why I feel as I do.

And often—though not always—I can "move" my feelings, carry them forward, by these self-therapy focusings.

Thus, I don't feel at the mercy of my feelings. Reynolds (1986) argues that feelings are simply 'givens' that cannot be changed, and so we all had best just get on with doing what we have to do, day-to-day, regardless of how we feel.

Focusing shows me that this simply is not so! These mini-focusings and focusing rounds help me experience over and over what Gene calls "an experiential effect"—a felt shift, some release or relief of feelings, and thus I feel better able to face the day. Typically, before these experiences, I felt worse, and afterward I feel better. These self-therapy focusings help me feel better.

Of course, there are times when focusing does not get me out of a bad feeling place; shifts do not *always* happen. (In psychology, nothing works all the time.) But even then I tend to live better with the feelings that feel heavy inside. I have more acceptance of them even when there is no release.

Focusing helps me experience on a daily basis the lines of the serenity prayer. "God grant me the serenity to accept the things I cannot change, courage to change the things I can, and wisdom to know the difference."

What things can be changed and what things cannot be changed differ from focusing to focusing. Focusing keeps these words experiential and up-to-date. They do not remain merely conceptual and timelessly abstract.

Notice: Unlike many other forms of self-therapy (e.g. yoga postures, diet, affirmations), focusing is a way of dealing directly with what affectively is right now. It is a different kind of self-therapy than many other kinds. This does not necessarily make it better than the others. It depends what one wants to be working on.

If what one wants to be working on is one's felt sense of now, or of an issue, then focusing is the route to take. Other roads lead to other places. Much psychological self-therapy methods are ways that purport to manipulate one into a better affective life.

Focusing is somewhat unique in that its emphasis is on what affectively *is*. That *is* shifts through the naming of it rather than by any forcing or tricking of oneself.

In sum, these focusings for self-therapy do two main things: They help me know my felt sense on a moment-to-moment basis. They often help me get felt shifts. They are not always enough. They are not always the best way to deal with things.

During a period of heavy depression ten years ago, I did self-therapy focusings regularly to no avail. They were not enough for the situation. They probably did no harm, and, now and then, some good. But they were not enough in and of themselves.

I know someone who has used focusing for self-therapy exclusively for over ten years. She is a very isolated person with a lot of distrust of people. She has been working on this issue by herself all this time. She has made no appreciable change. It is the wrong way to work on this particular issue.

These self-therapy focusings do not accomplish what a regular therapy session might—namely, a more intensive and extensive time period with another person devoted to my growth. They do not provide what a good therapeutic relationship provides: The unfolding of one's story in an atmosphere of growing trust in another person. They do not provide a longer "time-out" for self-reflection in the company of an experienced and trained other.

They are not a substitute for a therapeutic relationship. They are for knowing one's internal weather on a regular basis and helping partly cloudy skies move in the direction of sunlight. They are not enough in themselves during a heavy blizzard, a long bout of the mistral, a hurricane, a tornado, or other very threatening weather.

FOCUSING-ORIENTED HEMINGWAY-INFLUENCED THERAPY

Although my title—as you will see—is serious, let me share with you the playful way it came to me.

One day, as a way to instigate creativity, I was mischievously playing with conjoining dissimilars: "Spring Fashion, The Battle of Bull Run, and Life in Macedonia"; "Long Division and the Jewish Question"; "Vitamin A and the Dow Jones Average." I was also amusing myself by meditating Koan-style on one of my favorite Woody Allen aphorisms: "It is clear that there is an Afterlife. The questions are what hours it is open and how close it is to Midtown."

Suddenly, apparently out of nowhere, but no doubt stimulated by this ongoing wordplay, "Hemingway and Focusing" popped in. I immediately know I had become serious. Three months later I changed the title to what it is today.

Hemingway and focusing are like heads and tails. They are yin and yang. They are AM and PM. They are halves that fit together. They are "the outer act" and "the inner act."

Hemingway is the patron saint of "the outer act." Although in writing about writing he does observe how hard it is "knowing what you really felt," he quickly passes over this to identify "the [writer's] greatest difficulty," namely "to put down what really happened in action, what the actual things were which produced the emotion that you experienced." Asked how a writer can train himself to write, he replied, "Watch what happens.." He refers to fishing: "If we get into a fish. . . if you get a kick out of it while he is jumping. . . see exactly what the action was that gave you the emotion. [Was] it the rising of the line. . . or the way he smashed and drew water. . . Remember what the noises were and what was said. . . What the action was that gave you the excitement. Then write it down. . . that's a five-finger exercise." (in Phillips, 1984, p. 30)

Focusing is the "inner act." That is the title of Part One of *Focusing*. Focusers are virtuosi of the affective life. We know how to tune into a feltness, how to inquire of it to get further information. Focusing teaches a fineness of discernment in the inner life that precisely balances Hemingway's exhortation about how to observe the outer life.

Let me show how they go together in "Focusing-Oriented Hemingway-Influenced Therapy."

He comes in troubled. The night before he saw the spectacular Normandy beach invasion scene that begins "Saving Private Ryan." At a certain point, he is embarrassed to say, he yelled out in the crowded theater, "Ouch!" He does not care about the embarrassment. He wants to know—why the reaction?

Hemingway-like we slow down the action. What was happening on screen at the moment before his outcry? "The soldier was looking for his arm that had been blown off." What specifically was he observing right before the "ouch"? "The part of his insides which showed since he had no arm." What part of that was he gripped by? "The insides oozing out." What was it about that? There was the later scene when he was quiet and only grimaced when a soldier's guts were hanging out. What did the observation call forth inside him? Suddenly he remembered "witnessing the Caesarian birth where I saw the squiggles of a woman's intestines." More quickly now: a memory of a sexual situation "where I first saw a woman with a mastectomy. . . I tried to describe my feeling of awe to my therapist. She said, 'It was like seeing the face of God.' I did not know intellectually what the sentence meant. But it touched a string on some inner harp, it went right through me, and I burst into tears." He starts to sob. A minute goes by. He remembers reading a graphic description of open-heart surgery. Then he gets it: "It is not mortality. . . it is *invasive* mortality. I can accept the dying. I can't accept the 'being done to me' part."

We further explore the inner meanings of the 'being done to me' part. He has a shadowy memory of an incident in a barn when he was young. I get him to tell the story of the action in the present tense (gestalt) and in slow motion. We go frame by frame. The slowness allows him to find the exact moment, the real scene, the specific action where the feelings of shame, fear, arousal, and excitement begin. A man is touching his (the boy's) penis. But there is more. THE MAN HAS ONLY ONE ARM. The boy is looking fascinated at "the place where the arm should be." The sexual horror and thrill is matched to the "one-armed man scene."

He suddenly understands a repeated adult sexual experience which near perfectly mirrors that initial intensely felt invasive/ scene.

We are far beyond Hemingway now. But we used Hemingway to get here. Hemingway alerts us to watch, listen, taste, smell, and remember exactly the specificity of action or situation which gave rise to the feeling. Hemingway does little exploration of the feeling. Focusing comes along. It provides the same microscopic discernment of the inner experiencing that Hemingway has applied to the outer.

Together, they make for a rich, full, dense, finely discerned picture of outer actions and situations and the inner experiencings to which they give rise. Be it for writing or therapy the combination is satisfying and healing. Outer and inner are both given their due and brought into good connection with each other. They return to the oneness, the integrity, that they had before we cut them up into 'outer' and 'inner.'

BOOK REVIEW: BODY THERAPIES

The Body in Psychotherapy by Edward R. L. Smith. McFarland and Co., N. Carolina and London, 1986.
  The Hakomi Therapy Manual by Ron Kurtz. Hakomi Institute, Boulder, CO.
  Experiential Psychotherapy by Alvin Mahrer. Brunner/Mazel, New York, 1983.
  Therapeutic Experiencing by Alvin Mahrer. W.W. Norton, New York, 1986.
  These are four books that focusers who do therapy ought to know. Three mention focusing and one does not.
  The Body in Psychotherapy reviews the major contributions of Reich, Lowen, Pierrakos, Perls, Pesso, and other body-theorists to psychotherapy. It has excellent material on how to "read" bodies and on what the author calls "soft" (e.g. breathing, posture), "hard" (e.g. bioenergetic, Reichian), and "expressive" (e.g. gestalt, psychomotor) body-interventions. The book introduces very well the *other* body-oriented therapies with which focusing so well combines.
  The book makes no reference at all to focusing. This is significant. The omission highlights for me how focusing represents an entirely different approach to the body—entirely different from what is usually called "body-therapy." Focusing is the way that the Heideggerian and phenomenological approach to the body enters the world of psychotherapy.
  Hakomi is also omitted from *The Body in Psychotherapy*. Coming out of a bioenergetic tradition, Kurtz has put together, in *The*

Hakomi Therapy Manual, his own ingenious body-oriented therapy based on Buddhist principles of mindfulness and non-violence. Kurtz makes reference to focusing and it is an integral part of his work. I like Kurtz's whole attitude, which is very congenial to focusing. He communicates respect for the client and uses an impressive variety of therapeutic interventions (e.g. "probes," "taking over") which allow for the combining of expressive body-work and focusing.

Probes, for example, work like this. Clients have "nourishment barriers," good things that they have trouble taking in. The therapist says a sentence directed at the client's nourishment barrier; e.g., "You are fine just as you are," or "You really are welcome here." The therapist repeats the sentence a few times slowly with the instruction to the client to simply observe what happens inside. The aim is not to convince the client. The aim is for the client to see "what stirs inside" in response to the statement. I use this method frequently. It is a powerful way to stimulate an experiential effect.

Mahrer calls his system, described in his two books, "Experiential Therapy," the same thing Gene Gendlin has called his. This can be confusing, as the two systems are quite different. Every session of Mahrer's *begins* with focusing attention into the body. But then sessions move toward carrying experiencing forward through a variety of methods. The therapist has to have the same body sensations as the client and then the therapy takes off from there according to Mahrer's highly systematic principles. *Experiential Psychotherapy* introduces Mahrer's system and the early steps in therapy—the ones that make most use of focusing. *Therapeutic Experiencing* is the more advanced book on the later phases of the therapeutic session. Mahrer's work is quirky, pugnacious, and quite brilliant, and focusers will find fascinating the directions in which he takes his "experiential therapy."

Why do I single out these books? I continue to be intrigued with the relations between focusing, body-work, and cathartic interventions. I see focusing as basic to therapy. It will be remembered long after a lot of 1960's-1970's new psychotherapeutic methods are forgotten. But I keep wanting to deepen and intensify therapy—to turn up the volume—with methods that are expressive, cathartic, and full-bodied. These four books point in that direction.

THE INTEGRATION OF FOCUSING IN VERBAL FOCUSING THERAPY (1996)

I am often asked by other therapists how I introduce focusing into my therapy. These therapists have been exposed to focusing. They are intrigued by it. But they are unsure as to how to present it to clients. As one said, "It is something new. It seems useful. It can be powerful. How do I get clients to do it?"

Over time I have evolved the following answer to their question.

There are two main ways that I introduce focusing into therapy. They parallel how I use focusing for self-therapy. One way is "focusing rounds." I lead a person through the steps of focusing. The other way is "mini-focusings." I tuck invitations to focus inside other verbal exchanges. This may mean one, two, or three focusing steps embedded in some combination of listening, self-disclosure, asking questions, giving feedback, making interpretations, verbal gestalt experiments, etc.

I do focusing rounds when (a) a person has come to me explicitly for focusing therapy; (b) after I have had a person read FOCUSING; (c) when a client who knows something about focusing comes in with nothing pressing to work on and wants to practice focusing.

I do not do this very often. Two out of twenty sessions a week may look like the following:

She comes in, takes off her glasses, closes her eyes, gets comfortable in the chair, and we go through a whole round of focusing:

T: Take a few deep breaths... Imagine your attention is like a searchlight... you can turn the searchlight on and shine it down inside your body.... Just see what's there...
C: (30 seconds) There's a knot in my stomach... and I want to curl down over it (curls). I want to slump.
T: There's a knot, and you want to slump to curl over it.
C: Yeah.
T: Should we stay with it for a moment or put things out on the bench?
C: Let's put things on the bench.
T: OK... Imagine you're sitting on a park bench... you're going to stack, at a comfortable distance from you—down there on the other end of the bench— whatever is between you and feeling all fine right now... Just ask, "What's between me and feeling all fine right now?"
C: (after a minute of silence) There's this trouble with my child.
T: Trouble with your child.
C: Yeah... then there is this new thing with my boss.
T: The new thing with your boss.
C: Yeah... Then there is the whole thing about my job—whew—that's a big one.
T: There's the big one about your job.
C: (quiet for about 30 seconds) There are a few other minor things... my elbow... missing judo class... some trouble—small—with Martin (her husband)...
T: Whew! Let's slow it down... There's the elbow—
C: Yeah.
T: Missing the judo class—
C: Yeah.
T: And the small thing with Martin—
C: Yeah... (perks up) maybe it isn't so small!

T: Anything else? See if there is anything else that needs to go out on the bench.
C: (after a minute). No. I think that is all. Could you say them back to me?
T: (repeats each thing) . . . Now, first take a moment to feel that there is a "you" separate from all that stuff. . . (20 seconds). Then let yourself feel pulled toward the one thing in the stack that most needs your attention right now. . .
C: (quickly) Ha! I'm surprised. It's the thing with Martin.
T: Ah, yes. The thing with Martin. . . Now, hold it in front of you, this thing between you and Martin, picture it, say its name over and over. . . and give your body time to get the whole feel of it. . . let the whole feel of it form. . . .
C: (after about a minute) That's the knot, and the wanting to curl over it. . . I'm afraid I've hurt him and he'll leave.
T: So, it's the knot (yeah). . . and it's the wanting to curl over it (yeah), and you're afraid you've hurt him and he'll leave.
C: Yeah. . . (starts to cry, first a little then convulsively) I'm afraid he'll do what Faith did (a woman lover who left her).
T: Ah. . . there it is. . . you're afraid that it will happen again (yeah). . . he'll leave like Faith did. . . (yeah). (I hand her a tissue.) Does that feel like the crux of it?
C: Yep. That is sure it. (She is sitting up more erectly now, almost with a rueful smile on her face. There has certainly been a shift.)
T: Can we ask it some questions?
C: Sure. Why not?
T: Ask it. . . (I struggle to come up with what feels like a right question. I'm not sure and so pick a general one). . . Ask it—what's wrong?
C: (very quickly) What's wrong is I'm a scaredy cat! Once burned, twice shy! Every time I get mad at him—boom, Faith redux.
T: (I could repeat this, but she seems to be suddenly on a roll,

and I don't want to get in the way. So I move right to a next question) Ask it, what does it need?
C: It needs some courage, damn it. I'm no cowardly lion. (She is laughing by this point)
T: Ask it, what's a good, small step in the right direction?
C: I'm going to go home and tell him—you're not Faith! You're not Faith! That's funny. I feel like a character in the "Crying Game"! Hey, when I said that the knot left. . . Jesus Christ. . . I'm tired of being haunted by ghosts. . .
T: See if there is any other question the felt sense wants to be asked.
C: Yeah. How long does this have to go on?
T: Ask the felt sense—caringly—how long does this have to go on?
C: (slowly) It says— "Till you really get it."
T: Get what?
C: (breaks into sobs) That I didn't cause Faith to go away. . . (more tears)
T: Yeah. . . that you weren't responsible for Faith's leaving.
C: Yeah.
T: Yeah. . . . Does that feel like a good stopping place? (There is about five minutes left in the fifty-five minute hour, and she has begun to reach for her glasses.)
C: Oh, yeah, I guess so. Boy, I didn't know that was there. Thanks.
(We hug)

Notice: (1) The client is surprised by what she chooses to work on; (2) There is a real felt shift during the session; (3) I mostly pick and choose focusing questions to ask; (4) Often I reflect back what she has said; (5) There is a lot of emotional expression in the session; (6) I follow her lead and what I know of her over time so as to tailor the focusing round to her needs; (7) I ask whether we have reached a place to stop.

This is fairly representative of what a focusing therapy round looks like. The whole encounter has consumed about thirty minutes. (She was ten minutes late to start.)

And we covered a lot of ground in that thirty minutes.

Why don't I do focusing rounds more often? I'm not really sure. One thing is I think I would get bored if all I did all day was lead people through focusing rounds! It does not engage me enough if I do it too much. It would get too repetitious. Second — and more important—I like to start where a person is rather than impose a structure on the person. (This person came originally requesting focusing rounds after a weeklong focusing workshop with Gene.) I think that it is some combination of these two factors—plus some clients' reluctance or inability to do this much focusing—that keeps me from doing more therapy following this form.

Much more often, I introduce focusing into my sessions by tucking invitations to focus among other verbal exchanges.

Here are several examples. I will indicate in parentheses what the various therapist responses would be called, especially invitations to focus. The examples are varied so as to give a feel for the variety of focusing therapy as I was practicing it during the time period involved (about 1979 to 1985).

Some of these examples come from real therapy sessions, some from classroom demonstrations, and some from training groups. All of them together provide a flavor for the similarity and diversity of *verbal* focusing therapy sessions.

1. He has been talking abut various aspects of his life for the first fifteen minutes of the session. He seems to be trying to take stock of where he is. I invite him to close his eyes, breathe, let his attention come down into his body, and sense the whole feel of his life right now: "Ask your body to let form the whole feel of your life as you experience it right now." **(focusing invitation)**

After about thirty seconds he responds: "It's like I have this enormous duffel bag in my arms, and I have only a semi-secure grip on it."

There is a lot in this image that we could explore, but he has been asking me to help him take some real steps in life. So I say to him, "Ask the image—what does it need to make the grip more secure?" (**'asking' step**) (15 seconds)

He responds: "I need rest. I need to be alone. After being alone, I need a period of intense work. And I need to spend time at my summer house."

The rest of the session is spent in conversational interaction as he elaborates upon these realizations and makes concrete plans to put them into effect.

Only about five minutes of the session are spent focusing. The rest of the time is more interactional-conversational. Yet in those five minutes quite a lot has been accomplished!

2. The outstanding thing for me abut this next session is that I never learn what specific *content* the person is working on. She works on a feeling: it changes: She feels better. Neither therapist nor client feels a need to check in with content. (In this and in some other of the examples I will use extensive footnotes to consider alternative responses that could have been used along the way).

The session begins right after a training group exercise in which the background is Nina Simone singing, "I wish I Knew How It Would Feel to Be Free."

C: I think I want to stay with that music. . . Everything is so external. . .
T: You're very focused outwardly and your feelings get lost.[17]
C: Yes, that's right. . . I don't know if that's good or bad. . . this is a new place for me.[18]
T: So you feel a little **uncomfortable**. . . not quite able to decide if it's good or bad.[19]
C: Yeah. . . I wanted to **feel** the music. I didn't want to be in my head (points to her forehead). It seems like I'm dealing with everything up here right now. . .

T: You want to be really **feeling** what is going on, and you're somewhat unhappy that you're so much in your head right now.
C: I'm wondering what I did (voice trails off). . . . last week it was **all** up here (tapping her forehead again). . . I felt so miserable for so many days after. . . (she seems to be bouncing from thought to thought, leaving each unfinished). . . . retelling gets me in touch. . .
T: What are you feeling right now? (**invitation to focus**)[20]
C: Very uncomfortable about the subject. . .
T: Where in your body do you feel the uncomfortable?
C: Right here (puts her fist to her chest).
T: Put your attention right there, and see what that place is saying.
C: "I'm very frustrated". . . it's saying "I feel so frustrated!"
T: What do you experience in your body right now?
C: A sense of tears coming up (she looks weepy).
T: What does that feel like. . . just be with that. . .
C: I feel defeated (she slumps in the chair). . . like, it doesn't even pay to think about this problem. . . I just can't. . .
T: You're feeling like you just can't deal with it **at all**. . .
C: The frustration is that **it hasn't moved**! (she sweeps away with both her hands)
T: "I'm so **frustrated** with it. . . " Do that more. . . (therapist mirrors client's arm and hand movements)
C: (continues to push away with both her hands) It's old and moldy. . . I hate it. . . It's like an old dried up lemon in the back of a refrigerator. (pause)[21]
T: So. . . like an old, dried up lemon in the back of a refrigerator. . . old and moldy. (Pause)
C: It sticks in my craw! (Her hands begin to move more vigorously)
T: Do that again with your hands. . . breathe. . . Again.. more, some verbalization (**gestalt**)
C: Go away! Get out! Go away! Get out! (Client screams at the

thing stuck in her craw. This continues for a few minutes)...
I can't believe I did that. It was fantastic!

T: Yeah, **you** were fantastic...

C: ... that's what the problem needs—a good screaming at... I'm screaming at my stuckness...

T: What are you feeling right now?[22]

C: (she closes her eyes for 5 seconds) I'm mourning... the word coming up was "sad"... can I accept that this is the way it is.... I'm exhausted.

T: You're mourning the loss of your feelings?[23]

C: (in response to T's remark) I have lived **so long** with such rotten feelings... I can't change the situation... I'm **grieving**...

T: You're **grieving**... just let it happen...

C: (cries and sobs for 5 minutes)

T: What are you feeling now?

C: Real good... giggly... I'm in a much better place... I see now that I only have to relate to **my own** expectations and demands, not other peoples'.... Thanks.[24]

3. Here is another example from the same training group. This is from about 1983, and the emphasis is on a combination of listening, focusing, and verbal gestalt methods. That is where I was at the time.

In the check-in with which I start the training group each week, she has said that she is upset about a relationship thing that happened the past weekend. An interesting thing for me in the session is how an old place in her around her father looms on the horizon, and keeps insisting on being heard.

C: (She closes her eyes and goes inside. T sits, giving her his full attention. After about 30 seconds she starts talking.) It's kind of hard to get back to my original agenda because here, I feel good.

T: So it's hard to get back to that agenda... could you sort of

check inside as to what that was all about when you first came in? (**invitation to focus**)
C: I can tell you, but I'm not sure how much I'm feeling it. . . what was so sad for me is that I got a real sense of his being like a solid person who is in a place where he could give back to me. . . a whole different flavor to it than with other men I've been seeing. . .
T: What was the sadness?[25]
C: My expectations weren't met! (she lightens up and laughs) That's outrageous!
T: What's the sadness?[26]
C: First, that my fantasy didn't work. . .
T: And something else, too?
C: On the plane coming back, something about my father. . . (she breaks off and pauses and starts on another track) Today it is so **rare** for me to be with someone who can give me something. . . .
T: So the sadness came from being with someone who. . . [27]
C: No, it came from it being such a **rarity**.
T: Would you say that to the people in the group?[28]
C: (to X) It's rare for me to be with someone who is in a place where they can feed me.
(to Y) It's very rare that someone can give me something and I feel comfortable taking it.
(to Z) It's **very** rare that people give to me and I take.
T: Now close your eyes and check inside. . . see what is there now. . . [29] (**invitation to focus**)
C: I just realized that I'm so **tired** of having to **look** all the time. . .
T: You're so **tired**. . . say it again.
C: I'm **really** tired of having to look so hard for someone. . . . People who I can't get from are so **draining** —
T: It's **draining**. . . (breaks in)
C: I'm particularly angry with this woman, Rae. I'm going to talk with her (sets up an empty chair for Rae). I'm always

there having to listen to you. Everybody has to be there for you, and no one is there for me. Well, this is going to change. I'm not going to put up with you anymore![30]
T: Go inside. (**invitation to focus**)
C: I'm angry!
T: See what's all in that anger.
C: I'm not getting enough!
T: Say that again.
C: I'm not getting enough!
T: (After a too brief pause, I address her by name and start to say something.) Jean, I'd like to—
C: (Stops me) I want to stay with this a minute. . . [31] (T sits back; C starts to cry) In Cleveland this past weekend, he was almost **paternal**. . . doing things for me, to please me.
T: Where are you now?[32]
C: Not that badly. . . It doesn't feel as bad. The whole thing meshes with my father leaving.[33]

4. These are a client's notes on a session from 2/6/85. The example uses focusing, listening, gestalt and interpretations to help a feeling move forward and provide profound insights about a piece of troublesome past behavior—a long time spent in bed:

"Started session by saying things had gotten better as I had been more active, and outside of two days where I had to stay in bed due to severe cold, was fairly busy. N suggested that I go inside and see if anything would come up. (**focusing invitation**) I did, and was met by nothing. Finally, it looked as though there was just a small area of sadness, but the rest of the area was all right. Visualized the area as being cylindrical in shape to the rear of my neck. Felt stuck and complained of this. N suggested that I kneel down on the floor and address a large pillow (where the pillow was to be the sadness that I was trying to make contact with) (**gestalt**). I was surprised to see a mass of worms which were bundled up together and were very active. Rather than being repulsed by this, I interpreted the mass to mean that it was in motion and was very entangled and complex. As I tried to relate to the mass/pillow, the thought that the sadness would always be with me crossed my mind i.e., that I would always be carrying it around with me. Its function was to protect me. It was essentially saying, watch out, be careful. I must be careful. N was helpful during all of this as he reflected back to me what I was saying. When the word *convalescing* came up, tears really began to flow. That certainly was the right word. It seems that the sadness was using the tears to communicate with me (my interpretation) to tell me that *convalescing* was indeed the stage that I was currently in. I concluded that the tears are a way for the sadness part of me which is there to protect me, to communicate with me, principally acknowledgement.

"I tried to interpret my tears in this new light, i.e., a form of communication as opposed to one of self-pity. And that the form, or rather the meaning of the communication, was recognition or acknowledgement that the sadness part was being heard. I also interpreted my long siege in bed as the way that the sadness part had chosen to let me heal from a variety of disappointments. All these interpretations—verbalized to N who simply reflected them back—seemed right on. I could feel them. There was a lot in the session of what N calls "felt shifts" or "experiential effects." I felt much better and clearer when it was done; my whole long siege in bed felt different now."

5. In this next example a client is working on his "resistance" to completing a graduate school application. Notice how, through repeated invitations to focus, careful listening, and a gestalt dialogue, the whole shape of the problem changes. (The next week he finished the application.)

C: I want to talk about my resistance to doing the Columbia application.

T: Some part of you wants to do it, and some part of you is holding out from doing it.

C: Yeah. I'm pretty sure the resistant piece is afraid.

T: The resistance feels like fear.

C: Yeah. I'm afraid I can't say who I am.

T: 'I'm afraid I can't capture myself in words as I am.' Can you touch that fear place inside? (**invitation to focus**)

C: I don't know much about it.

T: It is terra incognita. . . . So, close your eyes, let your attention go to the fear place, just hang out there. . . Maybe ask, "What is this fear. What's the crux of it?"

C: (after 30 seconds, eyes closed) It feels like an old fear, like I never had confidence in my writing. I didn't know I could write till high school. My inside feeling place still has trouble believing. . .

T: . . . early fear.

C: I don't know where it comes from.

T: (taking his cue from C's words) Go inside. . . make contact again with the fear. . . . Ask it, "Where do you come from?" (**another invitation to focus**)

C: (really perks up!) This is really interesting! I just remembered I was afraid to talk as a child, to say who I was. So it doesn't come from school. I brought it to school. Wow, is that a revelation! I never really knew that.

T: It's a real discovery right now.

C: Yes. The fear is not of writing. *The fear is of saying who I am.* That feels like a big shift. There is something, though, about writing it down that makes it even scarier.

T: Ah. So there are two steps, not one.

C: Yeah.

T: The first is fear of saying who you are. The second is of writing it down. Could you touch that second fear place? (**invitation to focus**)

C: (30 seconds) If I write it down, that makes it permanent, and I'll have to live up to it... There is something in there about being right or being wrong.
T: It seems that at the base of the thing about writing is this thing about being right or wrong.
C: Right. Exactly. As if there is a right or wrong...
T: Go inside. Ask, "What is this whole thing about right or wrong?" (**invitation to focus**)
C: (30 seconds) It's all connected. I just saw it. There is something about not talking in the family and being right or wrong... wait... it's like I have to go through sending the application in and waiting and being judged like by my parents.
T: So, at its crux does the fear... are you saying the fear has to do with your reaction to your parents' being critical of your self-expression?
C: Yeah!! That is it right on the nose. Now I've transferred that fear to Columbia.
T: Put your parents right there and talk to them (**gestalt instruction**)
C: Fuck you! Who do you think you are? You really stifled me. You shouldn't have treated a little kid that way. It was abuse. You made me afraid. You made me keep my beauty and talents inside. You never affirmed me... and now I'm stuck on this sucking application!
T: See what's there now (**invitation to focus after gestalt expression**)
C: (30 seconds) Some tears for me... how I shut myself up... or down... how I buried my talent in the ground (biblical reference).
T: You shut yourself up—or down—rather than expose yourself to enemy fire.
C: Yeah. But now I have to remember that Columbia is not the enemy.
T: It could be a friend.

C: Yes. . . And I can do the application!

6. Focusing is very useful in therapy—as we have seen in self-therapy—when a decision needs to be made.

In this brief example a lot of work has already been done. I have listened to him talk for several weeks about the two women in his life. Mostly I have reflected back his feelings, asked questions, and disclosed some of my own struggles with the same issue. He has been getting closer and closer to what it is all really about. This is from my notes in my fourteenth session with him:

C: I really want to get to the crux of this issue.
T: So let yourself feel it. . . really feel the struggle. . . . Can you feel it? (**invitation to focus**)
C: Uh-huh.
T: Now, ask the feeling—what's the crux of it?
After about a minute, to his utter surprise, he gets a vivid memory of the Vito Antefermo-Alan Minter middleweight championship fight which he had seen the week before. "What relevance does that have?" he asks. I encourage him not to discard it, but to swim around in the image for awhile.
Pieces begin to come to him: The fight was very close. The fight was between a boxer and a slugger. **He** couldn't decide who had won.
An image of the Marvin Hagler-Vito Antifermo fight now comes to him. (By the way, he is Italian by birth.) That one was called a draw even though he was sure Hagler had won. He chuckles.
We talk. All these magnifications of aspects of the focusing image when empathically entered reveal important truths about the relationship issue—as does the fact that it is seen as a boxing match! They crystallize perfectly what he had only vaguely and fuzzily sensed as the trouble. At the end of the focusing he feels calm and knows he isn't ready to decide. It is a draw.

7. Kathy McGuire has been so kind as to publish this example from a demonstration I did in her focusing class.[34] I will quote from her use of it and from my own transcription of the session.

"This is a 10-20 minute vignette of focusing therapy that happened in a class-room demonstration situation. The client is a thirty-year old woman, a graduate student in counseling psychology. The therapist is Neil Friedman. . . ." (McGuire, 1991, p. 240)

C: Um. . . what I want to talk about. . . is a feeling that I'm . . . um. . . just beginning to recognize. . . I noticed it yesterday. . . so I thought "Great. . . work on it."
T: So it's kind of like a brand new bud that you noticed blooming just yesterday.
C: Yeah. . . but I knew it was coming. . . it's all around terminating from here [school]. . . um. . . with clients. . . internship. . . . so a lot of termination.
T: So, like, you knew it was on the way and you started feeling it just yesterday. (This is just a repetition; it does not add anything at all to what has been said. Probably it slowed things down, which might have helped. At least it did no harm.)
C: Yeah. . . and it's. . . there's sadness there. . . all of this ending. . . I'm in the graduate program and doing it in one year, it's intense. . . um. . . it's kind of like my whole life is here in a lot of ways. . . it's all going to be over really soon.
T: It's all going to be over really soon. . . just let yourself be quiet now and see what's there. . . (**invitation to focus**) Let your attention be like a searchlight and go down inside your body. . . Just breathe into it, just be in a friendly way. . . .
C: (long pause) I can really feel the loss (tearfully) and somehow it has to do with when my mother died.
Kathy comments: "This is the beginning of a bodily carrying forward. The events around termination at school had touched

upon the unresolved grief around mother. The client had not been conscious of this connection at the beginning [of the session], but only conscious of the vague, bodily felt discomfort around the ending. . . ". (p. 242)

We return to the transcription:
T: So the loss of school brings up the loss of mother.
C: (sniffling, tears) Yeah. There's real similarities there. Like she had cancer, and I knew, and I began here right after she died.
T: Um.
C: And I guess it's almost. . . when you said the words "loss of mother" or "loss of school brings up loss of mother" somehow, I had this whole other sense of how (tearful) nurtured I've felt here.
T: Uh huh.
C: (tearful)
T: The school has been like a mother to you.
C: (more tearful) Yeah. . . (very tearfully) I'm not ready to lose another one.
T: (softly) Not again. Not another one.
C: (sobbing, sighs) Oh God. . . now I'm getting more and more connections, like, I realize, I'm graduating in August and I don't recall the exact date, but it's within four days of when she died. . . I see more and more connection. . . losing my mother felt like I also lost my family. I'm the only (more tears) female really left, and she was the link, and kind of without her it's really dissipated. . . . and being here has been a family as well. . .
T: (here I shift gears to a Gestalt experiment) Let's try this. (I put three chairs in front of her to represent her mother, the counseling program, and her family.)
C: Oh (very tearfully), that feels like too much to look at all at once. (Cries off and on for several minutes. She does not talk to the chairs, yet I feel the 'experiment' has been a success as it

has brought forth still more catharsis. I'm aware we need to stop soon. I wait until her crying subsides on its own.)
C: God... I can't get over it. It feels like the final part of it [the graduation] is going to happen on almost the exact date that I lost her.
T: It almost sounds like somebody planned it.
C: (laughs) Yeah. It kind of feels like it.
T: (aware that time is running out) Could you ask the feeling, "What do you need? What can help things?" Go inside. (**invitation to focus**)
C: (10 seconds) Well, I got immediately, I need to start therapy again. And to do that now I would have something nurturing, sustaining... that would be... it wouldn't relate to the ending, it would be happening now.
T: Yes, yes.
C: And I really want to do that!
T: Does it feel OK to stop here? Do you know where to go with this?
C: Yeah, yeah.[35]

8. A final example: I want to include this one because it adds therapist sharings to the list of kinds of verbal expressions with which focusing invitations and listening responses may be interspersed. And this point deserves a few words of amplification.

As a therapist I do not attempt to be a blank screen. I attempt to be a real person. The session is not for me. The session is for my client. But my sharing about myself can help his process move forward. And it is even OK if every so seldom I talk about me even if it is — or seems — just for me. I keep this to a minimum. But at times it is fruitful in itself and at times it pays dividends — and keeps paying dividends — far beyond what had been expected.

He is recently divorced. I am less recently divorced.

C: I don't know. It is hard getting started.
T: Beginnings are difficult.
C: I meant, in particular, starting over.
T: Oh yes. I remember. 'Here we go again. Pick yourself up, Neil. Off the floor, back out into the world!'
C: Yeah. Sort of like that. But for me it is more stumble, get up, stumble; flat on face; get up.
T: Ram Dass describes his spiritual journey in exactly those terms.
C: But this does not feel very spiritual!
T: I know for me it has been… but maybe for you it isn't. We don't have to be both the same.
C: I don't have to do it your way?
T: No way! In fact… do it better!
(We both laugh.)
C: (long pause) I don't know that I can afford that luxury.
T: Go inside… be gentle with yourself…just ask your inside feeling/knowing place—do I have that kind of time? (**invitation to focus**)
C: (tears leading into sobs; words between convulsive bodily uprisings) The death thing… too close… no time to waste.
T: (leaves time for him to cry, for me to take this in, for me to be with him compassionately) Maybe you have to do it faster than I did. Check that inside. How does it feel? (**invitation to focus**)
C: (nodding his head positively) Yeah. Not as an 'ought to,' but as a—'this is the way it is.' There is a given or a belief.
T: Huh?
C: Either it is given or I believe I will die sooner rather than later and I accept that.
T: Acceptance?
C: Yeah. I have to do what I have to do. The time is now.
T: Will you do it? (Notice — a compassionately challenging direct question — another kind of verbal intervention.)
C: (30 seconds) Yes, I will. It helped to hear where you were.

It helped to see where I am and have to be, and now I want to be in a different place. I reserve the right to retrospective reluctance. And I intend to move forward.
T: Go for it!

We have now seen eight examples of what I will call verbal focusing therapy. What do I want to say about them?

First, notice how much reflective listening I do. I really try to say back the important things a client says and get them right. I vary the way I say things back, and I strive for either a kind of poetic evocativeness or literal exactness. I often tuck focusing questions in after reflections—and sometimes instead of reflections.

Second, notice that verbal gestalt experiments are a second kind of talking interventions I tend to do. I have been in three gestalt training groups and have always been enamored of the directness of gestalt techniques.

Third, notice that in these examples there is little self-disclosure, little interpretation, and little of what I now call asking direct pointed questions (e.g., Do you want to marry her or don't you?. . . Why are you so afraid to lose weight?) This may be a function of the time from when the examples come or just the luck of the draw. I think self-disclosure is underrepresented in the examples.

I would say, though, that the amount of combining of focusing invitations, listening responses, and verbal gestalt experiments was fairly representative of my work at that time.

But now it is time to move on.

THE INTEGRATION OF FOCUSING WITH OTHER BODY-CENTERED INTERVENTIONS (1996)

Since 1982 the major development in how I do therapy has been the addition of body-centered therapeutic interventions to my Focusing-Oriented Experiential Therapy. I still use the verbal methods chronicled in the previous essay. I have added to them body-oriented interventions.

I have learned these interventions primarily at Spring Hill conference center in The Opening the Heart workshop.[36] That is also where I often use them. In this essay I will cite both individual therapy and workshop examples of body-centered interventions.

What do I mean by body-centered interventions?

Robert E. L. Smith, in his 1985 book, THE BODY IN PSYCHOTHERAPY quotes approvingly from Jung: ". . . psyche depends upon body and body depends on psyche." (vii) He goes on to say that "A major trend during the past 15 years or so has been the bringing of the body into psychotherapy." (vii)

This trend has accelerated since the publication of Smith's book. Bioenergetics, gestalt, psychomotor, radix, Reichian orgonomy, and, most recently, hakomi—and the combining of these—are now, more than ever, one accepted part of the overall therapeutic landscape. I agree with Smith: "All of these approaches are of value, and not one of them is a complete system having a total perspective on psychopathology, growth, and learning" (1985, p. vii).

But, when these several approaches are integrated and—I would add most importantly, are integrated with focusing and other verbal methods—then one has what I will call a vibrant and effective body-oriented, focusing-oriented, experiential therapy.

It is the task of this essay to introduce such a therapy.

Notice that it is the *combining* of methods rather than a monogamous relationship to any one that is characteristic of this approach to therapy. The emphasis in the combining can vary. After introducing the concepts of "hard," "soft," and "expressive" body-centered techniques, Smith writes, "I do a body-oriented Gestalt therapy, integrating aspects of Reichian, neo-Reichian [hard], and other body-focused growth methods in the context of the therapist-patient relationship" (1985, p. vii). Whereas I would say I do a focusing-oriented experiential therapy integrating hard, soft, and expressive body techniques along with reflections of feeling, probing questions, feedback, interpretations, personal sharings, and statements of support and affirmation within the context of a Rogerian-like, person-centered therapeutic relationship.

II

There is no universally agreed-upon categorization of body-oriented therapeutic methods. I like the classification introduced in Smith's book. He talks of "soft," "hard" and "expressive" body-centered techniques. I want to take them up in turn, define and describe several of them, and show some ways to combine them with focusing.

Of "soft" techniques, Smith writes that they "tend to be gentle and allowing rather than forcing. . . [they] tend to be subtle. The things which happen, such as increased body awareness, psychological regression, increased experience of emotion, and expression of emotion, do not happen as quickly or as dramatically [as with the other two categories]. . . the soft methods are safe. . . ." (p. 115)

Hakomi probes, work with posture, touch, and work with the

breath are examples of "soft" technique (Smith, chap. 8,). (See Table 1)

Table 1 — Soft Technique

Characteristics:	gentle and allowing
	subtle
	safe
	may or may not include physical touch
Results:	increased body awareness
	psychological regression
	increased experience of emotion
	expression of emotion
	contact, empathy, nourishment
	access and deepening of inner experience
Examples:	posture
	touch
	breathing
	Rogerian listening
	focusing
	hakomi probes
	guided inner experience

I want to illustrate the combining of focusing with (1) touch and (2) hakomi probes.

1. Focusing and Touch[37]

Focusing-oriented therapy that is body-oriented grows naturally out of verbal focusing/listening therapy. It was Gene Gendlin's discovery that certain words, phrases, and images have an "experiential effect." When they are said by the client—or said back to the client by the therapist—they carry experiencing forward. The "talk therapist" tries to say such words. He directs his verbal articulations at the felt sense of the client. When his words "hit the mark," so to speak, verbal therapy moves forward.

It is only a small step to "hands on" body therapy. The link: Focusing involves the body. The felt sense is in the body. It is real. It is bodily felt. What distinguishes verbal focusing therapy from "just talking" (or "just imagery") is that it is bodily.

Since focusing is bodily, it makes sense that the focusing therapist would make use of body interventions.

For example, the "body-oriented focusing therapist" uses touch to:

a) anchor the felt sense
b) amplify the felt sense
c) help the felt sense move, thereby facilitating a felt shift

Anchoring the felt sense: The client has identified a felt sense in her chest. "It's here," she says, pointing to her chest. The therapist places her hand gently on the place the client has pointed to. This helps anchor the felt sense. It helps the client stay focused. The therapist's hand says, "Keep your attention right here."

Clients who are focusing do have difficulty in keeping their attention on the felt sense. They lose it. They wander. They get distracted. The therapist, by putting his hand on the felt sense, helps keep the client "on beam"—tuned into the felt sense.

Amplifying the felt sense: The therapist's touch also helps by increasing the "volume" of the felt sense. We all have energy. When the therapist touches the place where the felt sense is, she sends energy directly to it. This amplifies the felt sense.

For example, during focusing a client said he had a pressure in his stomach. The therapist asked if he could put his hand on the client's stomach. (Notice this "asking" way of introducing touch.) The client said yes. The therapist placed his hand on the client's stomach, waited, and then asked, "What are you experiencing?" The client responded, "The pressure feels sharper, clearer. I can sense it better."

Helping the felt sense move (shift): The therapist can use her touch to help the felt sense move. When a felt shift comes at the end of a round of verbal focusing therapy, some way that the body has been carrying its troubles actually changes, shifts, moves. It seems miraculous, at first, that words, distal as they are, can do this. Not surprisingly, touch, properly applied, can do it, too.

For example, the client's felt sense was something pushing down on his chest. The word for it was "burdened." The therapist used his touch to "imitate" the felt sense. He pushed down—hard—on the client's chest. The client reported he felt some "give" inside. Then, as he continued to push, the therapist gave the client the instruction, "Let your body do what it wants to do." The client pushed back against the therapist—that is, against the external imitation of the felt sense. The therapist pushed back. The client got angry. The therapist and client were soon wrestling. The client threw the therapist (i.e. the burden) off. "That feels better," the client reported. A big shift had occurred. The client felt lighter, energized, exhilarated, clear. With the burden off he now "saw" that he needed to mobilize his anger under his depressed/burdened place. The insight had come after the shift, just as focusing theory would predict.

In sum, I am suggesting an addition to focusing therapy in the direction of touch and the body. The body-oriented focusing therapist does everything that the verbal focusing therapist does, and also uses his or her touch to help anchor, amplify, and move the felt sense.

2. Hakomi probes and focusing

A second "soft" technique is the hakomi probe.

Hakomi purports to be a complete system of body-centered psychotherapy. (See Kurtz, 1994) It was begun by Ron Kurtz who was influenced by Al Pesso, Moshe Feldenkrais, and Eastern principles of non-violence and mindfulness. Turning away from the hard and forcing nature of his training in bioenergetics, Kurtz and his original trainees developed a body-centered therapy for the 90's—one that combines a background of Eastern teachings with a Rogerian respect for the person and powerful body-oriented interventions.

A hakomi probe is the kind of statement an ideal parent would make. For example, "You are perfectly welcome here. . . Your needs are OK. . . You are fine just the way you are. . . Everything is going to be all right. . . ."

The hakomi therapist delivers the probe in a ritualized way. He gets the person into mindfulness, eyes closed, attention inside his own present experiencing. (This is very akin to focusing.) Then, he puts his hand on the client's chest, says the first name, and very slowly delivers the probe: "Al, you are perfectly welcome here. . . ". He may repeat it—with the person's name each time—three times. Then he asks for the person to report his experience.

Here is how I combine focusing with a hakomi probe:

He has been talking about his distrust of people in general. The talking had started "off the top of his head" but has moved closer to feeling:

T: What are you feeling right now? Go inside. (**invitation to focus**) Let your attention come down into your body. See if there is a word, phrase, image, sound, or gesture for what's there.

C: It's funny. I'm feeling like I trust you!

T: Ha! A surprise. You trust me.

C: Yeah, but don't get cocky. . . I don't trust M, Z, or B! They aren't going to pull anything over on me.

T: Let's try something. (Client nods OK) Close your eyes. Breathe. Put your attention right here under the palm of my hand—is it OK if I put my hand here? (client nods yes) Now, pay attention to what you experience when I say these words: "Charlie, all people are your friends. . . Charlie, all people are your friends. . . Charlie, all people are your friends. . . ". Now, what happened?

C: (He had begun to cry on my second repetition of the probe.) I felt my **longing** to believe that. I know you've said things like that before; I remember when I read Angyal ("Neurosis and Treatment") and he said that. But I never really felt—I want to believe it! So just now I felt the wanting, the yearning. . . and also that I can't (sob). . . I just can't.

T: Focus again. Be friendly to yourself. Ask yourself, "Why

not? Why can't I believe it? Don't ask it judgementally. . . but with real caring for yourself.

C: (deep sobbing) Because they (his parents) beat me too much, and they were the first ones. The first models weren't my friends. I can't get beyond that—yet.

T: You can't get beyond that—yet.

C: Yes, but I did feel—there is some hope. It could shift.

Here is another example. I cannot overstate how valuable the combination of focusing and hakomi probes really is:

She has been talking about how she lives for others; how she doesn't take care of herself; how she is all worn out. The talk has been getting more and more feelingful.

T: Let's try something.

C: OK.

T: First, just go inside and see how you are right now (**invitation to focus**)

C: (closes her eyes, takes 30 seconds, tunes in to herself) I'm pretty OK, sort of feelingful, but calm, serene, even though I'm really feeling what I've been saying.

T: OK. Now keep your attention inside. If it's OK, I'm going to put my hand here on your chest (client nods OK). Put your attention right under the palm of my hand and now just listen inside and report to me what happens when I say. . . Chris, your needs are OK. . . Chris, your needs are OK. . . Chris, your needs are OK. . . . What happened?

C: That was fantastic!

T: Yeah. . . but what happened?

C: I saw the house I grew up in. I saw my parents in separate rooms. . . away from each other. I saw my four brothers all involved in doing things. . . and I saw—no one had any time for me! I even went from room to room trying to make contact (she cries here), but no one stopped what they were doing; no one paid any attention—

T: To your needs.

C: Right!. . . And they still don't. I go home and it is the same story. Damn! To this day. I'm invisible.

T: You live your life as if everyone were your family. (**interpretation**)
C: What do you mean?
T: As if your needs are unimportant to us all. . .
C: And, therefore, to myself! Damn. I'm going to change that.
T: You really have to, you know, or you are going to wear yourself out and ruin your health. (**feedback, said lovingly**)
C: (cries) I don't want to admit it—but you're right.

Notice that hakomi and focusing are quite similar. There is only a slight change in the energetic vibration of the session as one moves from focusing to a hakomi probe. They combine easily together and carry the session forward on a similar wavelength.[38]

As focusing itself is a "soft" technique, its combination with other "soft" techniques does not much change the overall feel of the session.

Our next examples of "hard" techniques will be quite different.

III

By "hard techniques" Smith refers to methods of body intervention which are neither subtle nor gentle. They may be, in fact, uncomfortable and painful. They "tend to be dramatic in their releasing of blocked emotion and memories." They are of "high potency and therefore require considerable judgment and caution. . . if they are to be used in growthful.. rather than traumatic ways." (1985, chap. 9) They can contribute mightily to unblocking and disinhibiting.

These are the kinds of techniques that helped me the most when I was a participant in the Heart workshop, and that is where I tend to use them the most.

Smith discusses hard techniques from Reichian, bioenergetic, and psychomotor therapy (see Table 2).

Table 2 — Hard Technique

Characteristics:	neither subtle nor gentle
	can be uncomfortable/painful
	can be dramatic
	high potency/high risk
	force/pressure
	use with care
Results:	dramatic breakthroughs
	release of blocked emotions/memories
	disinhibition
	resumption of flow
Examples:	deep pressure on various muscles (Reich)
	"limits structure" (Pesso)
	mimicking "hard" feelings inside body (Focusing)

The flavor of hard technique—what it is like, what the client thinks of it, what it accomplishes—is most charmingly captured in this long excerpt from Orson Bean's ME AND THE ORGONE. Bean describes his first session with Reichian therapist, Dr. Baker, who has just finished some opening chit-chat with him. I quote this at length as it beautifully captures the flavor of a kind of work that is not all that well known.

Dr. Baker sat down behind his desk and indicated the chair in front of it for me.... "Well," he said, "take off your clothes and let's have a look at you." My eyes went glassy as I stood up and started to undress—"You can leave on your shorts and socks," said Baker, to my relief. I laid my clothes on the chair against the wall in a neat pile, hoping to get a gold star. "Lie down on the bed," said the doctor. "Yes, sure," said Willie the Robot, and did so. "Just breathe naturally," he said pulling a chair over to the bed and sitting down next to me. I fixed my eyes on a spot of water damage near the upper left-hand corner of Dr. Baker's window and breathed naturally. I thought: "What if I get an erection, or shit on his bed or vomit." The doctor was *feeling the muscles* (italics mine) around my jaw and neck. He found a tight cord in my neck, pressed it hard and kept on pressing it. It hurt like hell but Little Lord Jesus no crying he makes. "Did that hurt?" asked Dr. Baker.

"Well, a little," I said, not wanting to be any trouble.

"Only a little?" he said.

"Well, it hurt a lot," I said. "It hurt like hell."

"Why didn't you cry?"

"I'm a grown-up."

He began *pinching the muscles* in the soft part of my shoulders. I wanted to smash him in his sadistic face, put on my clothes and get the hell out of there. Instead I said "Ow." Then I said "That hurts."

"It doesn't sound as if it hurts," he said.

"Well, it does," I said, and managed an "Oooo, Oooo."

"*Now breathe in and out deeply,*" he said and he placed the palm of one hand on my chest and pushed down hard on it with the other. The pain was substantial. "What if the bed breaks?" I thought. "What if my spine snaps or I suffocate?"

I breathed in and out for a while and then Baker found my ribs, and began probing and pressing.

I thought of Franchot Tone in the torture scene from *Lives of a Bengal Lancer*. I managed to let out a few pitiful cries which I hoped would break Baker's heart. He began to jab at my stomach, prodding here and there to find a tight little knotted muscle. I no longer worried about getting an erection, possibly ever, but the possibility of shitting on his bed loomed even larger. He moved downward, mercifully passing my jockey shorts. I don't know what I had expected him to do, measure my cock or something, and began to pinch and prod the muscles of my inner thighs. At that point I realized that the shoulders and the ribs and the stomach hadn't hurt at all. The pain was amazing, especially since it was an area I hadn't thought would ever hurt. Notwithstanding, my feeble vocal expressions were nothing that would have shamed Freddie Bartholomew.

"Turn over," said Baker. I did and he started at my neck and worked downwards with an *unerring instinct for every tight, sore muscle.* he pressed and kneaded and jabbed and if I were Franchot Tone I would have sold out the entire Thirty-first Lancers. "Turn back over again," said Dr. Baker and I did. "All right," he said, "I want you to breathe in and out as deeply as you can and at the same time roll your eyes around without moving your head. Try to look at all four walls, one at a time, and move your eyeballs as far from side to side as possible." I began to roll my eyes, feeling rather foolish but grateful that he was no longer tormenting my body. On and on my eyes rolled. "Keep breathing," said Baker. I began to feel a *strange pleasurable feeling in my eyes* like the sweet fuzziness that happens when you smoke a good stick of pot. The fuzziness began to spread through my face and head and then down into my body. "All right," said Baker. "Now I want you to continue breathing and do a *bicycle kick* on the bed with your legs." I began to raise my legs and bring them down rhythmically, striking the bed with my calves. My thighs began to ache and I wondered when he would say that I had done it long enough, but he didn't. On and on I went, until my legs were ready to drop off. Then, gradually, it didn't hurt anymore and that same sweet fuzzy sensation of pleasure began to spread through my whole body, only much stronger. I now felt as if a rhythm had taken over my kicking which had nothing to do with any effort on my part. *I felt transported and in the grip of something larger than me. I was breathing more deeply than I ever had before and I felt the sensation of each breath all the way down past my lungs and into my pelvis.* Gradually, I felt myself lifted right out of Baker's milk chocolate room and up into the spheres. I was breathing to an astral rhythm. Finally, I knew it was time to stop. I lay there for how many minutes I don't know and I heard his voice say, "How do you feel?"

"Wonderful," I said. "Is this always what happens?"

"More or less," he said. "I can see you on Tuesdays at two.

Ideally I'd like to see you twice a week but I don't have the time and once a week is more than sufficient."

I stood up shakily and began to pull on my clothes. "I'm a bit dizzy," I said.

"You'll be all right," he said. "Just take it easy. Actually you're in pretty good shape. It shouldn't take too long."

We agreed on a price per hour, I finished dressing, shook his hand and walked out into the waiting room. A bald-headed man sat there reading *Life* magazine. He didn't look up. I wondered how long he had been there and if he had heard my noises in the other room. I walked out the door and down the hall. It seemed as if my feet barely touched the carpeted halls. I came out into the air and crossed the street into the park. I looked up into the sky over the East River. It was a *deeper blue* than any I had seen in my life, and there seemed to be little flickering pinpoints of light in it. I looked at the trees. They were a *richer green* than I had ever seen. It seemed as though *all my senses were heightened*. I was perceiving everything with *greater clarity*. I walked home feeling *exhilarated* and *bursting with energy*. That night I went to work at the theater and got through the show somehow. I didn't know if I was good or bad. I got home sometime after midnight and I knew there was no remote possibility of going to sleep. Far from settling down, the energy coursing through my body had increased as the night went on, moving rhythmically up and down from head to toe. There was no doubt in my mind that it was *orgone energy* or whatever the hell name anyone wished to give it. It was like nothing I had ever felt before and I knew that I had tapped into the strongest force in the world. I sat by my window on the river, watching the debris float by. I thought about life and people and kids and sex and my ex-wife and psychoanalysis and how in the name of God human beings had gotten themselves into the shape they were in and finally, about five-thirty in the morning, I fell asleep. (Bean, pp. 31-36)

Let me say right away that I don't have clients take off their clothes, and that the eye-rolling segment and bicycle kick segment are soft and expressive techniques rather than hard techniques. But most of the session is a good example of Reichian hard techniques. Notice both Bean's comments on what the client is saying to himself *during* the work (an equivalent of—what is this shit!), and how he feels after (an altered state of ecstatic consciousness). Both the client's inner comments on his experience of hard technique *and* the remarkable after-effects of hard technique need to be given careful, respectful, and due consideration. There can be no doubt that something very powerful has occurred here—as it did for me in the application of hard techniques in the Heart workshop.[39]

One might think that the combination of focusing and hard technique is unlikely. After all, Dr. Baker does not sound like a focusing therapist. He sounds like just the opposite, just the kind of therapy and therapist focusing is the antidote for!

Yet, empirically, it turns out that focusing and hard technique *can* be combined. This is surprising. Even with its philosophical opposite—violent, therapist-directed, pushing— focusing can be combined.

If focusing work is the ground, the foundation upon which therapy sits, then moments of hard technique combined with focusing are quite possible: The combination is *very* powerful. Consider these examples:

1. C: When I close my eyes and go inside I feel like throwing up. There is an image of a hand over my mouth, keeping me from speaking.
   T: May I do that?
   C: (surprised) What?
   T: (matter-of-factly) Put my hand over your mouth. I'll try to do it like it is in the image. (Notice that I ask permission to initiate hard technique.) Let me know when I get it right, if you want to do it. Then, breathe. . . and let your body do whatever it wants to do. OK?
   C: (a bit warily) OK.

T: (puts hand over client's mouth; adjusts force until C nods head "yes" as in "yes, that's it.")

C: (muffled)

T: Let your body do whatever it wants to do.

(At first C collapses. I keep my hand over her mouth. For about a minute she is rolled up in a fetal-like ball, and I am leaning over her with my hand over her mouth. She signals to stop. I take my hand away.)

C: It's moved. It's in my throat now, squeezing at me.

T: May I?

C: (gives me an "oh my God, this too?" look) Sure.

T puts his hand over her neck and squeezes—not as hard as he can, but hard enough. Suddenly she starts to stir and to fight. She grabs at my hand to pull it away from her neck, and I don't let her.

T: No you don't. Keep it in. I won't let you out. (By now we are in a violent tussle rolling around the room—this is in my private office, and it is rather large. We keep wrestling for a few minutes until she finally uses both her hands and all her force and pulls at my bracelet. . . and gets me to let go. We lay a few feet apart from each other. She is crying and laughing wildly. I am laughing.)

In exchange for a reduction in fee, this client wrote me two or three pages of her reflections on each session. Hence we have her own words about this interaction.[40]

"The neck thing was interesting. Actually, I knew the block has been there for a very long time. . . on and off since I was about 16. Maybe even way before that.

"Interesting that when Neil held his hand hard over my mouth. . . I felt it familiar and bearable (on one level). If that is what you [her partner] want to do to me, why resist? And then as I tried to take his hand away. . . I really didn't! I thought about pushing it away, and it felt premature, like, I'm not ready. It is as if I don't want to come out mean and harsh and bad!. . . Some part of me at 16 pulled back. . . the sexuality part. . . and became held in. . . and has been there all this time. . .

"And then when Neil started to press hard against my neck. . . it was different from my mouth. Ah ha! You want to squeeze the life out of me! That I will not take!

"That is when I pushed his hand away. Hard.

"So I'm willing to be shut up in a relationship, but not to give up my life. Interesting. . . I felt OK during the session. I'm ready to move, to get unstuck."

2. Here is another example of focusing and hard technique. Remember: much of the background of our sessions are focusing, listening, and other verbal methods. What I am highlighting, however, are some of the breakthrough sessions which often combine focusing with body-centered techniques.

This is another session that this client wrote up for me:

"2/21/89 — When I went in I didn't know what I wanted to work on. Neil gave me focusing instructions. I wasn't anxious—which I've been feeling lately—but I could feel something pushing out—and being held from within at the same time.

"Feel that," said Neil. Definite bondage. And since it was being held from within, I knew I had everything to do with it. I felt it particularly in my legs! That was new. It had something to do with who I am and who I am not. A lot of weight on my legs. . .

"Neil sat on my legs. Hard. It felt normal. So I pushed him off (I'm glad I'm as big as he is!) Not really knowing why I did. Then I was suddenly sobbing and crying. Out of nowhere. This went on for maybe five minutes.

"After the tears, the insights: Like this is my facade, but I won't tolerate you really believing this is who I am. I mean the wanting to be liked. It isn't who I really am. Where does this whole thing about being liked really come from, and why is it so important to me? It is like a dead weight holding me down [on my legs] so I cannot move. I mean, it is an overwhelming factor in my relationship with the world.

"Near the very end of the session. . . my legs felt very different [**felt shift**]. . . I don't mean just from getting his weight off them. . .

I mean from the inside. I started to get the feeling. . . maybe I am getting ready to move."

3. Another example of focusing and hard technique: This one comes from an Opening the Heart workshop. It is a seven-minute segment of work with a participant in the sharer role. (This one has elements of hard and expressive technique, which we will take up next).
T: Go inside and see what is there. (**invitation to focus**)
C: (after 30 seconds) I don't know if I can tell you.
T: You don't know if you can tell me.
C: The image is so horrible. . . and I have it so often.
T: There is a horrible image there, one you have quite frequently.
C: Yeah. . . OK. . . I see myself holding a knife and stabbing myself in the stomach with it. The feeling with the image is—disgust. But it is what I want to do.
T: Would you be willing to try something?
C: (looks at me warily) Maybe.
T: Make a fist like you are holding a knife in your hand. (C does this) Then let me grab you by the wrist. (She agrees) Now, you try to stab yourself, and I'll hold you back. I'll make sure you don't do it. [In hakomi terms, this is an example of "taking over"]
C: Are you sure you can keep me from doing it?
T: I'm sure. . . but we can try it for a minute so you'll see.
C: Let's try it.
We try it out. She struggles to "stab" herself. I am able to keep her from doing so. We stop.
C: OK, you can do it. I'm game.
T: See how you are inside right now.
C: Excited!
T: OK, whenever you are ready.
She tries to stab herself and I stop her. I also verbalize what I imagine are the voices she hears when she has this image: "I want to be dead. Life isn't worth it. I want out." I scream these words,

and she throws herself more and more into the self-destructive effort. She pulls me all around the room. . . but she never "stabs" herself. Her face looks fiercely angry, and I hold her wrist very hard. After seven minutes the bell rings, and we fall to the ground—three-quarters of the way across the room—in a heap.

The rest of the morning she was very alive and present. She thanked me twice for the experience. I had never seen her so relaxed as I did later that day.

4. One more example. This, too, is from a Heart workshop. It is similar to the example I used in the focusing and touch section.

T: What is happening inside you? (**invitation to focus**)

C: There is all this tension. . . I'm carrying it on my neck and shoulders.

T: Can I be the tension?

C: What do you mean?

T: Get on your knees. (C does this) I'll get on your neck and shoulders with my hands leaning on you like the tension does.

C: Oh, I see, OK, why not?

I lean all my weight on the palms of my two hands digging into his neck and shoulders. At the same time I tell him to breathe and to let his body do whatever it wants. He is a little smaller than me, and I am feeling very powerful and energetic this morning. He starts to struggle and fight to get from under the pressure (me). . . and I won't let him.

C: Wait a minute.

He takes off his glasses. Now he really goes at it. I'm yelling, "You can't get out from under me," and he's yelling, "I'll get you off me you son-of-a-bitch." We wrestle and roll around the floor. . . and just as he throws me off. . . I climb right back on—just as I imagine his pressure does. We are back at it again, maybe for five minutes altogether, and in the end we are laughing uncontrollably after he does, for good, throw me off.

C: My shoulders sure feel better!

T: How about **you**? How are you? How are you inside? (**invitation to focus**)

C: I feel exhilarated! I haven't had so much fun in years. And I feel relaxed—boy, do I put a lot of pressure on myself. But it is not there now. I really see how I do it to myself, and how I have to stop doing it to myself.

T: Will you?

C: Time will tell.

T: Yes. It always does.

We hug.

I want to repeat. **I do not use hard techniques often. Focusing and listening are the staples of my therapy. But the careful use of hard technique can really propel things forward.**

IV

Smith says that "the essence of the expressive techniques is taking action, concrete musculoskeletal movement." He adds, "the action to be growthful, however, must carry symbolic meaning." (Smith, 1985, p. 135)

The expressive techniques, then, involve the client's taking symbolic action beyond the point of usual self-interruption. "The expressive work involves movement of energy into the musculoskeletal system. . . support is given to the patient's acting on what he or she is organismically experiencing as growthful or natural, rather than self-interrupting and continuing the old pattern of avoidance. The patient is invited and encouraged to act in spite of the voice of the toxic introject, to act in the face of catastrophic expectation." (Smith, ibid.)

Much psychotherapeutic expressive work is verbal, and Smith singles out the gestalt therapy literature for this (I would agree, and add the psychodramatic.) Smith makes the case forcefully for the need for body-oriented expressive work to really finish the unfinished business:

"When there is self-interruption, there is some body part that has not been put to full use. There are an arm and fist that have not hit, a jaw that has not bitten, tear glands which have not secreted, a throat which has not screamed, a belly which has not chuckled, a pelvis which has not thrust. . . the expressive work. . . involves the reowning of the 'missing' body part." (Smith, p. 136)

Gene explicitly acknowledges the need to combine focusing with expressive techniques:

> Many events, especially in childhood, generate strong emotions and at the same time block their expression. If a child can cry, shake, and scream, it is sooner done with a painful event. But along with bad events children are usually also prohibited from expressing anything [that the parent or caregiver does not want to hear]. One meaning of 'completing' an incomplete experience is to let these long-missing expressive sequences happen. (Gendlin, 1991, p. 265)
>
> Another kind of completion concerns the interaction: what one could not tell the original people, how one could not fight back. Incomplete interactions need to be completed. . . in therapy there needs to be room and welcome to cry the uncried tears, to sob, shake, or move to express old pain and fury in more than words. (ibid.)
>
> Therapy must involve more than focusing on inner data in reflective inner space. there also needs to be a movement outward, into interaction. . . . Moving out, rolling out[his words for expressive action] is an essential dimension of therapeutic change that is not provided by inward process dealing only with inner data." (Gendlin, ibid., p. 267)

However, I do not feel that he goes far enough in providing for this expressive rolling-out. He says:

> Cathartic therapists are right to tell other therapists not to stop expressive discharge, however, intense it may be. . . I welcome discharge when it has already come. The next ques-

tion is whether it should be deliberately engendered. . . . On that question agreement is not so easy, and I am not sure of the way I have chosen. . . . *I believe that catharsis should be an open, known, and included possibility. Beyond that I don't believe I should engender it. (italics mine)* (Gendlin, 1991, p. 265-6)

My own experience both in private practice and group workshops is that clients often need a lot of encouragement and cheerleading in order to get into cathartic, expressive, or intense feeling work. The work is unusual. It breaks certain taboos. ("Don't ever raise your voice at me; big boys don't cry; big girls don't hit.") In my experience, if the therapist really wants expressive work to happen, he has to lend it his energy and also find the way that helps each particular client into it. Simply mentioning that it exists as an option is not, in my experience, enough. The dice are too loaded against intense expressive emotional release. The therapist needs to "point" the client towards it.

Here are several examples in which focusing and expressive work are combined.

1. This is one of my all-time favorites. Both for aesthetic reasons and in terms of its overall effect it seems to me picture-perfect.

The context was a Spring Hill Opening the Heart workshop. Laury Rappaport was doing the overall timing of all the healing circles, and I was leading one.

I had worked earlier with this woman. She had made reference to a terrible trauma when she was 11. Her mother had set fire to her favorite doll's clothes. She mentioned especially a Barbie's blue dress.

When she lay down on the mat she mumbled that she wanted to work on "the doll dress thing." I asked her to close her eyes and tell me what she felt (**invitation to focus**). She said, "apprehensive, scared, terrified."

I asked her to keep her eyes closed and, speaking in the present (gestalt) tell me the story of the doll dress.

She began: "I'm 11 years old. I'm sitting on the porch playing with my Barbies. My mother has just come home from the crazy hospital. She is upset about something. She sees my Barbies. My favorite has on a blue dress."

At this point, as she is talking I signal to Laury, "bring over the old blue bataka that is falling apart and a box of matches." Laury doesn't know what is going on, but she catches my drift and brings over the props.

Back to the story: "Mother is mad at me for some reason. She tells me she is going to get rid of my doll clothes." (The story is told with increasing agitation.) "I cry and beg her not to, but she grabs my Barbie and takes off the blue dress. Then she takes a match...."

At this point I have Laury stand above her with a lighted match about to touch the old blue bataka.

"And she sets fire to the blue dress."

At this point I instruct her to open her eyes and look straight up. At this moment Laury sets the bataka on fire.

The woman makes a piercing shriek that is heard throughout the workshop room, above the din of everyone else. She loses it. She is moaning and groaning, and moving all around, and I get down real close to her to keep her company. This goes on for five minutes. The group surrounds her lovingly but also gives her room as she screams, yells, punches, and kicks. Finally, as she seems to settle down I invite her to talk directly to her mother (Laury), who has been standing there the whole time.

"How could you have done that? Why were you so sick? I hadn't done anything bad (tears). That was my favorite dress. That Barbie was my real friend (sobs). You burned her favorite dress. What kind of a mad woman were you?"

She continues to cry for another ten minutes, those old, ancient, forbidden tears; and then, by the time the bell rings, she is quiet, taking in the love from the group. Her face is transformed. She is glowing. I feel fully contented.

In a letter after the workshop she thanked us profusely and

told us of the real life changes she made in the following week. They were many and included—buying herself a Barbie with a blue dress!

2. The second example also comes from a healing circle at a Heart workshop.

It was a mens' workshop, and I had in my circle five men who had known each other for some time. Two were twins. They asked if they could take a turn together.

I was agreeable. They told me they wanted to re-enact their birth. (They were both quite "warmed-up" and had previously done considerable work individually and together in psychotherapy.)

I had them lay on a mattress and had a second mattress placed over them. The group held the second mattress in place—not forcefully—just enough for it to be womb-like.

They both must have been inside there about five minutes. There was no big noise—just little whimpering sounds. Then one (the older by five minutes) started to come out through an opening we gradually gave him at one end of the mattress. He cried, like a baby, and the group held him.

Then there were moans and movements and crying from inside. The other twin stayed in another five minutes and was very agitated, moving around, whimpering more. Finally, he too came out and was also helped by the group.

The twins lay there, side by side, held by a bunch of men.

I asked the second twin to focus and tell us what he had been experiencing when he was by himself in the womb.

He said one word— "abandonment," and broke out crying, his twin held and embraced him, and we all cried. "I'm sorry. I didn't mean to leave you. I still loved you and I always have." The older twin told all this to the younger. They held each other, and there wasn't a dry eye in the circle. We all sang to them:

> Like a ship in the harbor,
> Like a father and child,

> Like a light in the darkness,
> I'll hold you awhile.
> We'll rock on the water,
> I'll cradle you deep
> And hold you while angels
> Sing you to sleep.

A beatific smile came over the face of the younger twin as the older stroked his beard, mustache, and thinning blonde hair. It was an unforgettable scene.

3. Here is one more example from another healing circle. (The healing circles at Spring Hill often lead into expressive work. Kurtz calls it, nicely, "riding the rapids.")

She has identified herself as a survivor of childhood sexual abuse although she has no clear memories of the event—just a feeling. She lays down and immediately identifies my assistant (Louis Mezei) as looking like her father. "I can't get his face out of my bed," she says.

I have Louis lay so that just his face is on the mat facing her. There is no time (or need) to ask her how she feels. She begins to cry, scream, moan, shriek, and kick. Another assistant, Selig, puts a kick bag at her feet and she kicks away.

Then she stops, and I can see she is feeling something that is difficult to say. I lean over very close to her, remind her where we really are; "We're at Spring Hill and this is a healing circle, and no one is going to really hurt you. Tell me what is happening for you." She confides in me, "There is a burning pain in my vagina." I nod my head, yes. I ask her if it would be OK if I had Louis try to pull her legs apart while she tried to keep them together. I tell her that if she does it, she can, at any time, say "STOP, I MEAN IT" and Louis will stop. Louis hears my same instructions and nods his head. She rolls her eyes and nods her head yes. (I got this idea from Al Pesso's paper on Abuse) I had Louis start pulling her legs apart. I can't describe the sounds that came out of her. The whole room is filled with them. Louis plays his part to perfection.

He accommodates (Pesso) exactly the role she needs. I am the director. After a very short while she motions for him to stop and rolls up into a fetal ball and cries some more. The whole group—mostly women—stays close to her, very caringly and unobtrusively. The bell is about to ring. I'm not sure what reality she is inhabiting so I ask her to tell me her social security number (this is a trick I learned fifteen years' before from Armand DiMele as a way to bring a person back to "present time.") She starts to laugh, recites her number, we de-role Louis, and I have never seen her looking so present. I ask if she would like a song. She would and tells me the one she wants. She wants it to be like her husband is singing it to her. We sing to her:

> How could anyone ever tell you, that you're anything less than beautiful?
> How could anyone ever tell you, that you're less than whole?
> How could anyone fail to notice that your loving is a miracle,
> And how deeply you're connected to my soul.

We hum the verse to her four times, and she seems almost to doze off. Louis and I exchange a nod of mutual respect and collaboration.

4. This one comes from my private practice:

He is in the midst of deciding to finally separate from his wife after several months of ambivalence. He is carrying a lot of rage. I invite him to place his wife's face on the pillow in front of him and take the bataka. I tell him to close his eyes and remember the last seven months of their marriage. "Just let the memories cross the screen of your awareness, one by one, whatever ones want to walk through." I notice that a few tears drop, and his hands enfold the bataka handle more forcefully. "When you feel ready, open your eyes, see Amanda's face on the pillow and let your body do whatever it wants to do." Soon he is beating up the pillow with gusto as I cheer him on. Days, weeks, months, years of anger, rage, and frustration come pouring out. After awhile he stops beating the pillow and collapses into long-suppressed tears.

When he has had enough time with the tears by himself, I move toward him gently and slowly and cuddle him. He puts his head in my lap and cries even more.

When the tears subside, I ask him to focus. We are both surprised by what he "sees." "I see the 1954 All-star Baseball game. My father and I are at it together. Gil McDougal has just made this wicked wonderful play at second base." He is smiling. "Where did that come from?" "Beats me—what is the feeling?" "Like, peaceful. (tears) Like I need to spend time with him and other men (more tears). Like I need to go to a baseball game." "Tomorrow is Opening Day." "Maybe I'll go to Fenway, play hookey from work. . . Amanda never liked baseball."

By this time he is grinning from ear to ear, and it is time for the session to end.

Notice in these expressive sessions how much and what variety of previously blocked emotion is released! I don't want you to think every session is like this. It isn't. But when it is—there is little doubt that something very powerful has happened.

5. One more example from my private practice. This one allows me to at least allude to my work with focusing, expressive work, and couples. In my practice these days about three out of twenty sessions a week are with couples. I have a particular way I begin a first session with couples. After listening to each person talk for awhile about what has brought them to me, I ask them each to close their eyes, imagine their attention is like a searchlight, and first, just see how they each are inside. (This is the first step, of course, of focusing.) After they have done this, I ask for a nod of the head when they are ready to move on.

I wait until they are both ready. Then I ask them to hold their relationship in front of them, picture it, say their partner's name over and over—whatever will hold it in front of them. And then I say, "And let your attention come down into your body and see what is the whole feel of the relationship for you. . . (**invitation to focus**) let a word, phrase, image, sound, or gesture form that will match or act as a handle on the feeling inside. . . when you get a handle, say it b ack to yourself, check it against your body, see if it fits. . . . Take your time. . . you don't have to do it as quickly or slowly as your partner. . . . Give me a nod when you are finished."

When they have each nodded, I may ask them a further one or two focusing questions -Ask the feeling—what's the crux of it? What makes it this way?" "Ask it—what does it need? What does it need to have happen?" Or I may simply say, "now I want you to open your eyes, turn your chairs to face each other, and take turns—like sharer and witness—telling each other what you have just experienced."

This lesbian couple has come in because one member wants a child and the other does not. They have done the focusing and now are ready—more or less—to talk.

T: Decide who wants to talk first. Talk directly to your partner—unless you want for some reason, at some point, to talk to me. Then turn your chair so it is facing me. You two decide who goes first.

C1: (the one who wants a child) I saw us holding a baby girl. . . (tears) and the feeling was in the song lyric, "We Are Family." It was warm (more tears), warm in a way my family never was.

C2: (she looks flabbergasted) I saw us holding a baby girl, too. (C1 now looks shocked) And we were playing with her, and suddenly she wanted to go into your arms, and I felt left out—just like I always did growing up. I also heard the lyric, "We Are Family" in my head, and I saw—who was it?—The Staple Singers singing it?— (none of us can remember who sings it!) But they all had their tongues sticking out at me (cries).

There is an embarrassment of riches here. Remember: It is just a first session. I decide to go for gestalt expressive work. That is, I focus, and see inside how to set up a gestalt expressive experiment.

T: OK. Let's bring that doll over from the corner of the room. I'm the doctor so I'll go get it. (laughter. . . I bring the doll over) Now I want you to each hold it and talk to it as if it were the baby you may or may not have.

C1: (tears throughout) I love you, my darling. You are the little girl I always wanted to be. I'll take good care of you. I'll never forget you. I'll never forsake you. We are all going to be family. (Gives the doll to C2)

C2: (can hardly hold her) You are going to come between us. If we have you, I'll be the outsider— the father who stays down in the cellar watching TV. You'll prefer her to me. . . and you know what? (this comes like a revelation to her). . . I won't like you so much either. (She hands the doll to me.)

T: (to doll) Well, I guess we see where we stand at this point (C1 and C2 nod their heads in agreement). But don't worry. Remember: this isn't about you; it's about them. Now, this is just where we will all start. Let's keep an open mind—and open hearts—as to where we will end up.

I saw them for seven months, once a week. They never missed a session. This was three years ago.

Last month I got a postcard with a baby shower announcement from them.

Table 3 summarizes the characteristics of expressive work, its results, and a sampling of kinds of expressive work I make frequent use of, and where each comes from.

> **Table 3 — Expressive Techniques**
>
> | | |
> |---|---|
> | **Characteristics:** | symbolic action; use of arms and legs and other body parts |
> | **Results:** | finishing unfinished business; going beyond point of self-interruption |
> | **Examples:** | **Gestalt:** repetition; amplification; exaggeration; presentification; "let me feed you a sentence. . ."; "speak directly to _____. |
> | | **Psychodrama:** role-playing; re-creation of crucial scenes |
> | | **Bioenergetics:** "abandonment" stress position (this is expressive and hard) |
> | | **Pesso:** accommodation |

V

I hope the last three sections have given you a feel for what body-centered focusing-oriented therapy is like as I practice it nowadays.[41] Please remember that these examples are illustrative, not exhaustive, and, obviously, I have chosen to share the ones I feel particularly good about.

Not all my sessions are like these. I make mistakes. Things don't work. I can't get a handle on what is happening. People refuse to follow my invitations. People aren't sufficiently warmed up. There is reluctance.

Therapy is not an unending string of successful, dramatic, and stirring interactions. It is, at times, hard work—but it is the best work I know.

Let me conclude with a final question: How crucial to psychotherapy is focusing?

I want to look at Gene's answers to this question in historical perspective as they somewhat parallel my own, and they are fascinating in themselves. I also want to look at his attitude toward catharsis and emotion, a place where we differ.

In the beginning, Gene saw focusing as "the motor" that powered all successful therapy. I heard him use this analogy frequently in discussing the relation of focusing to therapy. He saw one process (focusing) as underlying all successful therapy: ". . . we have found that all the different ways of doing therapy, [old and new]. . . come down to one central question: does the person spend some time directly attending to something bodily sensed, implicitly complex, but unclear? [i.e., focusing]. When any of the other methods work, this happens. When it is not happening the methods don't work." (Gendlin, 1971, p. 4)

This was what I would call the conquistador phase of focusing. In another place, Gene wrote, "Every situation and every problem is lived with one's body. . . . Psychotherapy could not be successful if it were not for the role which this bodily lived complexity plays. . . the 'edge,' the sensed but not yet known, must be brought into the therapy process in some way [or else it will not work]." (Gendlin, 1971, p. 2)

Gene at times still lapses into language which suggests this "focusing is the motor that drives all psychotherapy" position. Consider this brief excerpt from a recent chapter:

A felt sense is a vague, implicitly complex, physical feeling that can come in your body in regard to any situation or any aspect of life. . . in psychotherapy one *must* (italics mine) focus on the felt sense. (Gendlin, 1991, pp. 255)

But notice what has happened more recently to the "motor" analogy. Gene has kept the analogy but complicated his usage of it considerably:

> Focusing is like a motor. It powers all the other methods like a motor powers a car. Wheels and chassis don't move without it. But who can drive anywhere in just a motor?
> *This analogy overstates the case for focusing. No single way can be the only way for human beings. It also overstates the need*

for other methods; one can go far with focusing alone. (italics mine) (p. 265)

What are we to make of this? On the one hand, Gene is very seductive with the analogy of focusing as the motor of therapy. On the other hand, he now undermines the analogy from both sides. Focusing cannot be the only motor of therapy. Yet one can go far with it just by itself!

And I think Gene is right here! As we have seen in the examples of the use of focusing rounds, you don't always need more than just focusing to "motor" therapy. At times focusing will *do the job all by itself.* But, on the other hand, you can "motor" therapy without focusing. I have one client who abhors focusing. His mother was always asking him what he was experiencing and then denying the validity of his responses. We never use focusing in our sessions, yet, he makes progress.

Paradoxically, I think the analogy with its caveats states the case better than the analogy standing on its own. And, as I read him, Gene's claims for focusing are getting less conquistador-ish—on the whole—as I believe they ought:

> Focusing is an entry into a crucial mode of sensing. Every other method of therapy works much more effectively when focusing is added. But, one cannot gain this advantage if one uses only focusing and not the other methods! Focusing improves other methods by letting them work as they are intended... [for example] focusing enables clients to do gestalt role playing as gestalt therapists intended, not as a play that is thought up and then acted, but as arising directly from sensing the body. And so it is with all the methods. They intend and wish for it, but they lack the specific differentiated steps to find the felt sense...
>
> On the other hand, if we use only focusing by itself, we lack almost everything. I have never proposed focusing as a

method of therapy by itself. Why miss anything that is helpful?. . .

. . . let us always ask, 'What can we learn from the other method?' as well as 'How would that method work better with Focusing?' (Gendlin, 1991, pp. 264-5)

On that note, let us end with the observation that I do not think Gene has learned enough from the other methods of body-oriented psychotherapy and, especially, from the cathartic methods. His attitude towards emotion in therapy has always been (to me) surprisingly skeptical.[42]

For example, in the 1971 paper he writes (and I have heard him say the essence of this many times):

> Only in this physical way [i.e. by focusing] does real change occur [the conquistador position again]. Our difficulties are physically in our bodies, we live our lives with our bodies, we take in any situation in a total bodily way. That is why intellectual answers are usually so ineffective. *That is why feeling and suffering the same emotions over and over again doesn't help.* . . . (italics mine) (1971, p. 5)

I have heard Gene on several occasions speak derisively about pillow-pounding as if it will do nothing to help change happen. The person will just repeat and repeat what will become a "used" feeling.

But of course, the recycling of a habitual emotion is not the only kind of catharsis. Gene knows this (see his 1991 chapter). Yet he does not give adequate representation to the other side. He does not give the good use of catharsis its real due.

Here my experience of seventeen years with the Opening the Heart workshop tells me something different. I have staffed over one hundred workshops. I have seen a few thousand people pound pillows, kick kick-bags, scream their lungs out, choke batakas, throw themselves headlong into a stack of mattresses, punch punching bags, cry for seven straight minutes, stamp on pillows, stab pillows with imitation knives, arm wrestle, throw people off their backs—etc. Believe me: it works.

Emotional release works. Intense feeling therapy works. Focusing helps it work better. But Gene does not give a fair enough evaluation of the value of a marathon-like group experience utilizing body-centered and heart-centered therapies over and over for the purpose of liberation. To quote one Spring Hill staff member who put it so beautifully: "The crying is not the pain. The crying is the release of the pain. We are going to a liberation party."

I hope that I have demonstrated in this essay the power of combining focusing with other body-oriented therapeutic interventions. When these are artfully intermingled with a predominantly verbal focusing-oriented experiential therapy, the results are satisfying indeed. People get better. It is wonderful to be a fellow-traveler with them. It is quite a trip.

PART FOUR
FOCUSING AND MEDITATION

PROLOGUE

As we have seen, **focusing** is the name of a process originated by Eugene Gendlin for psychological growth and development. It is a very specific and very special process useful both for self-therapy and in psychotherapy. It is a quiet, gentle, and powerful way to listen to one's whole Felt Sense of a problem, issue, or situation, and, through specific steps, to achieve a Felt Shift, a piece of bodily resolution of the matter. Focusing enables one to accurately name one's felt experience and thus help it unfold. Focusing training frees one from the tyranny of the mind and mental constructs and returns one to the wisdom of genuinely felt experience. Focusing shows one how to listen to the small, still voice of the felt sense, ask it open-ended questions, help it to shift, and thus receive both new information and a sense of greater psycho-physiological well-being. The readings that I most recommend for learning the focusing process include those by Gendlin (1969; 1978) Amodeo and Wentworth (1986; part II), Cornell (1990, 1996), Campbell and McMahon (1985), and three of my own (1982a; 1986, 1996).

Meditation is the name given to a variety of practices originated for spiritual growth and development. More recently, they have also been cited for their contribution to psychological well-being (cf. LeShan, 1974; Benson, 1976). There are various kinds of meditation, and it is probably best to say that what they have in common is a family likeness. This "family likeness:" to quote again the beautiful lyric of Molly Scott, seems to be about freeing oneself from "the confines of the mind:" and taking one to "the silence beneath thinking."[1] Meditation is practice in doing one thing at a time. "It's like coming home [to] our fullest 'humanhood.'" LeShan elaborates: "We meditate to find, to recover, to come back to something of ourselves we once dimly and unknowingly had and have lost without knowing what it was or where or when we lost it" (1974, p. 1). The writings that have been most useful to me as a meditator include those by LeShan (1974), Ram Dass (1978), Levine (1976),Shiarella (1982), Goldstein (1976), and Tollifson (1992).

Most often both the focuser and the meditator are sitting with their eyes closed engaging in some kind of inner act in inner space. To the outside observer what they are doing may very well look the same. Hence, questions arise: Is focusing a kind of meditation?[2] If not, what about the relationship between focusing and meditation?

In this section I want to look from several angles at relationships between focusing and meditation. In the first essay I present a formal comparison of focusing and meditation in terms of where one places one's attention and what one then does with it. The second essay describes what I call "a focusing approach to meditation." In the third essay I indicate three places in a round of focusing where I may move away from focusing into meditation. The fourth essay lets me look back at the first three and add further thoughts especially about meditation.

I write from the perspective of twenty-five years' extensive experience with focusing and ten years experience with meditation. I think of myself as a more accomplished focuser than meditator. I write for both focusers and meditators and especially for those who do both. The first three essays in this part were assembled over the course of two years during which I had been focusing less regularly and meditating more regularly. If I were to graph them against each other, the line representing my focusing practice would start higher and decline; the line representing my meditation practice would start lower and ascend. These essays come out of a time and space in which these lines were crossing.

MEDITATION AND FOCUSING: ONE COMPARISON

As meditation becomes more and more popular, it happens increasingly often that I am asked in focusing workshops, "How does focusing compare with meditation?" At times the comparison implied in the question seems naive (as in, "Oh, focusing, yeah—it's a lot like meditation, isn't it?"). Sometimes it is based simply on the notion that both happen with one's eyes closed. At other times, the implied comparison speaks to the experience of both focusing and meditation. I find it best to answer that question by describing what happens when I meditate and what happens when I focus.

But there are times when experienced students of meditation seem to be asking for what might be called a formal comparison between meditation and focusing. Gradually I have evolved this answer to their question:

Comparing focusing with meditation can be useful, but it can also be confusing. It helps to speak of different kinds of meditation. One may contrast mindfulness approaches and concentration approaches.[3]

In mindfulness meditation one closes one's eyes and then simply watches—thoughts, feelings, sensations, memories, whatever—as they pass the screen of awareness. One dis-identifies with the content of these inner percepts. Imagine a subway station platform. Trains pull in and trains pull out. In mindfulness meditation, thoughts, feelings, sensations, etc. are these trains, and when one finds that one has gotten on a train, one gets off and returns to the platform One watches. There is no selectivity and no owning.

In concentration meditation one fixes one's attention on some specific object—a mantra, a spot in the room, a mandala. The aim is to blot out all save the object of concentration.

Now, focusing combines aspects of the two approaches, but it is not exactly the same as either.

Focusing *concentrates* one's attention on one's flow of experiencing. So it is not just a matter of being mindful of whatever passes the screen. There is a selectivity. And there is a going-into, a working-with what is in the flow. One gets on the train. So one feels and allows oneself to feel; e.g., one's whole sense of sitting just now at Coki Beach: A serene sense of emptiness in the chest area and some flickering of lights behind the eyes. One identifies this in-flux state as one's own for now: I'm mellow and energized.

But the *contents* of this object of concentration are in flux rather than static (like a mantra), and it is much of the mindfulness attitude which most helps in going with the flow. That is, a nonjudgemental, letting rise and fall relation to the experiential flow. The subway station platform now has become our experiential flow, and we return to it over and over again after delving into its contents as needed.

Hence, one can say that focusing is not just like either mindfulness or concentration schools of meditation. But it tends to use a mindfulness-like attitude in concentrating attention on the flow of experiencing.[4]

I have found that this comparison helps students of meditation better understand focusing. It helps them know where to put their attention, what to do with it, and what to allow it to do. Less explicit comparisons tend to be more confusing than helpful, especially when the kind of meditation being spoken about is not made clear. One must know what question one is answering before launching into a comparison of meditation and focusing.

A FOCUSING APPROACH TO MEDITATION

There are lots of different kinds of meditation. How shall I choose mine? How decide which one is right for me right now?

Here we come to the application of focusing to meditation. The focusing attitude can be used as one way to choose and evaluate one's meditation practice.

To repeat, by "the focusing attitude" (as contrasted with "the focusing technique") I mean a reverence for bodily felt experiencing. It is Gene Gendlin's basic discovery that there is in each and every one of us a way of knowing that we all too easily neglect to make use of. Many of us don't even know it exists! In fact, this important resource has been neglected in the philosophy of knowing. Gendlin writes:

> A vast amount of information is sensed [by each person] . . . as a global, bodily sentience. In the history of thought this bodily sentience is a crucial, forgotten dimension. . . Bodily sentience always implies a next move. We should not say of sentience that it just is; rather, it is—for a next move. (Gendlin, 1991, p. 258).

What does Gendlin mean?

At any moment I can stop what I am doing, turn my attention inward and ask—what is my felt sense right now? I can ask—what is my felt sense of _____? Many things can fill in the blank: e.g., my work, my health, my primary relationship, my friendships, my immediate situation at this very moment. As we have seen, the focusing attitude is being friendly to this felt sense, embracing it, opening to it, tapping into it, and using it as a source of guidance and wisdom for a next step. The focusing attitude is—"Felt senses, y'all come! Y'all welcome! Show me my next step!"

For example, if I pay attention to my bodily sentience right now I find a sensation in my belly that the label "hungry" fits. I also feel a very slight shakiness in my arms and legs that I know often accompanies hunger. I'm hungry. This hungriness implies a next move—stopping this writing shortly and going to lunch. This next move follows from my listening to my bodily felt sense.

Tapping into this level of knowing leads us to what I am calling "a focusing approach to meditation."

These days I practice five different meditations. I count my breaths; I repeat a mantra; I visualize Spring Hill, a place that gives me good energy; I visualize a ball of golden healing light radiating down over me; I watch whatever thoughts, feelings, sensations, images, memories, reveries go by. The first four are concentration meditations; the fifth is mindfulness.

How do I choose which form of meditation to use at any one sitting? As I may switch forms in the course of a sitting, how do I choose when to switch and to what?

I ask my body/being, "What would feel right right now? What meditation is my body/being calling for?"

When I get an answer, I try that meditation out. I try it on for size. If it fits, I go with it. I go on with it for as long as it feels right. If after a trial period it doesn't feel right (i.e. it doesn't deepen, I get twitchy and distracted), then I switch. I let my body/being decide to what I switch.

This is what I am calling "a focusing approach to meditation." It seems to me to be analogous to Gendlin's approach to dreams (Gendlin, 1986). Gene is respectful of all vocabularies of dream interpretation. I read him as saying that we don't have to search for and identify the right and true path to dream interpretation. We don't have to declare allegiance to the one absolutely correct school.

Each school can be right—some of the time. We let our body/being decide which is right *this* time, for *this* dream.

The parallel: we don't have to choose absolutely and finally among schools of meditation. We don't have to decide which is the true and right path. Today's right path—the right path right now—that is what we discover experientially and evaluate experientially. I might say, paraphrasing, Gene, let your body choose your meditation.[5]

An alternative approach to meditation often encountered in the spiritual literature is the exhortation to find a guru and a tradition and surrender. There is a way to follow, a right way to meditate. The focusing approach to meditation is different. In the spiritual literature Krishnamurti is the teacher most in resonance with what I am suggesting. He writes, "Truth is a pathless land. . . . Be your own guru and your own disciple. . . ." I take this to mean: Truth is the monopoly of no particular path (including focusing!). Evaluate all traditions and received wisdom against your own experience.

Focusing gives me the tool with which to do this. It gives me access to bodily felt experience that can act as a touchstone by which to evaluate in the moment forms of meditation in terms of their rightness-for-me-right-now. Focusing provides a way to do that of which Krishnamurti speaks.

HOW I COMBINE FOCUSING AND MEDITATION

How do I combine focusing and meditation?

I almost never go from a period of meditation into a period of focusing. It doesn't seem right to me. It seems backwards. I may, on occasion, sit down to meditate, notice quickly that I'm getting nowhere, that agitated emotion is in the way, and then I may decide to focus instead of (or, before) meditating. But this is "instead of" or "before" rather than a movement from meditation to focusing.

I do sometimes go from focusing into meditation. In fact, there are three specific steps in a round of focusing where I may choose to move into meditation. This to me has proved the optimal way to combine the two processes in a planned way.[6]

Let us look at these three places:

1. Sometimes in the *initial* step of focusing (How am I from the inside right now?) I find a felt sense that a handle like "open," "calm," "expansive," "meditative," "up," fits. There may be a serene energy. There may be an "up" and finger-popping energy.

I may choose to go directly into meditation from either of these energies. When I say, "I may choose. . ." I mean that my body/being may want me to meditate at this point.

It is not that, were I to step back and carefully scrutinize it, my life is all fine. There are, as always, problems and issues. It is that right at this moment it feels either "all fine" or "fine enough!" Nothing in my life—no content, no issue—requires my working on it at this very moment.

"OK, let's meditate." When I propose this to my self, my self says "yeah!"

2. A second place where I may move from focusing into meditation is after the step called, *clearing a space*. The scenario goes something like this:

In the first step of focusing I have found a felt sense that a handle like "anxious," "upset," "depressed," "angry," or "heavy" fits. In the second step I have stacked on a bench a comfortable distance from me the stuff that is between me and feeling either "all fine" or "fine enough" right now.

After having done so, I find that I am feeling clearer, lighter, more spacious, more peaceful. At this point I may decide to leave the stack on the bench and meditate from the peaceful place. Again, I will do so when my body/being is calling for meditation.

Nothing on the bench is frantically waving its hand, desperately clamoring for my attention. It says it is OK staying on the bench for now. This does not happen very often for me. It happens either when not much is really bothering me or when the "clearing a space" step has worked particularly well. Then staying meditatively with the cleared space feels like the thing to do.

The third place where I tend to move from focusing into meditation is at a particular question in the *asking* step. By this point I have been working on something via focusing through several steps. I have asked the felt sense some exploratory questions (e.g. what is the crux of it?) and some forward-looking questions (e.g., what does it need?). Now I ask it, "how would my body be if this thing were all better, all resolved?" I move my body into the position it would take if I had magically looked up the answer to this trouble in the back of a book, found the answer, and successfully applied it. Now, for the moment, I'm all fine.

I may at this point choose to go into meditation from this "all fine" place. (In fact, in focusing workshops this is the place where I have people move into meditation. Several experienced meditators have reported that it has been a very useful way to enter meditation.)

What do these three places have in common?

I tend to choose to go from focusing into meditation at a good-feeling place. This is not always the case. But it is a tendency. I tend to use focusing to work on things—to clear up issues, to fix places inside—and meditation to stay with and enter more fully into a space where my mind has been quieted and I am mostly beyond it. I don't find that I get that much from meditation when I try to enter it directly from a place of nagging emotionality and consequent mental chatter.[7] At such times (which are many) focusing is the indispensable service road that leads me from the heavily-trafficked street of ordinary consciousness out onto the open highway of meditation. It is very difficult, bumpy, and often unsatisfying to try to go directly from the street to the highway without using the service road.

MICHAEL JORDAN, IMPROVISATIONAL ACTING, AND NONTRADITIONAL MEDITATION: FURTHER REFLECTIONS ON MEDITATION (ESPECIALLY) AND FOCUSING (1999)

For me, meditation is about (1) being fully in the present; (2) doing one thing at a time; and (3) stillness. The three go together. If I am fully in the present, I am fully doing and only doing what I am now doing. I am not preoccupied. I am not distracted. I am not forcing myself to be in the present. (If I am, then I am in 'forcing myself' and not the present.) I am not in the past or the future. I am not AWOL. I am not partialed out. There is no 'this part' and 'that part.' I am not both here and there. There is only the whole of me doing wholly whatever I am doing.

If what I am doing is closing my eyes and going inside, there is — stillness. *No mind-chatter*. Nothing. There is simply a darkness behind my eyes. If I stay with it for awhile, it is refreshing. All of me is closing my eyes and going inside. None of me is left outside.

Meditation is about awareness, efficiency, and effectiveness.

Four times this year I have tripped over my feet, a stoop, or an obstacle in my path. In each instance, part of me was somewhere else. I was preoccupied with where I had been. I was anticipating where I was going. I was not fully where I was. I tripped.

II

Since writing the three preceding essays, I have gone further with meditation. My journey has taken unexpected turns. I have had one new extensive practice and been influenced by two new books. I will get to them shortly. First I want to look backwards and amend in three places what I had written about focusing and meditation.
1. I no longer 'sit' as much as I did. My present meditations are mindfulness, improvisation, and 'just listening.' I will talk about them later.
2. In the second essay, I overemphasized switching meditations moment-by-moment. In a book to be reviewed shortly, *Bare Bones Meditation* by Joan Tollifson, for most of the book she vacillates between Zen and another form of meditation. Her Zen teacher, Mel Weitsman, advises her:

> You have to find the thing you really want to do. . . the thing you can't not do. And then you have to stick with it. . . You have to let go of the paths not taken, and really allow yourself to deeply penetrate the one you've chosen. . . You have to make a choice and then commit yourself. . . Nirvana is seeing one thing through to completion. Otherwise life just becomes a lot of mental ideas about an imaginary future. (Tollifson, 1996, pp. 32-33)

This is sound advice. Joan Tollifson has difficulty committing. For such a person my previous statement needs amendment. Find a practice that seems to work for you. Give it at least a three months' trial period. Do not switch during that time. *Then* use focusing to

evaluate your choice. Stay with it or change as your focusing suggests.
3. In contrast to what I said in the third essay, at times I now do go from meditation into focusing. I have been one of a three-person focusing group. One member cannot get to it on time. The other two of us meditate while awaiting her. Then the three of us do a focusing check-in.

I find that meditation does the job of clearing a space. So long as I change my posture and take a short break, I can then go into a very useful focusing. The meditation seems to quiet the static that may get in the way of focusing. This finding has surprised me and contradicts what I had previously written.

III

> If your mind isn't clouded by unnecessary things, this is the best season of your life.
>
> — Wu-Men
> (in Jackson, 1991)

Now we come to more recent developments.

The second best book on meditation that I have read since 1991 is Phil Jackson's *Sacred Hoops* (1995).

Jackson may be familiar to you either as the former coach of Michael Jordan and the Chicago Bulls basketball team, or as advisor to former Senator Bill Bradley.

Jackson is a meditator. He sees basketball in terms of mindfulness:

> In basketball—as in life—true joy comes from being fully present in each and every moment, not just when things are going your way... Things are more likely to go your way when you stop worrying about whether you're going to win or lose and focus your full attention on what's happening *right this moment*. (his italics)

> When players practice what is known as mindfulness. . . not only do they play better and win more, they also become more attuned with each other. And the joy they experience working in harmony is a powerful motivating force that comes from deep within, not from some frenzied coach pacing along the sidelines, shouting obscenities at them. . . The group imperative takes precedence over individual glory, and success comes from being awake, aware, and in tune with others. (Jackson, 1995, pp. 4-6)

Jackson teaches his players meditation. He introduces them to mindfulness meditation and then brings in a colleague of Jon Kabat-Zinn to lead a meditation retreat. The players hear:

> Focus your attention on your breath as it rises and falls. When your mind wanders. . . note the source of the distraction. . . then gently return the attention to the breath. This process of noting thoughts and sensations, then returning the awareness to the breath, is repeated for the duration of the sitting. . . (p. 119).

Jackson is refreshingly honest about the players' reactions. "Bill Cartwright once quipped that he liked the sessions because they gave him extra time to take a nap" (p. 119). The first time Jackson introduced meditation, "Michael Jordan cocked one eye open and took a glance around the room to see if any of his teammates were actually doing it" (p. 173). They were.

For Jackson, his players learning mindfulness meditation is the exactly right practice for how he wants them to play basketball. He uses something called "the three post" or "triangle" offense. Don't worry; I'm not going to go into the intricacies of this offense. Suffice it to say that everyone on the team is moving at the same time and by no single pre-arranged script. Every Bull has several options. The idea is to "break down" the defense. That is, to get one or more players open. The defense does not know who is going where. If the ball-handler is mindfully aware, if he is totally present, he will see who is open at any moment. (If he doesn't, he can always give the ball to Michael Jordan.)[8]

This "form" does not look like what we usually identify as meditation. We usually identify meditation with sitting. But that is just a form. The Bulls are meditating and Jackson explicitly evaluates games in meditative terms.

> Basketball is a complex dance. . . The secret is *not thinking* (his italics). . . The point is. . . precise attention, moment by moment. . . we show players how to quiet the judging mind. . . (p. 115)
>
> Winning is important to me, but what brings me real joy is the experience of being fully engaged in whatever I'm doing. I get unhappy when my mind begins to wander, during wins as well as losses. Sometimes a well-played defeat will make me feel better than a victory in which the team doesn't feel especially connected. (p. 201)

Jackson's book is about taking the practice of meditation into the world—into daily activity. Here the activity is basketball. The emphasis is on getting off one's cushion and being in the world meditatively.

IV

For three years (1995-1998) I took Improvisational Acting and Movement classes with a gifted teacher, Daena Giardella. The essence of Improvisation is to be on a stage without a script. In Improvisational warm-ups Daena will suddenly send you an instruction once you are on stage: (for one) "Be a person in a hurry to get somewhere"; (for two) "Be a person in a hurry to get somewhere who bumps into a person who desperately wants to talk with you"; (for three) "One of you is in a hurry; one wants to stop and talk; one is distracted. Okay. Go."

Improvisation is wonderful for people who feel in life that everyone has read the script except them. Here—no script at all. This can be dramatic/traumatic for those who feel the need for a script. I was about to write that "improvisation is meditation-in-action." But to put it that way is again to identify meditation with one "form" of meditation: sitting. Improvisation is meditation. Full awareness in the moment is necessary. This includes the awareness of other people and their offerings—i.e., gestures towards you. This brings in an interpersonal dimension to meditation—as does basketball.

Daena says:
> Improvisation is a practice of active meditation similar to what the Sufis call 'meditation (samahdi) with open eyes.' The improvisational actor practices a state of awakening where she/he is both in the moment in tune with individual impulses and simultaneously aware of 'the larger context.'

She continues:
> I think we are on the edge of a paradigm shift in what we define as meditation. Solitary meditation practice will always be essential. However, as our world unfolds with greater and greater interdependency issues among people, nations, and systems, it may not be enough for us to simply sit alone in meditation. In improvisational practice one has to face oneself as well as others in a mutual practice of developing awareness. We learn to listen and collaborate with the impulses of the mind, body, emotion, and intuition, in both ourselves and others. The actor/meditator learns to harmonize in relationship even as he/she is embracing conflict. Improvisation is a practice of generosity—an invitation to open to the deliciousness of the whole banquet. (personal communication)

A time when I failed to improvise is worth noting. There was an open stage. That means whoever goes up first starts a scene. I go up on stage. I am very much into the book, *A Civil Action*. I am the lawyer in the book. I am talking about how the toxic water has hurt this neighborhood in Woburn. A woman in the class has read the book. She joins me on stage. She plays the main woman character in the book. We are talking together about the toxic water. We're grooving. We're on a roll. A third person joins us. He mimes taking a glass of water. He says, "This water tastes fine."

I'm non-plussed. I'm thrown. I'm in a scene from *A Civil Action*. The water it toxic. No one would drink it and say it is good. This character does not appear in my script.

But that is the whole point. *I am not in the present.* I am in *A Civil Action*. I cannot adapt to the newly-created reality. I cannot incorporate seamlessly this new input.

More frequently improvisational actors are spaciously aware of the here and now. Complex scenes evolve as each new element is added to the moment.

He and I are at either end of the stage. There is no direction. I see a line of tape on the floor. I start walking on it as if it were a tightrope. I put my arms out as if holding a balance stick. He does the same. We approach each other. As I step around him, I say, "I remember yesterday." We go around each other. He is nettled. "What about yesterday?" "The way you tried to push me off." "You're crazy." "Am I?" We are moving towards each other again. This time there is tension between us. There is no script. We are jointly making this up as we go along. "I know you want to replace me with him." "You're paranoid." "Oh really, well let's see." I imagine a third person on the ground holding a net below us. I yell to him—"take away the net." I nod. He has done it. The two of us on the rope look at each other again. There is no net below us now. We both tense up. We move towards each other slowly. We stop two feet apart. The hostility, the mistrust, the doubt between us is palpable.

Daena calls "scene."

Our scene has been a meditation. We stay in the present. It

changes moment-by-moment. Our relation to the tightrope, the net, and each other changes with each change in the present. We co-create an ever-changing now.

V

The best book on meditation that I have read since 1991 is Joan Tollifson's *Bare-Bones Meditation* (1996). It is sub-titled, "Waking Up from the Story of My life." The book is about both the story of that life and her awakening from it.

Joan Tollifson was born with one arm. She became a one-armed radical lesbian substance-abuser. She was living in a "radical ultraleftist anti-imperialist communist organization" when she began sitting at the Berkeley Zen Center.

She began missing demonstrations in order to sit. She went on to massage school, studied karate, and got a degree in creative writing.

Something about Zen always bothered her. She called the ritualized sittings "a macho endurance test." She wondered about how the emphasis on posture was experienced by a quadriplegic. Zen was full of foreign trappings. "Why do we act like we are in medieval Japan," she asked.

Then she took a workshop with Toni Packer.

Toni Packer is the main teacher at a non-traditional meditation center called Springwater outside Rochester, New York. It was originally the Genesee Valley Zen Center. But under Toni's leadership Zen began to disappear: "Over time the Zen forms, names, and ideas were dropped. . . It had gotten much, much plainer. All the trappings of religion had been stripped away. . . There are no rituals or ceremonies. Just the bare bones of ordinary life. . . " (p. 44).

The rest of the book chronicles Joan's vacillation between Zen and Springwater and her vacillation about entering a love affair with a quadriplegic.

I am most interested in Springwater. At Springwater awareness does not depend on any practices, procedures, or traditions. There is no "trying." During retreats, people sit on cushions, chairs, the floor. They go to their rooms. They take naps. There is no prescribed clothing. No dictated sitting style. During retreat some people even read books or magazines at times. There are no trappings of any particular path—no Hinduism, no Buddhism, no Christianity.

In this way Toni Packer is a female Krishnamurti: Springwater is pathless. "No formal practice is recommended (following or counting the breath, labeling thoughts, working on Koans, visualization, mantras). When meditating, don't do anything at all, Toni advises. Just listen. Just be with the moment itself, no props or extras, no authorities, no beliefs" (p. 45).

Don't "meditate." Just be.

Joan has her ins and outs with Springwater. On the one hand, she says, "I have never been anywhere in my whole life where silence was this resonant and bottomless" (p. 47). Then, she thinks, "I'm a childless, careerless female living in an unauthorized meditation center in the middle of nowhere with a bunch of belching men who watch television" (p. 110). Finally she comes to feel that, "There is something special happening here at Springwater. There's a different body-mind feeling, experientially, to working in this way (without a 'practice'). . . It has to do with completely effortless seeing rather than imposing something, however subtly. It's somatic as well as mental" (p. 133).

Joan refers to the work at Springwater as "radical subtraction." She applies it to even her most cherished identity:

> I begin to see how quickly ideas and identities form around our experiences. The idea that I'm 'a lesbian,' for example. Actually, there's certain activity that occurs, and then from that experience and its historical repetition we draw a conclusion—an identity—and project a future 'I am a lesbian,' or 'I am heterosexual.' We identify with this image of ourselves, it becomes fixed; we see ourselves in opposition to

others who are different and perhaps out to destroy us." (p. 134)

Joan remains a lesbian. But all forms do get questioned at Springwater. Sometimes Toni attends a retreat not as teacher but as participant. Other people give talks. Some retreats have no leader. Springwater moves away from a hierarchical structure.

The most radical notion of all is the questioning of the separate, solid self.

Joan notes the way Toni talks: "Nothing is personalized. 'There is wanting,' she says, rather than 'I wanted.'"

Listening to Toni, Joan says, "It was as if the lights had been turned on. I realized that the whole story of 'me' is imaginary, that 'I' exist as a separate, discrete individual only when I think of myself. Without this thought of me and my story, everything is permeable, spacious, without division. The thought of 'me' is so powerfully conditioned, so seemingly real, so socially accepted, that we take it as an unquestioned fact. We exist, in our thoughts, as separate selves by telling stories to ourselves and each other" (p. 41).

Joan struggles with the question of identity. She does not simply yea-say Toni's point of view. (See pages 152-156 especially.)

This is a profound, beautifully written, transformative book. It provides questions. It does not provide answers. Perhaps the last word about it should be Toni's: "In the midst of everything, can there be simple awareness, not knowing any answer?" (p. 156)

VI

As of 1991, meditation for me meant sitting. I would sit with eyes closed in the Spring Hill workshop space. Forty of us would be sitting together. I identified meditation with this practice and expected it to continue unceasingly. Since then I have come to see that meditation is not restricted to sitting. It is not about who can sit the straightest or the longest. Sitting can help. But meditation is a way of life. It is about being fully in the present, doing one thing at a time, and stillness. It is about "showing up" to life. It is no particular path. It is the pathless path.

PART FIVE
FOCUSING AND MIRACLES

PROLOGUE

The gist of this section is summarized in Hamlet's famous assertion to Horatio that "there are more things in heaven and earth, Horatio, than are dreamt of in our philosophy."

This section is about that "more."

"A miracle... is really just a name for something [good] we cannot explain" (Shermer, 2000, p. 95). It has not been dreamt of in our philosophy. It eludes comprehension within our dominant explanatory paradigm. The dominant explanatory paradigm of our time is some mixture of scientific materialism, belief in rationality and logic, and "common sense." What is real can be seen, heard, touched, smelled. It is tangible. It has substance. It conforms to scientific laws. It is intersubjectively replicable.

If it is an idea or thought, it has to follow the rules of rationality and logic. It has to make sense.

Furthermore, it has to conform to that summation of unconscious beliefs known as "common sense." Thus, individuals are separate from each other. They have individuality. They stand over against something called the environment. Persons and environments are separate from each other and interact.

Some things are not possible. A person cannot be in two places at once. One person cannot peer into another person's being. So-called paranormal phenomena are unreplicable hoaxes. I cannot know what someone in Tokyo is thinking. Such notions "make no sense."

These essays concern experiences that elude this explanatory paradigm. They bespeak, therefore, the inability of that model to explain everything without remainder.

II

The first essay tells the story of the most amazing focusing experience I have ever had. There is much in it that I cannot explain. What stands out for me most is the experience of "no boundaries." This is not a concept. It is an experience. It violates our common sense notions about the relation of person and environment.

The second essay tells the story of the diagnosis of my kidney cancer and the surgical removal of my left kidney. It reports what my focusing revealed about the experience. There is no way the cancer could have been caught when it was. It was a miracle.

The final essay is my review of an extraordinary book (*The Future of the Body*) about the extraordinary potentials of human beings. The author, Michael Murphy, echoes Hamlet: There is much more in the life we are given than most of us realize. He collects "specimens of extraordinary functioning" from territories as diverse as sports, esoteric religions, and the study of the paranormal. His examples show the existence of things and events inexplicable within the dominant explanatory paradigm. In my review I mention some modest and mundane ways in which focusing has given me at least a brief glance in the direction to which Murphy points.

III

I like ending the bulk of this book with a nod in the direction which Abraham Maslow has called *The Farther Reaches of Human Nature* (Maslow, 1971). I think those "farther reaches" and the relation of focusing to them are part of the territory into which the psychospiritual Lewises and Clarks of the 21st century will take us much further inland. If my view from the shoreline can be of use to future cartographers of this uncharted wilderness, I am happy.

FOCUSING, TOPISTICS, MEDITATION, AND ALTERED STATES: ONE EXPERIENCE

I have been using focusing now for twenty-five years. During that time I have grown accustomed to what may be called the everyday miracle of focusing: the way a previously unclear bad-feeling state will sometimes open up and shift into a clear good-feeling state. Such remarkable improvements become commonplace to experienced focusers. I hardly record them anymore.

But every now and then I have a focusing experience that knocks my socks off. That blows me away. That leaves my mouth wide open. Often these awesome experiences occur when focusing leads over into other inner processes that take me into altered states.

Here is one such experience. I've recorded it pretty much as I experienced it. Fortunately, I had paper and pen ready when it began, and when I saw where it was going I followed it along. My report as jotted down in the moment—dressed up just a bit to go out in public—makes up the bulk of this article. It is preceded by a little background and followed by a little commentary in which I relate the experience to the expressive energies of places and to altered states.

The experience took place at Coki Beach in St. Thomas on September 1, 1990. Coki Beach is one of my two favorite places in the world. The other is Spring Hill, in Ashby, Massachusetts, which used to be the home of the Opening the Heart workshops which I helped facilitate. My former wife, Laury Rappaport, and I were the Directors of Spring Hill for three years. Our retirement gift was plane tickets to St. Thomas. At the time we had an almost three-year-old daughter. It was a full year before we could get away. When we did, it was our first trip together to St. Thomas in exactly three years.

The trip represented a convergence of my two favorite fields of energy and a homecoming for my wife and me. It was very brief: two full days plus travel. The experience followed my first swim of our first full day in St. Thomas—which was also our next to last full day before leaving.

9/1/90. I'm sitting in the shade leaning against the bath house wall drying off. I'm seeking an example of focusing for some writing I'm planning. I close my eyes and put my attention in my chest area. The words "I feel *very* still" come to me and fit. The "very" is underlined.

After these words comes a strong sensation like the current of the water running down the outside and inside of my body from shoulders to feet. I get an image of the blue-green water off Coki with the tide coming in. When I say to myself, "The tide is coming in," I feel a shiver and hear inside the words, "death. . . going home (from St. Thomas). . . coming home (to myself)." The words in parentheses are not actually heard but are clearly implied.

I sit. I feel calm. I ask inside, "What is the crux of this?" The old man carrying the scythe appears. OK, I think, it is about death. That isn't what I was wanting or expecting—but here we are.

As if carried by the current, my process is moving very quickly. I start to ask a focusing question, "What. . . ," and before I can finish, there is an image of my father, who has been dead twenty-one years, and I feel. . . sadness and regret that he feels far away from me.

Suddenly I see the first moment I saw him dead. The image is vivid. My mother is kissing his eyelids, and as I watch I feel a lump in my throat, tears well up and I cry.

Up to this point, I have been struck by the vividness of the sensations and images, but there has been nothing other than focusing going on. Now the experience takes a sudden turn: in the image, my father sits bolt upright from his deathbed. Laury and I are standing at the foot of the bed. My mother is at his side. My father looks angry, points in my direction, shouts, "You," and falls backwards.

I am shaken and stunned. My first thought is, "He is mad at me." My analytic mind wants to start telling a story from my case history about my father and me. Instead, I stop, study the image, and return to focusing.

It does not really feel like he is mad at me. His eyes are more vacant and glassy. He is looking through and beyond me. It is more like he is recognizing someone—Death?—behind me.[1]

That feels more like it.

I am calm again in my chest and there is now a lot of energy behind my eyes. My eyelids first begin quivering and then wildly jumping up and down. I know this means that I am in an altered state.

When I go inside again, there is Robert Gass, musician and creator of the Opening the Heart workshop, singing, "It's about time; it's about changes; it's about time." There is a sadness again, a calm sadness, with just a hint of tears. The tears feel different from the earlier tears—more philosophical, less personal.

Now I remember that it was at this beach some years before that I had finished Hemingway's *For Whom the Bell Tolls*. I remember the passionate intensity with which I had read the ending—as if carried along by a current. I remember my tears at the wonderful line when the hero, Robert Jordan, knows he is going to die and regrets only (as I recall the line), "The missing of it all."

And now I know that I am dying (not soon, but eventually), that I am leaving St. Thomas (tomorrow), and that it is the "missing of it all" that is with me.

When I close my eyes after writing the above paragraphs, there is the feeling of the current again and a lyric from the Heart workshop. It is the song that was sung to me when I received the laying on of hands in my first workshop back in 1981: "I am a bubble/make me the sea/make me the sea, Lord/make me the sea/I am a bubble/make me the sea." At the end of the song, I hear my own voice inside, "I'm preparing to leave. . . *all leaving is a little death.*" I heave a Big Sigh. Two revelations whiz by: There is an instant of knowing that leaving St. Thomas and dying are being equated, and that both the personal and transpersonal levels of dying are being explored. Then, there is an insight: this equation of leaving (or being left) and dying has always stood behind my stuff about endings. This insight grabs me; I have "known" it before, but it seems like this time I have felt it to the core. I realize that I am feeling no fear of death. The peace and clarity inside me feel very spacious. I also realize that something very interesting is happening in this experience.

I want to describe what happened next without it seeming too weird. I did not experience it as weird. It is an experience I have at times while sitting in intense energy fields. To some it looks weird.

I sit and have three quick experiences of inner imagery leading to a repeated physical movement. First, there is an image of two cymbals in an orchestra crashing together. Then there is a locomotive racing from the back of my head out the front. Then there is a jet plane breaking the sound barrier. At the apex of each image my head jerks violently from left to right and back in a kind of semi-swivel. No feeling accompanies the movement. There is no personal meaning attached to the imagery. I like the movement; it seems like a kind of releasing. It is a sign for me of something good happening. There is a shudder in my body along with the head motion, and after the third time I am perfectly still and go back to focusing.

There is a new sensation. It is not easy to describe. I remember having had it once before: *I would say that it is as if I have blended into the scene in which I am sitting and there is a complete flow between "internal" and "external," except that there is no sense of an "internal" and "external." I hear the words "no boundaries." I am reminded of something I once wrote about a French impressionist painter.*

He used the same brush strokes for the people and the scenery in his painting. They blended.

That fits. That is how I now feel. It is a wonderful feeling. Beyond wonder. It is awesome. I sit in it and cry for a few minutes, tears that have no words to go with them.

And then I get up and go for another swim.

There are two main points I want to make about this experience. The first has to do with focusing and altered states. The second has to do with the expressive energies of places and focusing.

1. I have heard Gene say that focusing stands at the doorway to spirituality and altered states. The interesting thing about this experience is that I went (or was drawn) through that doorway... and back... and through again... and back, etc. The experience goes back and forth between focusing and other inner processes and between the personal and transpersonal levels of being.

Focusing can lead one into altered states. Altered states can be very useful for change.

For hours after this experience, I was very quiet and deep inside. During the rest of the trip I was very alert and present. Nothing fazed me. I needed little sleep. I had a lot of energy. I wrote several chunks of what I was working on. I had a great time.

10/20/90. As I write this, it is seven weeks since the experience. I remain in a state I call "high-level wellness." My life situation has not been easy, but I have had a clear, strong energy with which to meet it. There have been brown-outs, and there have been a few jolts to replenish the energy. But it was this experience that provided the spark and that I continue to draw upon, like money in the bank.

2. It is not accidental that this experience happened at Coki Beach.

Topistics is the study of the expressive energies of places. E.V. Walter (*Placeways*) introduces it: There are archways at either end of a public housing complex. According to a computer print-out, they are identical. Yet under one there is a lot of crime and under the other very little. Why? Walter says that it is by standing under each, by feeling the energy—rather than computer comparison—that one can answer the question.

Places have energies. Visit a gambling casino, a meditation hall, a waterfall, a locker room, a school for wayward adolescents. Stand there. Feel the energy. That is what I mean.

That is why it is useful to have a focusing place—a place primarily or solely given over to focusing. The focusing energy will build up there and provide a current to help the process flow along. It is much easier to focus with the current than against it.

Some places have such energy naturally. For me, Coki Beach is one. Spring Hill is another. The energy of the place carries along and accelerates my own process. Its current helps mine flow.

I do not know why this is. I do know that it is.

For this, all I can do is be grateful.

Thank you, Coki.

Thank you, Spring Hill.

Thank you, focusing.

CANCER. FOCUSING. MIRACLE

There is a growing literature on cancer and focusing. My contribution will be from the perspective of a patient. I am a focuser. I have had kidney cancer. I want to share with you the two hours of focusing I did the morning after my kidney cancer surgery.

In this account I highlight what I will call here the "exquisite sensitivity" or the "radical honesty" of the *handle*, the symbol that matches the felt sense. You will see how a word that is not usually part of my vocabulary becomes the handle and then resists efforts to alter it, to make it more "spiritually correct."

BACKGROUND

I had been urinating excessively at night for some time. I told my primary care physician, Dr. Maurice Martin, about this. First he said what I had expected to hear: it probably indicates a benign, enlarged prostate. "But," he added, "there is another long-shot possibility." There is a rare condition, he told me, where the bladder does not empty completely. "Let's get a sonogram of the bladder."

I tripped off to Somerville hospital singing happy songs to myself. I was on a lark.

I was told that the sonogram would include the kidneys. I had the sonogram. I was not even bothered that the left side had to be taken twice.

Afterwards I sat in the visiting room. By chance, Dr. Martin was in the hospital at that time. He waved to me as he disappeared behind the curtain into the darkened room.

When he came out, his face was scrunched up and his brow furrowed.

I knew something was very wrong.

He sat down beside me. He told me the pictures showed a renal mass in my left kidney.

He said, "It's cancer."

I was flabbergasted. I was in shock. I couldn't speak.

The next three weeks included a CAT-scan and MRI. All indications were that the cancer was contained to the left kidney. Just in case, I took a three-day trip to St. Thomas. I wanted to say good-bye to my favorite island.

On Monday, April 28, 1997, I had a radical neferectomy in which the left kidney and its surrounding environment were removed. A week later it was confirmed that 100% of the cancer had been excised. I would not need radiation or chemo follow-up.

FOCUSING

On Tuesday morning, April 29th, I awoke in an interesting state. I focused. I could sense the after-effects of the anesthesia. I could sense the feeling of pain-killers at work. And I could sense. . . something more.

My overall state was mellow, at times a little woozy, but with great clarity in one place that was not woozy.

I kept my attention on my "something more" place.

Words wanted to come. They seemed to come from some faraway place. I imagined them travelling through a long tunnel. They then had to kick open a large wooden door.

Sometime in the first hour, a sentence came through.

"It's a miracle."

The sentence fit the felt sense.

During the hour, the sentence expanded into a paragraph of felt-thought.

I had had no symptoms of kidney cancer. I had no family

history of kidney cancer. I would not have gotten a routine checkup for kidney cancer. There was no reason for a kidney scan. It was a throw-in. It was only because of the thoroughness of my doctor and because bladder scans include the kidneys that the cancer was detected when it was, before cells had migrated anywhere else in my body. If cells had migrated, I would not have chosen to have chemotherapy.

"It's a miracle."

My body resonated with this sentence.

I did try some others. I tried, "good fortune," "lucky," and "a fluke."

Each of these phrases would be volunteered by someone to whom I later told the story.

None of them fit.

I got the image of a cruise ship, like the ones that dock at St. Thomas. "Miracle" was given a cabin. "Good fortune," "lucky," and "fluke" were thrown overboard. But... I don't use the word miracle. This "m" word is not part of my ordinary vocabulary. I don't hang out in the vicinity of miracles. I don't watch *Touched by an Angel*. I don't like answering machine messages that say "Today is the first day of the rest of your life." I don't expect miracles. My world is more mundane.

"It's a miracle."

The sentence still matched the felt-sense.

The second focusing hour was taken up with the experience of gratitude and gratefulness toward my doctor, Maury Martin.

Given my condition, I did not jump up and down. Rockets did not go off. There was simply a beatific silence and the words, "Maury Martin's miracle." That was the phrase that fit. I resonated it over and over. The beatific calm deepened.

But again, a part of me was dissatisfied. What about God? Miracles come from God. I knew intellectually that that was so. I could even think through the tie-in between my doctor and God— the sense that each of us is but a point on a string that stretches from everlasting to everlasting (Angyal, p. 243).

All that was terribly interesting and spiritually correct. But my felt-sense would not co-operate. It would not be altered by my intellectual analysis. It said, "Maury Martin's miracle." The rest it called, "unfelt-sense verbiage."

I was both amused and annoyed with my felt sense. "I" did not like the handle "miracle". . . but if it had to be a miracle, then at least it ought to be a full-blown spiritually correct miracle! The felt sense said, "no dice."

AFTERWORD

Throughout the entire experience of cancer, every step, every choice, every decision was made by focusing on it. Which doctor? Which hospital? Second opinion? Which test? How spend the day before the operation?

Each decision was made via focusing. The entire experience went very well.

It is now more than a year since the surgery. As I was getting ready for a follow-up CAT-scan, I focused on the whole experience again.

Once again, loud and clear, without hesitation, with a certainty that would not yield to questioning, the felt sense said, "Maury Martin's miracle."

So be it.

FOCUSING, METANORMAL CAPACITIES, AND TRANSFORMATIVE PRACTICE

In his brilliant book, *The Future of the Body* (Tarcher, 1993), Michael Murphy, co-founder of the Esalen Institute, argues that human beings possess "metanormal capacities" which can be enhanced by "transformative practices."

By "metanormal capacities" Murphy refers to such things as clairvoyance, telekinesis, remarkable athletic feats, telepathy, feelings of oneness and union with God, etc.

For "transformative practices" Murphy reviews literature on hypnotic suggestion, autogenic training, biofeedback training, structural integration, martial arts, yoga, and Zen Buddhist practice and meditation.

Murphy's remarkable 589 pages of text is itself an example of the "farther reaches of human nature." The quotes range from Sri Aurobindo, William James, and various Christian mystics, to Sandy Koufax (baseball), John Brodie (football), and Ingemar Johanssen (boxing).

I want to argue that focusing is a transformative practice that can release metanormal capacities. I will cite only metanormal occurrences that I myself have experienced during and just after focusing sessions. I invite readers to respond with experiences of their own.

METANORMAL OCCURENCES DURING FOCUSING SESSIONS

1. For several months each time I focused I had the sensation of myself sitting in a barber's chair which would take me up to the ceiling, where I might stay for all or part of the focusing session. I think this meant that I was getting a bird's eye view of whatever I was working on that day.
2. I have described in detail elsewhere (*Focusing Folio*, Winter 1991) an extraordinary focusing experience in which, among other things, an image of my father seemingly took on a life of its own. In the image, he sat up from his hospital bed, shouted "You!", and pointed at someone or something right over my shoulder. I have conjectured that the "you" referred to a visitation of Death, because one year after this experience I had to have an operation for the same condition from which my father had died.
3. I have had the experience, while focusing, of an image of a typewriter located somewhere in my abdomen, sending out automatic writing. For the fun of it, I asked it, "Is there a God?" It typed back "yes" at a time in my life when I would have consciously said either "no" or "I don't know."
4. For several months during weekly focusing sessions I experienced quite regularly a female mannequin's head coming straight at me from a distance. It would scare me and I would wince. Over time the fear subsided and the mannequin was soon replaced by a domestic scene of my father's female relatives sitting in our living room. A little later my father started to come down the steps from the floor above to join the scene.
5. Eventually—over the course of eight months—the entire scene disappeared and has never returned. I never felt a full understanding of it, but my sense of my own maleness and my relations with women improved markedly during this time.
6. After a very important financial transaction in which I helped to save a piece of property which was very special, spiritual, and dear to me, I focused. I felt as if I were melted into my

surroundings. There was no place where I began and where things on either side of me left off. There were no boundaries. I remembered reading about a French Impressionist painter who used the same brush stroke for his people and their surroundings. They blended and interpenetrated. That was how I felt, and I wept for joy.

**METANORMAL OCCURRENCES
AFTER FOCUSING SESSIONS**

1. One evening I went directly from my focusing session to the bowling alley. I bowled five straight strikes. After the fifth I said to myself, "Aha! The focusing session has sharpened all my senses." The rest of the game was ordinary.
2. After an especially powerful focusing session for myself, I did a therapy session where I could not shake the sense of an outline of another person sitting on the left side of my client. There was no one there. The dotted line of the other person would not go away. I mentioned it. My client was shaken. He had been abruptly separated at age 16 from an identical twin brother. The brother had always walked on his left side.
3. After a visit with an extraordinarily kind and gentle doctor who had had me informally focus on my experience, I felt very strange—like I had entered a twilight zone. I sat down at an outdoor café. For about fifteen minutes, I was visited by sense impressions of another old-fashioned-looking doctor of whom I had no conscious memory. I could just almost see him. When I later described what I had seen to my mother, she said, "That is an exact description of Dr. Tasman who operated on you and saved your sight when you were four."

On page 374 of his book, Murphy makes one minimal reference to focusing. There could be a lot more! In particular I would guess that focusing veterans have felt sense/emotional experiences that far exceed the norm. I would bet that focusing practice increases sense-memory of distant past emotional events, leads focusers over into other kinds of altered states, and allows access to felt/emotional experience that far exceeds what we usually consider "normal" for past, present, and future experience.

We would do well to collect and document these focusing explorations into the future evolution of human nature. I am sure that they will reveal focusing to be valuable for transcendental self-work as well as remedial work.

CONCLUSION

"Sunday, September 26, 1971: Alone in my apartment on a dank, gloomy day... I completed the book a few minutes ago. I'm strangely, idiotically near tears. So many completions are involved, my own and Black Mountain's, that they blend into some indistinguishable sadness. Is it really over? Do I want it to be over—the place, my writing about it...

"I'm glad of the tears. They lead me back to [Charles] Olsen's phrase: 'Now Arise!'"

Duberman, 1972, p.413

I am going to keep this brief.

Whether or not he knew it in 1971, Martin Duberman was focusing. He included in his conclusion his own experiencing. In fact, he did this throughout Black Mountain (1972). Duberman is a well-respected professional historian. Duberman included himself in his book. No wonder I admire it so much. That is what I do.

Duberman's final words remind me that this is not just *a* conclusion. It is *my* conclusion. It may also be *your* conclusion. I have a little more to say in conclusion about focusing. But first there is the possibility of *my* focusing and *your* focusing on the feltness that is there in conclusion.

Whether or not you do is up to you. For me, I will stop now, put my black felt tip pen down, and focus...

When I do, I find relief, gratefulness, and satisfaction.

Relief: Whew! There were so many obstacles. I've overcome them.

Gratefulness: to Gene, for being the Johnny Appleseed of focusing; to all those who have helped me along this way; to myself for staying on course.

Satisfaction: I've taken some steps forward with this book. I feel good about it.

That is how I am. How is focusing?

II

As the century turns, focusing is alive and well and flourishing.

Consider these numbers:

From 1950 to 1964 there was one focuser— Gene Gendlin— who was discovering and developing it.

Between 1964 and 1968 there was a small nucleus of focusers— perhaps ten— helping Gene give the first focusing workshops in Chicago. People from Japan, Germany, Belgium, Holland and French and English-speaking Canada visited.

By 1970 some members of the nucleus had scattered. They took focusing to new places. Visitors took focusing back to their native lands. Gene travelled. A lot. Soon, others did too.

Fast-forward: Focusing is an international phenomenon. As of 1999 there is at least one representative of focusing in each of thirty-one countries, six provinces of Canada, and thirty-five of our United States, and Puerto Rico. In Japan alone there are ninety-one focusing trainers and trainers-in-training. FOCUSING has been translated into ten languages— including a pirated Chinese edition. It has sold over 450,000 copies. It continues to sell. The last page of the September, 1999 Focusing Connection newsletter lists thirty-one upcoming focusing workshops, classes, and trainings in eight countries.

Ann Weiser Cornell has written of five reasons why focusing is not yet better known (1996). Some of her words are wise. I will make use of them. But I would suggest a different emphasis. Perhaps it is amazing that focusing is as well-known as it is.

Focusing is not slick. It lacks pyrotechnics. It is not a cure-all. There is no mass mailing on "Five Minutes of Focusing for Health, Wealth and Happiness." No one would ever accuse Gene of diluting focusing to pander to popular taste. Focusing has none of the trappings that make for instant success.

I love focusing. It has integrity. It has clarity. It is a human process. It is both simple and complex. It is subtle and powerful. It takes time to learn. It does not work all the time. It rewards serious study.

To better appreciate focusing, let me suggest an analogy to movies.

Movie Y comes out with a lot of fanfare. Big-budget. Lots of publicity. Big name stars. Easy plot. It grosses a lot of money the first weekend. But it is superficial, over-hyped, insubstantial. Negative reviews catch up with it. It disappears from the first-run theaters. It is not heard from again.

Movie Z opens in only a few theaters. Minimal publicity. No big name cast. Low-budget. No well-financed organization to back it. Not flashy. It starts slowly at the box office. It breaks no weekend records. But it has substance. It grows on you. It stays around. People return to see it more than once. It spreads by word of mouth. It plays worldwide. It becomes a classic.

Focusing is movie Z.

III

Our task now is to continue to get focusing out to more and more people and places without diluting its special qualities. It is more than a matter of numbers. Quality control is very important. Focusing is out there in the world. We need to stay true to its essence. How well we continue his work may be the next test of the greatness of Gene's legacy.

END NOTES

INTRODUCTION: AN OVERVIEW OF THIS BOOK

1. Ironically, one she turned down, "Focusing, Topistics, Meditation and Altered States: One Experience" is an all-time favorite of mine.
2. This is why I got into self-publishing my books. It began as a creative response to the situation. I did not want to go through all those rejections. Daniel Shapiro, Lynn Koerbel, Annie Bissett, Bill at Porter Square Press and Mulberry Studio have been essentially helpful in this endeavor.
3. My favorite 'plump' sentence is: "…focusing is the indispensable service road that leads me from the heavily trafficked street of ordinary consciousness out onto the open highway of meditation."
4. I would read the whole ending starting with page 463 in the Scribner's paperback. The key sentences for me are "He looked down the hill slope again and he thought I hate to leave it, is all. I hate to leave it very much and I hope I have done some good in it . . . It is only missing it that's bad."

PART ONE: IN THE BEGINNING

1. The titles of further lectures: The Four Families of Psychotherapy; How People Change: The Role of the Experiential in Therapy; Dimensions of the Experiential in Therapy; Alienation, Experiencing, Psychotherapy.
2. At the International Focusing Conference in Wisconsin in 1998, Gene announced that his only PhD was in philosophy. He

had no degree in psychology. Walking him to the elevator after his talk, I said playfully that I wanted a refund. I had assumed I was seeing a psychologist. We shared a good laugh. He said now I know what was wrong with the therapy (i.e., that he was a philosopher.)
3. I do not support this position anymore. I do not believe Gene does either. See especially FOCUSING-ORIENTED PSYCHOTHERAPY. See also Leijssen (1999).
4. May's full quote: "Presence is not to be confused with a sentimental attitude toward the patient but depends firmly and consistently on how the therapist conceives of human beings . . . Any therapist is existential to the extent that with all his technical training and his knowledge of transference and dynamisms, he is still able to relate to the patient as 'one existence communicating with another' . . . In my own experience, Freida Fromm-Reichmann particularly had this power in a given therapeutic hour . . ."
5. Psychodrama, gestalt, co-counseling, primal therapy, and body-centered techniques could be added to the list of instances of and influences on the experiential orientation.
6. But notice: This is not yet about a certain brand of therapy called Focusing-Oriented Therapy. It is about the Experiential as a meta-orientation which many schools can adopt. It is not yet a new school in itself. I think this distinction is significant. Over time Gene moved from emphasizing the Experiential meta-orientation to therapy to writing about his own.

PART TWO: FOCUSING-ORIENTED EXPERIENTIAL THERAPY.

1. As in all the clinical examples in my writings, certain identifying features have been changed so that in all probability only the person in the example will recognize his/her self. Permission has been obtained for the use of these examples.

2. I am persuaded by Ann Weiser Cornell's work to make Clearing A Space an optional step. So far, in my practice, about 85 percent of the time focusers use it.
3. I think of 'sound' and 'gesture' as my contribution to the standard list of possible kinds of symbols. However, in my own work, I find focusers use them no more than 5 percent of the time. So I do not include them all the time anymore.
4. For more on focusing partnerships see Cornell, Ann Weiser, 1996, chapter nine, "Focusing With a Friend," and Simpkinson, C&A, 1999, pp. ix and 32.
5. At times Gene is adamant that the felt sense has to come there, in the trunk, in the center of the body. I do not feel so absolute about this. I find working with wherever the feltness is better than asking how the center of the body feels about something that is felt somewhere else.
6. As you read this please remember that I have been focusing—not continually—for twenty-five years. For the first ten I seldom focused on my own. When I tried I usually failed. I began to practice and appreciate self-guiding around 1987. Many times—but not always—I can get a lot of mileage out of it these days.
7. See my chapters in Part Three on the integration of focusing with both verbal and body-centered therapeutic interventions.
8. For more on the focusing attitude see Hinterkopf (1998), chapter 4, "Focusing Attitudes."
9. I have borrowed the skeptic from my favorite book on couples and couples therapy: Dan Wile, AFTER THE HONEYMOON (1998). See especially chapter seven, "Using Communication Errors as Clues." I usually give this chapter to couples to read—one copy for each partner.
10. Curiously, in the index to FOCUSING-ORIENTED PSYCHOTHERAPY (1996), there is no entry for 'felt shift.'

11. I think much of Kevin Flanagan's EVERYDAY GENIUS is really about this form of listening. I do not believe that it is really focusing.
12. See "How I Use Focusing for Self-Therapy" later in this volume for the introduction of this distinction.
13. For the controversy over Clearing a Space, see THE FOCUSING FOLIO volume on Clearing a Space and Ann Weiser Cornell, "The Trouble with Teaching Clearing a Space as The First Step of Focusing." TFC, Jan. 1991, p. 1-2, 5.
14. I do not do any of these other activities. I seem to be allergic to affirmations. However, one could combine focusing with one or more of these activities to move towards what Michael Murphy and George Leonard call a 'transformative practice.' If I had it to do over again I would combine focusing with other methods as per their model to create a transformative practice.

PART THREE: FOCUSING AND PSYCHOTHERAPY

1. On Rogers as listener cf: "Rogers was a great listener. This was one of my first impressions of him. I had driven across the country to visit him and [his wife] Helen …. When I arrived, Helen was occupied with a friend, so Rogers and I went into his study to talk for about forty-five minutes. When he came out to join Helen, he summarized our conversation for her by reviewing all the major points I had made during those forty-five minutes. I remember my astonishment, thinking, 'My God, this man **really** heard everything I said! What an incredible listener he is!' Then I laughed at myself for reacting this way, remembering why I had traveled across the country to meet him …"
"Norman Rice … remembered … 'I came to Carl and asked him if he might be able to work me into one or more counseling interviews, since I had never experienced him directly as a therapist. He managed to work in four. At the end of the first

session with Carl, I came out to Virginia Hallman, his secretary, and practically shouted, "Now I know the secret ingredient!" She was kind of low-key and gave me a "What's with you?" response. I told her I have never felt so deeply and fully understood and so completely respected in all my life, and that the effect on me was electrifying" (Kirschenbaum, 1979, p. 178) And: "What is obvious about Rogers, in the Gloria films for example, is that he listens: he really tries to understand Gloria and accept her without conditions. What is most obvious in Rogers is **the self-transcendent quality of his empathic attitude.** It almost seems that he disappears. He himself has said that it is difficult for him to describe afterwards what happened in a therapy session" (in Levant and Shlein, 1984, p. 219, emphasis mine).

2. From a slightly different angle, Cf. Mathieu-Coughlin and Klein:
"The history of the experiencing construct forms an interesting lattice between the work of Rogers and Gendlin ..."
"... Rogers defined pathology as 'incongruence' between awareness and experience, but he lacked a way to define the term 'experience' in observable terms, so that 'congruence' with it could be measured. The hidden storehouse could not be observed and compared with aware experience. This problem was solved by Gendlin's definition of implicitly complex experiencing... as the basic felt datum or referent of awareness" (in Rice and Greenberg, eds., 1984, pp. 214-215).

3. Listening is a very subtle art. On paper it can look deceptively easy and resistible. Invariably, when I teach listening someone says, "I don't want to just say back a person's words. Anyone can do that. And what good would that do anyway?"
Two points: try out both listening and being listened to.
Doing it well is much harder than the simplistic (and inaccurate) description "say it back" indicates.

And the experience of being listened to is most important. One must experience how it feels to be on the receiving end of listening. I continue to be surprised at how special it feels and how useful it is when I get well listened to.
4. With regard to selectivity in listening (or, when to paraphrase) remember: "We are experience [Gendlin would say 'experiencing'] oriented. Not every statement of the client receives equal attention. We always try to shift from the narrative to the feelings, from the theoretical-abstract level to what is concretely lived through" (Lietaer, in Levant and Shlein, eds., 1984, p. 51).
5. Gendlin encourages therapists to allow themselves mistakes (1996). And he has a beautiful image for what a therapist ought to do when he finds he has made a mistake: "The way to respond is simple. It is something like discovering that you are standing on someone's toes. You do not argue; you just move your foot off the person's toes. But you do not go home, or sit down and cry, or apologize overly profusely, as if what you did is more than you can stand. You just say you did not intend to stand on their toes, and then you do not go right back to standing on their toes again …. This is true with most mistakes a therapist can make. It is not the mistake itself that matters. It is what the therapist does about it afterwards." (pp.. 110-111)
6. Reflection is not the only way to be empathic. See Bozarth, "Beyond Reflection: Emergent Modes of Empathy" in Levant and Shlein, op. cit., pp. 59-76.
7. In doing Experiential Focusing-Oriented Therapy, I use listening in conjunction with other methods including focusing, gestalt, bioenergetics, interpretation, personal sharings, etc. So I move in and out of the listening mode. In some other modes, I do take a more directive stance. Hence, my own therapy allows for a zig-zag in therapeutic stance from the less to the more directive position. Gestalt and body-centered therapeutic interventions are more effective when combined with lis-

tening. This essay is about listening, not experiential therapy. Were it about listening as part of experiential therapy it would include sections on when to listen, when not to listen, how to combine listening with other therapeutic methods, and a section called "beyond methods." Such a work is in progress.
8. My writings on The Heart Workshop, YOU CANNOT STAY ON THE SUMMIT FOREVER (1987) and A REMEMBRANCE: SPRING HILL AND OPENING THE HEART (1998) are available from me.
One form of focusing and listening is not considered in this book. See Janet Klein, INTERACTIVE FOCUSING: THE PATH OF HEALING THROUGH EMPATHY AND COMPASSION. The Center for Interactive Focusing, Skokie, Illinois: 1998.
9. I hardly ever ask it "more sharply" anymore. This sentence is a left-over from the impact of my therapy with Leida Berg.
10. Ditto to note 9 above.
11. This sentence is certainly presumptuous. There is always the possibility that I am wrong. But at these moments that possibility is about 1%. I imagine many therapists have this experience. I may be wrong about that.
12. One of Gene's best papers, "The Experiential Response" could be read in conjunction with this section.
13. Thanks to the internet, this sentence is dated. Please read Angyal. Skip the first part. Go back to it after you are well into the book.
14. I apologize for using this example again. If I had a better one, I would use it. I don't.
15. For more on Angyal see my "The Genius of Andras Angyal," essay four in THERAPEUTIC ESSAYS (1987).
16. As I just formulated this in 1999, some references to "self-help" may have escaped detection in previously written essays.
17. I might have said "and your feelings get lost?" with the question mark, tentatively, as it does seem to be an interpretation (that proves to be right on target). The important thing though

is that the client accepts the interpretation and it carries forward her experiencing.
18. I could have reflected, "Oh, so you are in *a whole new place…*" The rule here would be: Always reflect forward movement; don't be too pain-centered.
19. A good example of "listening for the implicit." The "uncomfortable" is the therapist's reading into the client's words. The therapist needs to check carefully that the client is *really* accepting the therapist's explications rather than merely agreeing to be polite.
20. Alternatively: "So *retelling* helps get you in touch… what's there now?" This would be an example of a reflection followed by an invitation to focus, an invitation that seems to follow well in the direction of the reflection.
21. The preceding interactions illustrate focusing followed by listening. Staying with this image I could have in a gestalt way invited her to be the old dried up lemon and see what she experiences as it. Instead I notice that the client is holding her throat as she is talking at this point and this awareness guides my next intervention. Notice how the therapist is aware of the client's body movements and makes use of them.
22. Notice that after a gestalt action segment, T invites C to focus.
23. I might have reflected here just what the C says: "You're mourning… there's a sadness and a question 'Can I accept that this is the way it is?'" It is not clear to me whether my interpretation here is correct. The C may be thrown off by it, but then returns to her own track.
24. Some new insights ("I see now…") have come to C as a by-product of deeply experiencing feeling which at the start of the session ("everything is external") she was far away from.
25. Alternatively: "So you got a sense of his *not being like* most men you've been seeing… he could *give* to you… can you stay with that sadness place?" This would combine a listening response with a "stay-there" focusing direction.

26. Alternatively: "Ah, something in that sadness about his not meeting your expectations around men... like you're just seeing that now ... can you stay with that and see what *that* all is?"
27. Nicely, C corrects this reflection. Unfortunately, we don't find out whether T was going to bring the reference to "father," above into her reflection, as, for example, in "the sadness comes from being with a solid person who can give to you... and there was something about your father in all that..."
28. Another example of using a gestalt action technique to deepen a feeling place.
29. A good example of following up a gestalt technique with focusing. The gestalt technique has the person relate in the here and now with the people in the group. Focusing now sends her back inside to see what is there now that the gestalt round has been done. This could be a guideline: follow gestalt action methods with focusing steps. This is an experiential use of gestalt.
30. I always feel good when a client *initiates* a gestalt experiment. This seems to me to be an example of gestalt done in a Rogerian way: in gestalt work in a Rogerian mode the T aims to be no more directive than seems absolutely necessary. The T does not eschew directiveness but works to maximize client self-direction so that over time fewer experiments are being T initiated and more are being C initiated. The T aims to work him/her self out of the director role.
31. T's intervention here is not timed right for C. No harm is done because she stays with what she senses she needs more time on. I follow her lead. This is most important: C takes the responsibility to sense where she has to go next and to interrupt the T if he is in the wrong place for her. (Given that T is male and C female and the content of the session, this is probably also an example of her working on her issue *in vivo*.) T quickly drops his intervention and follows C.
32. I don't know why I didn't pick up on "paternal." Just missed it, I guess. Notice how this is the second time it has come up.

33. We ran out of time here, unfortunately, as I would have said "So it meshes with your father leaving" which I believe would have finally opened that whole avenue.
34. Joan Klagsbrun initiated my annual visit to her Focusing class at Lesley College—kind of "meet the author and watch him work" night. Thanks, Joan, for the opportunity. This particular year Joan was on sabbatical and Kathy taught the class and kept the annual visit going.
35. I want to say that I think my listening responses were especially sharp and poetic in this session and that really helped carry it as far as it went.
36. See my pamphlet, "Opening the Heart." It is also chapter one of my book THERAPEUTIC ESSAYS, (1987).
37. This entire section follows closely the article, "Focusing and Bodywork," which I wrote with Laury Rappaport for the Focusing Connection (vol. III, No. 2, May 1985). I want to acknowledge and thank Laury for her collaboration with me on this article. It was very much a mutual piece of work.
38. I want to add at length about what Focusing and Hakomi have to offer each other:

Of all the body-oriented therapies, Hakomi is the most congruent with Focusing, Hakomi and Focusing meet in their core principles.

Both therapies are very respectful of and supportive to the specific client. They are tailor-made rather than off-the-rack therapies. They are both non-violent and utilize some eyes-closed processes to help the person into a state of consciousness in which inner data can be accessed and processed.

What does Focusing have to offer hakomi: Just this: Kurtz calls hakomi "assisted meditation." That is, the therapist does something (e.g. says a probe) which the client is then invited to process in a meditative state. This is not totally unlike Pesso or the bioenergetic therapist "doing" something to which the client responds.

But the Focusing therapist does something less than the

Hakomi therapist. He is less active in the creation of experience. His activity is more restricted to asking focusing questions and receiving and reflecting clients' responses. The Hakomi therapist has more input in the form of a probe or a "little experiment." The Focusing therapist does less evoking than does the Hakomi therapist. He asks: "What is there?" (Of course, the very asking can be seen as evocative, but less so than a Hakomi probe.)

And what does Hakomi have to offer when it is combined with Focusing? Just this: Focusing therapy can tend to be too passive, too reactive. The pure Focusing therapist has to wait till the client brings up X upon which to focus. The Focusing therapist waits and reflects, but what if the client does not bring up, say, his tendency to miss appointments or her cocaine habit or wonderings about incest? The pure Focusing therapist wants to be in the position to ask, "What is the whole feel of X?" but tends to be constrained by whether or not the client brings up X.

The Hakomi therapist is not so constrained. He can choose to use a probe to evoke an experience about which there are behavioral cues or about which he simply has a hunch; e.g., "what happens for you when I say…it is OK to have needs," even though the person has never directly said, "I can't have any needs." The Hakomi therapist can "go fishing"; he has latitude to be more expansive and creative than the strictly Focusing therapist would be… and the Focusing therapist reminds him how dangerous over-use of such latitude can be.

39. I want to digress for a moment about the suspicion many therapists (and clients) have about body-oriented therapy. Of course, the most basic reason for this suspicion is that sex is of the body, and therefore, to bring the body into treatment means to have to confront sex. It is absolutely crucial that there be no erotic element in the touching at all. Yet there is another reason, historically, for the wariness of many therapists to body-oriented therapy. That is that Wilhelm

Reich is really the historical personage most identified with body-oriented therapy. That does not give it a great pedigree. Reich finished out his life in prison, and, while he worked, as a sympathetic biographer has written, "In therapy, as in most of his other endeavors, Reich was a man of extremes. At his best, he played in a league all his own. At his worst, he made mistakes a first-year psychiatric resident . . . wouldn't make." (Sharaf, p. 243) I think that this reputation for inconsistency has fallen over body-centered therapies as a whole and contributes to the distrust of them. I think some of this distrust is well-merited. The abuse of body-oriented therapies can be even more harmful than abuse of verbal therapy—although that abuse can be plenty bad, too! And the training of body-oriented therapists has not tended to be as rigorous or professional as that of verbal therapists. (But this is changing, and training is not everything!) For more on the ethics of body-oriented therapy, see Smith, 1985, chapter 10).

40. Technically, the hands-over mouth and squeezing-neck interventions are examples of "taking over." They come out of my reading of Hakomi.

41. Notice how focusing often fits at the start and the end of hard and expressive sessions. This is when the sessions go easily and really flow. Many don't. The examples I've quoted are among my all-time favorites—times when we "rode the rapids" with little obstruction. When there is more obstruction, more reluctance, more resistance, more unclarity—then there is more focusing and listening off and on during the session—whenever they are needed to help us get back on track.

42. Kathy McGuire has similar things to say re Gendlin and emotion in her valuable chapter, "Affect in Focusing and Experiential Psychotherapy" (in Safran and Greenberg, 1991).
She had Gendlin read and comment upon a draft of her chapter and then write his own free-standing chapter ("On Emotion in Psychotherapy").

She writes, "Gendlin... does not give value to the changing, healing quality of the tears, sobbing, and laughter.... He equates this kind of catharsis with the non-productive repeating of the emotion.... This author would like him to give more attention to the qualitatively different nature of these two forms of emotion." (p. 233)

"Gendlin emphasizes the slow steps of direct reference and not dramatic moments of catharsis...." (p. 236)

And Gendlin writes back to her:

"If you want it to be me, do not move from emotion to felt sense. The hardest way to get a felt sense is from emotion—one has to pull the whole thing out first, usually, *pull out of the emotion* (ital. in the original), then get a felt sense directly, or from an image of the whole thing." (p. 248)

McGuire writes that her dialogue with Gendlin indicates to her, "the need for the creation of a new conceptual category, one that distinguishes between emotion that repeats in an unchanging fashion and emotion that is part of a healing change process." (p. 248)

She goes on to say, and I agree with her, that Gendlin is really most interested in what she calls quite nicely "a... nonemotional felt event," —the felt sense. This leads him to undervalue the emotional felt event—catharsis.

The dialogue (of sorts) between McGuire and Gendlin is fascinating although not always clear, and, to use a phrase impishly, "well-focused." But it is well-worth reading as a starting place to see where the important issues of focusing, emotion, catharsis, and psychotherapy stand within the focusing therapy community as of 1999.

A further source of difficulty: Gene says that "at times" the felt sense might "best be described in words that are also the names of emotions, for example scared, shameful, or guilty. Even so," he continues, "it contains a whole intricacy of elements, not only what the emotion of the same name would contain." (Focusing-Oriented Psychotherapy, p. 59) This is very important. To me it means that "emotion names" can be the names both of emotions and felt senses. In other words the culprit, so to speak, is not the emotion name but *how it is dealt with by the therapist and client.* If they treat it like a felt sense, i.e., look for the 'moreness' of it then the emotion name itself can be considered a felt sense and the previously black vs. white discrimination of emotion from felt sense becomes more gray.

PART FOUR: FOCUSING AND MEDITATION

1. The lyric is from the song, "Jesus of the Colors," which can be found on Molly Scott's tape, *Sumitra, Honor the Earth*, Philo Records, 1980.
2. Is focusing a kind of meditation? Tein calls it "a very meditative process" (1986, p. 33). Don refers to focusing as "a meditative-like process" and says it "bears many striking similarities to certain Buddhist meditations, although it grew out of psycho-therapy research," (1977-78, p. 147). I have been known to refer to focusing in flyers advertising workshops as a "quiet, gentle, meditative-like" process. But is focusing a form of meditation? To answer this question it is important to note that there is no official box located in, say, Paris, which is labeled "meditations" and into which one could simply look and see if focusing is to be found there. Nor is there any universally agreed upon exhaustively official listing of the characteristics of meditations against which focusing can be measured. In other words, there is no objective way to answer the question: is focusing a kind of meditation? The answer has to be more subjective and creative. It is a *decision* whether or not to call focusing a meditation. I would propose using focusing criteria to make that decision: does it feel right to call focusing a meditation? To me it doesn't. There isn't a feeling of rightness of fit. When I feel my way into the non-fit, I find it has to do with focusing being *primarily* for me about *psychological* issues and their bodily-felt

resolution while meditation is *primarily* about *spiritual* development. For me, then, focusing does not feel like it fits into the category called meditation and thus in this paper I talk of relations between focusing and meditation rather than focusing as a kind of meditation.
3. There are several different categorizations and typologies of meditation. Two that I have found useful are those of LeShan (1974), and Naranjo (1989). My description of mindfulness follows Naranjo (1989, chapter 5), and also Ron Kurtz' usage (1990, chapter 5).
4. Some weeks after writing this section, I reread an article by Joe Tein that I had read five years before. I was struck by the similarity between what Tein and I are saying. Tein writes, "In focusing, you turn off the chatter of the mind by centering your awareness in the body and keeping it there. You can't be paying attention in your body and planning, analyzing or criticizing with your mind at the same time (try it and you'll see). This makes focusing a very meditative process, but different from meditation techniques that use the same [i.e. unchanging] object of attention like a mantra, koan, or breathing each time. In focusing, you turn your attention in this meditative, letting-go way to the felt sense of the actual specific issues in your life, then. . . give up the ego's efforts to control and manipulate, and surrender to a greater process within." (Tein, 1986, pp. 32 and 37).
5. Compare LeShan:
"A good program of meditation is, in many ways, quite similar to a good program of physical exercise.... Both programs should be adapted to the particular person using them with the clear understanding that there is no one right program for everyone.... One of the reasons the formal schools of meditation practice have such a high percentage of failures among their students... is that most schools tend to believe that there is one right way to meditate for everyone and, by a curious coincidence, it happens to be the one they use. . . " (p. 3.)
LeShan goes on to categorize meditations in terms of four major

routes: "the path through the intellect; the path through the emotions; the path through the body; the path through action." (p. 32)

He goes on to speak further about how to choose a path. Notice his emphasis on how the path *feels*:

"How does the individual choose which path to follow? There are no absolute rules.... which path feels most natural for you as an individual?... One teacher of the mystic way, Rabbi Nachman of Bratislava, wrote, 'God chooses one man with a shout, another with a song, another with a whisper.' There is one additional test of... a meditation program that should always be kept in mind. It generally should make you feel better when you do it than when you do not do it." (p. 33).

Of course, what needs to be added to LeShan's wonderful words is that it is focusing that allows one to know how a meditation feels and thus do the evaluation that LeShan recommends.

6. In this section I make reference without full elaboration to the "steps" in a round of focusing. Fuller descriptions of the focusing steps can be found in Gendlin (1978), Amodeo and Wentworth (1986), Campbell and McMahon (1985), and Cornell (1990). There are differences among these descriptions. And I have my own sheet of focusing instructions (1982b) which tends to follow Gendlin's original description of the steps. For an interestingly different point of view, see Cornell (1992).

7. I am told that it was for this reason that Bhagwan Shree Rajneesh developed "dynamic meditation" which includes 15 minutes of intense emotional catharsis followed by 15 minutes of complete silence.

8. And how does Michael Jordan relate to what he calls "all this Zen stuff"? Jackson refers to him as "Michaelangelo in baggy shorts" (p. 172). Jackson says of him that "In the process of becoming a great athlete, Michael has attained a quality of mind few Zen students ever achieve. His ability to stay relaxed and intensely focused in the midst of chaos is unsurpassed. He loves being in the center of a storm. While everyone else is spinning madly out of control, he moves effortlessly across the floor, enveloped by a great stillness." (p. 174). This season we will see whether Jackson's meditative approach to the game can help Shaquille O'Neal shoot foul shots!

PART FIVE: FOCUSING AND MIRACLES

1. From my journal:
10/24/91: It is very eerie rereading this example today. I have not looked at it in six months.
On Friday, September 13th this year I had open-heart surgery for a tear in my ascending aorta. This is the very same operation that my father had at the same age for the same condition. Does this experience in any way prefigure that I will be visited just as he was ("You!")?
Also eerie: I walked around with the tear for about ten days. I tore the aorta late in August. That Labor Day weekend I was trying to get plane tickets to visit Coki! Had I gotten tickets I would have gone not knowing I had the tear. Planes were all booked. I could not go.

REFERENCES

Allen, F. "Therapy as a Living Experience." In Clark Moustakas, *The Child's Discovery of Himself*. New York: Ballantine Books, 1966.

Alter, R. "When Cries, Do What?" *Mothering Magazine*, Winter, 1981, pp. 24-27.

Amodeo, J. and Wentworh, Kris. *Being Intimate*. London: Arkana Press, 1986.

Angyal, A. *Neurosis and Treatment*: A Holistic Theory. New York: Viking Press, 1965 and Da Capo Press, 1982.

Back, K.W. *Beyond Words*. Baltimore: Penguin Books, 1973.

Bean, O. *Me and the Orgone*. New York: St. Martin's Press, 1978.

Benson, H. *The Relaxation Response*. New York: Avon Books, 1976.

Bozarth, J.D. "Beyond Reflection: Emergent Modes of Empathy." In R. Levant and J. M. Shlein (Eds.) *Client-Centered Therapy and the Person-Centered Approach*. New York: Praeger, 1984.

Campbell, P.A. and McMahon, E.M. *Biospirituality*. Chicago: Loyola Univ. Press, 1985.

Cornell, Ann Weiser. *A Guiding Manual*. Berkeley: Focusing Resources, 1990.

Cornell, Ann Weiser. "The Trouble with Teaching Clearing a Space as the First Step of Focusing." *TFC*, Jan, 1991.

Cornell, Ann Weiser. "Being Friendly With What is There." *TFC*, Sept., 1991.

Cornell, Ann Weiser. "Focusing is Not a Six Step Process." *TFC*, May, 1992, pp. 1-4.

Cornell, Ann Weiser, "How to Use Focusing to Release Blocks to Action." *TFC*, Jan., 1993, p. 5.

Cornell, Ann Weiser. *The Focusing Student's Manual: Part Two, Listening*. Focusing Resources, 1993.

Cornell, Ann Weiser. "Five Reasons Why Focusing Is Not Better Known (Yet)." *TFC*, Nov., 1996, pp. 2-3.

Cornell, Ann Weiser. *The Power of Focusing*. Oakland: New Harbinger Pubs., 1996.

Dass, Ram. *Journey To Awakening*. New York: Bantam Books, 1978.

Dom, N.S. "The Transformation of Conscious Experience and its EEG Correlates." *Altered States of Consciousness*, Vol. 3, No. 20, 1977-78, pp. 147-168.

Dorfman, E. "Play Therapy." In Carl Rogers, *Client-Centered Therapy*. Boston: Houghton-Mifflin, 1951.

Duberman, M. *Black Mountain*. New York: E.P. Dutton, 1972.

Eastman, P.C. "Consciousness-Raising as a Resocialization Process for Women." *Smith College Studies in Social Work*, Vol. XLIII, June 1973, No. 3, pp.153-180.

Ferenczi, S. and Rank, O. *The Devlopment of Psychoanalysis*. New York: Dover, 1926.

Fisch, Dorothy. "The Dance of Freedom: Focusing and Action." *TFC*, March, 1993, p. 2.

Flanagan, K. *Everyday Genius*. Dublin: Marino Books, 1998.

Freud, S. "Further Recommendations in the Technique of Psycho-Analysis: On Beginning the Treatment, ETC." In Sigmund Freud, Collected Papers, Vol. II. New York: Basic Books, 1959, pp. 342-365.

Freud, S. Beyond the Pleasure Principle. New York: Horton, 1961.

Friedman, N. *The Social Nature of Psychological Research*. New York: Basic Books, 1968.

Friedman, N. "Inequality, Social Control, and Educational Reform." Unpublished Manuscript, 1972.

Friedman, N. "From the Experiential in Therapy to Experiential Psychotherapy: A History." *Psychotherapy: Theory, Research, and Practice*, Vol. 13, No. 3, Fall, 1976, pp. 236-243.

Friedman, N. Review of Eugene T. Gendlin's FOCUSING, *New York Chapter Assoc. for Humanistic Psychol. Newsletter*, Spring, 1979.

Friedman, N. "Harold and Maude: My Experiential Therapy with Leida Berg." *Review of Existential Psychology & Psychiatry*, Vol. XVII, Nos. 2 & 3, 1980-81.

Friedman, N. *Experiential Therapy and Focusing*. New york: Half Court Press, 1982a.

Friedman, N. "Holistic Insight and Focusing: Angyal and Gendlin." *Journal of Humanistic Psychology*, Summer, 1982b.

Friedman, N. *Opening the Heart* (pamphlet). Ashby, MA: Spring Hill Press, 1983.

Friedman, N. "How I Do Experiential Therapy." *TFF*, Fall, 1983, pp. 1-16.

Friedman, N. "On Focusing." *Journal of Humanistic Psychology*, Vol. 26, No. 2, Winter 1986, pp. 103-116.

Friedman, N. *Therapeutic Essays*. New York: Half-Court Press, 1987.

Friedman, N. "Focusing and Body-Work." (with Laury Rappaport), *TFC*, March, 1987, pp. 3-4.

Friedman, N. "Benefits of Focusing." *TFC*, July, 1988, pp. 3-5.

Friedman, N. "The Man Who Never Said What It Was About." *TFC*, Nov., 1988, pp. 1-4.

Friedman, N. "How I Use Focusing for Self-Help." *TFF*, Vol. 8, No. 1, 1989, pp.33-44.

Friedman, N. "Focusing and Meditation: One Comparison." *TFC*, Nov., 1990, p. 4.

Friedman, N. "Going From Focusing Into Meditation." *TFC*, May, 1991, pp. 1-2.

Friedman, N. "How Focusing Came Into My Life." *TFC*, July, 1991, p. 2.

Friedman, N. "A Focusing Approach to Meditation." *TFC*, Sept. 1991, p. 4.

Friedman, N. "Focusing Topistics, and Altered States," *TFF*, Vol. X, No. 4, Winter 1991, pp.59-65.

Friedman, N. "Focusing Therapy." *TFC*, Jan., 1993, pp. 3-4.

Friedman N. "What Focusing Is and What It is Not." *TFC*, March, 1993, pp. 2-3.

Friedman, N. "Focusing, Metanormal Capabilities, Transformative Practice." *TFC*, July, 1994, p. 5.

Friedman, N. *On Focusing*. Porter Square Press, 1996.

Friedman, N. "Small Changes: Innovations in How I Lead a Round of Focusing." *TFC*, 1998, pp. 1-2.

Friedman, N. "Hemingway Influenced Focusing-Oriented Experiential Therapy." *TFC*, March, 1999, pp. 1-2.

Friedman, N. "Fundamental Concepts of Focusing." *TFC*, Sept., 1999, pp. 1-3.

Friedman, N. "Focusing and Meditation." Porter Square Press. (n.d.)

Fromm-Reichmann, Frieda, *Principles of Intensive Psychotherapy.* Chicago: University of Chicago Press, 1950.
Gass, R. with Brehony, Kathleen. *Chanting: Discovering Spirit in Sound.* New York: Broadway Books, 1999.
Gendlin, E.T. "Existentialism and Experiential Psychotherapy." In C. Moustakas (ed. *The Child's Discovery of Himself.* New York: Ballantine Books, 1966).
Gendlin, E.T. "Experiencing: A Variable in the Process of Therapeutic Change." *American Journal of Psychotherapy,* Vol.15, No. 2, 1961.
Gendlin, E.T. *Experiencing and the Creation of Meaning.* New York: Macmillan, 1962.
Gendlin, E.T. "A Theory of Personality Change." In P. Worchel and D. Byrne (Eds.) *Personality Change.* New York: John Wiley, 1964.
Gendlin, E.T. "Existentialism and Experiential Psychotherapy." In C. Moustakas (Ed.), *The Child's Discovery of Himself.* New York: Ballantine Books, 1966.
Gendlin, E.T., Beebe, J., Cassens, J., Klein, M. & Oberlander, M. "Focusing ability in psychotherapy, personality, and creativity." In J. Shlein (Ed.), *Research in Psychotherapy III.* Washington, DC: American Psychological Association, 1967.
Gendlin, E.T. "Therapeutic Procedures with Schizophrenics." In Carl R. Rogers (Ed.), *The Therapeutic Relationship and Its Impact: A Study of Psychotherapy with Schizophrenics.* Madison, Wisconsin: University of Wisconsin Press, 1967.
Gendlin, E.T "Values and the Process of Experiencing." in A. Mahrer (Ed.) *The Goals of Psychotherapy.* New York: Appleton Century Croft, 1967.
Gendlin, E.T. "The Experiential Response." in E. Hammer (Ed.) *Use of Interpretation in Treatment,* New York: Grune and Stratton, 1968.
Gendlin, E.T "Focusing." *Psychotherapy: Theory, Research, and Practice.* 1969, Vol. 6, No. 1, pp. 4-14.
Gendlin, E.T "The Use of Focusing in Therapy." 1971, unpubl. manuscript.
Gendlin, E.T. "Experiential Psychotherapy." In R. Corsini (Ed.) *Current Psychotherapies.* itasca: F.E. Peacock, 1973 and 1979.
Gendlin, E.T. "Client-Centered and Experiential Psychotherapy." In D.A. Wexler and Laura Rice (Eds.) *Innovations in Client-Centered Therapy.* New York: John Wiley, 1974.
Gendlin, E.T. *Focusing.* New York: Bantam Books, 1981.

Gendlin, E.T. *The Client's Client: The Edge of Awareness*. In Levant and Shlien, op. cit., 1984.

Gendlin, E.T "Making A Space." *TFF*, also in A.A. Sheik (Ed.) Imagination and Healing. New York: Baywood, 1984.

Gendlin, E.T. *Let Your Body Interpret Your Dreams*. Wilmet, Illinois: Chiron Press, 1986.

Gendlin, E.T. "On Emotion in Therapy." in Safran and Greenberg (Eds.) *Emotion, Psychotherapy and Change*. New York: The Guilford Press, 1991, pp. 255-279.

Gendlin, E.T. *Focusing-Oriented Psychotherapy*. New York: The Guilford Press, 1996.

Goldman, P. *Making Do*. New York: MacMillan, 1963.

Goldstein, J. *The Experience of Insight: A Natural Unfolding*. Santa Cruz: Unity Press, 1976.

Gordon, T. *Parent Effectiveness Training*. New York: Signet, 1975.

Green, Hannah (pseudonym). *I Never Promised You a Rose Garden*. New York: Signet, 1964.

Hart, J. "The Development of Client-Centered Therapy." In J. Hart & T. Tomlinson, *New Directions in Client-Centered Therapy*. Boston: Houghton Mifflin, 1970.

Hart, J., Corriere, R., and Binder, J. *Going Sane*. New York: Delta, 1975.

Hendricks, Mary. "Research Basis of Focusing-Oriented/Experiential Psychotherapy" in Cain D. and Seeman, J. (Eds.) *Handbook of Research and Practice in Humanistic Psychotherapies*. APA, in press.

Hesse, H. *Siddhartha*. New York: Dover, 1999.

Hinterkopf, Elfie. *Integrating Spirituality in Counseling*. Virginia: American Counseling Association, 1998.

Hobbs, N. "A New Cosmology." In B. Berenson and R. Carkhuff, *Sources of Gain in Counseling and Psychotherapy*. New York: Holt, Rinehart, & Winston, 1967.

Horney, Karen. *Neurosis and Human Growth*. New York: W.W. Norton, 1950.

Jackins, H. *The Human Side of Human Beings*. Seattle: Rational Island Press, 1965.

Jackson, P. *Sacred Hoops*. New York: Hyperion, 1995.

Jacobsen, S. *Characterological Transformation*. New York: Norton, 1985.

Janov, A. *The Primal Scream.* New York: Dell, 1970.

Kempler, W. *Experiential Psychotherapy Within Families.* New York: Brunner/Mazel, 1981.

Kirschenbaum, H. On *Becoming Carl Rogers.* New York: Delacorte Press, 1979.

Klein, Janet. *Interactive Focusing.* The Center for Interactive Focusing, Skokie, Illinois, 1998.

Kogel, Laura and Wurman, Vicki. "Consciousness Raising and Psychotherapy: A Case Study of a Woman's Group." Unpublished MSW Thesis, School of Social Welfare, SUNY Stony Brook, 1975.

Krishnamurti, J. *The Flight of the Eagle.* New York: Harper & Row, 1971.

Kurtz, R. B*ody-Centered Psychotherapy: The Hakomi Method.* Mendocino: Life Rhythm, 1991.

Kurtz, R. *The Hakomi Therapy Manual.* Boulder, CO: Hakomi Institute, n.d.

LeShan, L. *How to Meditate.* New York: Bantam Books, 1974.

LeShan, L. *Clairvoyant Reality.* Northamptonshire: Turnstone Press, 1980.

Levant, R.R. and Shlein, J.M. (Eds.) *Client-Centered Terapy and the Person-Centered Approach.* New York: Praeger, 1984.

Levine, S. *A Gradual Awakening.* New York: Harper & Row, 1976.

Leiissen, Mia. "The Power and Limitations of Focusing: A Few Research Findings." In Feurestein, H.J., Muler, D and Comell, Ann Weiser (Eds.) *Focusing in Process,* 1989 in review.

Lietaer, Germain. "Unconditional Positive Regard: A Controversial Basic Attitude in Client Centered Therapy." In Levant and Shlein, op. cit.

Mahrer, A. *Experiential Psychotherapy.* New York: Brunner/Mazel, 1983.

Mahrer, A. *Therapeutic Experiencing.* New York: W.W. Norton, 1986.

Maslow, A. *The Farther Reaches of Human Nature.* New York: Pengula, 1971.

Mathieu-Coughlan, P. and Klein, M. "Experiential Psychotherapy: Key Events in Client-Therapist Interaction," in Rice, L. and Greenberg, L. (Eds.) *Patterns of Change.* New York: The Guilford Press, 1984.

May, R. *Existence.* New York: Basic Books, 1958.

May, R. *Existential Psycholog*y. New York: Random House, 1961.

McGuire, Kathleen. "Listening and Being Listened To." *Building Supportive Community.* Cambridge: Supportive Community Project, 1981.

McGuire, Kathleen. "Review of Ron Kurtz' BODY-CENTERED PSYCHOTHERAPY." *TFC,* March, 1990.

McGuire, Kathleen. "Affect in Focusing and Experiential Psychotherapy." in Safran and Greenberg (Eds.) *Emotion, Psychotherapy, and Change*. New York: The Guilford Press, 1991, pp. 227-255.

Mullan, H. and Sanguillano, Iris. "The Subjective Phenomenon in Existential Psychotherapy." *Journal of Existential Psychiatry*, Vol. 11, No. 5, Summer, 1961, pp. 16-34.

Mullan, H. and Sanguillano, Iris. *The Therapist's Contribution to the Treatment Process*. Springfield: Charles C. Thomas, 1964.

Naranjo, C. *Techniques of Gestalt Therapy*. Berkeley, CA: The S A T Press, n.d.

Naranjo, C. *How to Be*. Los Angeles: Jeremy Tarcher, 1989.

Pearce, J. & Newton, S. *The Conditions of Human Growth*. Secaucus, NJ: Citadel Press, 1963.

Perls, F., Hefferline, R. and Goodman, P. *Gestalt Therapy*. New York: Delta Books, 1951.

Pesso, A. "Abuse." Franklin, NH: PS Press, 1988.

Philips, L.W. (Ed.) *Ernest Hemingway on Writing*. New York: Scribner's, 1984.

Rank, O. *Will Therapy*, New York: Knopf, 1950.

Raskin, N. "Studies on Psychotherapeutic Orientation: Ideology in Practice." *AAP Psychotherapy Research Monographs*. Orlando, 1974.

Reich, W. *Character Analysis*. New York: Noonday Press, 1945.

Reynolds, D. *The Quiet Therapies*. Honolulu: Univ. Press of Hawaii, 1980.

Reynolds, D. *Even in Summer The Ice Doesn't Melt*. New York: William Morrow, 1986.

Reynolds, M. *Hemingway: The Final Years*. New York: W.W. Norton, 1999.

Rice, Laura. "The Evocative Function of the Therapist," in Wexler and Rice (Eds.), op. cit.

Rogers, C.R. *On Becoming a Person*. Boston: Houghton Mifflin, 1961.

Rogers C.R. *On Personal Power*. New York: Delacorte Press, 1977.

Rogers, C.R. *A Way of Being*. Boston: Houghton Mifflin, 1980.

Rogers, C.R. and Meader, Betty. "Person-Centered Therapy," in Corsini (Ed.) *Current Psychotherapies*. Itasca: F.E. Peacock, 1979.

Sanguillano, Iris. "The Experience of Psychotherapy." Journal of Existential Psychiatry, Vol. III, No. 11, 1963, pp. 255-263.

Scheff, T. I have misplaced this reference to an unpublished paper.

Schuster, R. "Empathy and Mindfulness." *Journal of Humanistic Psychology*. Vol. 19, No. 1. Winter, 1979.

Sheiner, Sara. "The Importance of Emotional Experiences in the Analytic Process." *American Journal of Psychoanalysis*, Vol. XXVII, No. 1, pp. 88-90.

Sharaf, M. *Fury on Earth*. New York: St. Martin's Press, 1983.

Shiarella, R. *Journey to Joy*. New York: Matrika Press, 1982.

Shermer, M. *How We Believe*. New York: W.H. Freeman and Co., 2000.

Simpkinson, Charles and Anne. *Soul Work*. New York: Harper Perennial, 1999.

Siroka, E.K. and Siroka, R. and Schloss, G. *Sensitivity Training & Group Encounter*. New York: Grosset & Dunlap, 1971.

Smith, R.E.L. *The Body in Psychotherapy*. North Carolina: McFarlane, 1985.

Snyder, W.U. *Casebook of Non Directive Counseling*. Boston: Houghton Mifflin, 1947.

Stetson, Jan. "Letter to the Editor." TFC, Vol. V, No.2, 1988.

Sullivan, H.S. *The Interpersonal Theory of Psychiatry*. New York: W.W. Norton, 1953.

Tein, J. "Focusing: A Psychological Approach to Spirit." *Meditation Magazine*, Spring, 1986, pp.32-37.

Thoreau, H.D. Walden and Other Writings. New York: Bantam Books, 1981.

Tollifson, Joan. *Bare-Bones Meditation*. New York: Bell Tower, 1996.

Walter, E.V. *Placeways: A Theory of the Human Environment*. Chapel Hill: Univ. NC Press, 1988.

Welwood, J. "Unfolding of Experience." *J. Humanistic Psych.*, Vol. 22, No. 1, 1982.

Wheelis, A. *The Seeker*. New York: Signet, 1960.

Wile, D. *After the Honeymoon*. New York: John Wiley, 1988.

Note:
TFC= The Focusing Connection
TFF= The Focusing Folio

ACKNOWLEDGEMENTS

- Harvard Student Agency and, especially, Mulberry Studio for word processing.
- Xlibris for a joyful publishing experience.
- Annie Bissett for work on the front cover.
- My focusing partners.
- Gene, for focusing, therapy, and friendship.
- Laury Rappaport for help with various essays.
- The Focusing Institute (www.focusing.org) for the Focusing Folio and other network support.
- Ann Weiser and Focusing Resources (www.focusingresources.org) for the Focusing Connection.
- Little Joe's Coffee House in Somerville, Massachusetts for providing me with an office.

ABOUT THE AUTHOR

Neil Friedman has a Ph.D. in Clinical Psychology from Harvard University.
He has written the books:
- Focusing: Selected Essays 1974-1999
- Focusing and Listening
- A Remembrance: Spring Hill and Opening the Heart
- On Focusing
- You Cannot Stay on the Summit Forever: Talks and Stories from the Opening the Heart Workshop
- Therapeutic Essays
- Experiential Therapy and Focusing
- The Social Nature of Psychological Research

And the pamphlets:
- Focusing and Meditation
- Opening the HEART

And popular and scholarly articles including:
- "Has Black Come Back to Dixie?"
- "Harold and Maude: My Experiential Therapy with Leida Berg"
- "Africa and the Afro-American: Changing Black Identity"
- "James Baldwin and Psychotherapy"
- "The Tale of the Five O'Clock Clients"

Neil has taught at:
- Lesley College
- SUNY: Stony Brook
- Brandeis University
- The New School of Social Research

Tuskegee Institute
Miles College (Birmingham, Alabama)
He has presented focusing workshops at places such as:
Spring Hill
Interface
Omega
The Open Center
Association for Humanistic Psychology Conferences

For seventeen years, Neil was on the Opening the Heart Workshop staff and for three years was co-director of Spring Hill (former home of The Heart workshop). He remembers with special fondness Miles and Spring Hill and AHP.

Neil can be contacted at:
259 Massachusetts Avenue
Arlington, MA 02474
(781) 646-4481 neilheart@mediaone.net

Printed in Great Britain
by Amazon